FAR FROM THE SHORT GRASS.

Kildare Men In The Two World Wars.

FAR FROM THE SHORT GRASS.

Kildare Men In The Two World Wars.

JAMES DURNEY.

JAMES DURNEY.

ISBN No. 0 9530521 2 5
ISBN No. 0 9530521 3 3

ALSO BY JAMES DURNEY.

THE MOB.

THE HISTORY OF IRISH GANGSTERS IN AMERICA.

PRINTED BY
THE LEINSTER LEADER LTD.
NAAS, CO. KILDARE.

COVER DESIGN   JOHN LALLY

CONTENTS.

PART I.   Page

1. CALL TO ARMS. CILL DARA ABU.   1
2. FIRST BLOOD. MONS.   11
3. GALLIPOLI.   31
4. THE GREEN FIELDS OF FRANCE.   56
5. PATHS OF GLORY.   77
6. GUESTS OF THE KAISER.   87
7. THE SEA WAR.   100
8. ATTACK! THE MARCH OFFENSIVE.   107
9. ALL QUIET ON THE WESTERN FRONT.   116

PART II.   Page

10. HERE WE GO AGAIN. WORLD WAR II.   121
11. BALKANS INTERLUDE.   139
12. THE DESERT WAR.   147
13. THE LONG HAUL. SICILY AND ITALY.   166
14. BOMBER COMMAND.   196
15. FORTRESS EUROPE.   210
16. THE FAR EAST.   229

APPENDIX i   248

APPENDIX ii   258

*Dedicated to Mickser Mahon and Jackie Sheridan
and all the men from the Short Grass who
served and died in the two World Wars.*

ACKNOWLEDGEMENTS.

This book would not have been possible without the help of the many who contributed to it. I would like to thank all those who helped. A special mention to Mrs. Charles Clements, who made available the war diaries and papers of her late husband, Lt-Col. Charles Clements. Special thanks to Frank 'Yonkie' McCormack, who provided photographs, memories and organised interviews with families of veterans. Special mention also to Paddy Gorey, who provided photographs, interviews and memories of men from his locality.

Also to FAS, Naas, who provided typed pages of the Kildare Observer 1914-16, which made my research so much easier; Josephine Cashman, who made available all of her own research and pointed me to many other sources; Rosie Wilson, for photographs and memories of her family through the two wars; Elizabeth Trapp, for Fr. Murphy's story; Sandy Gallie, of the Kildare branch of the British Legion; Mark McLoughlin, of the Athy Heritage Centre; Patrick Hogarty and Tom Burke, of the Royal Dublin Fusiliers Association; Stan Hickey, Philip Higgins and John Lally of the *Leinster Leader*; Sally Mahon; Mary Byrne; Michael and Peter Sheridan; Lieut. Col. Con Costello; Tina Treacy; Liam Kenny; Jim Marsh and May Walsh; Noreen Dowling; Maurice Cullen; Bridget Martin; Declan Furlong; Jimmy Casey; Ken Mahon; Kevin Donnelly-Swift; Noreen Burke; Tom Doran; Ann Delaney; James Kelly; Ann Doran; Robert Jocelyn, for allowing me to quote from his excellent tribute to Major John Kennedy; the Commonwealth War Graves Commission and John Delaney of the Imperial War Museum and cartographer Brian Durney.

A special mention to the veterans who contributed so much to the book and to history in general; Major John de Burgh; Joe Walsh; Michael Coady; the late Mickser Mahon; Dennis Carroll; the late Jim Cullen; Brendan Conlan and Tom Dillon.

FOREWORD

It has been estimated that 206,000 Irishmen served in the British Army during the First World War, of whom over 40,000 were killed. County Kildare was a good recruiting ground as the presence of the major military encampment on the Curragh, and barracks in Newbridge, Naas, and Kildare, and the loyalty of the county gentry and professional class enhanced the role of the soldier. It is estimated that 567 men from the county died in the 1914-18 war.

However, historical events here during that war and immediately afterwards, did not ensure that the returning soldiers were always received as heroes. While many of the men opted to join *Óglaigh na hÉireann,* most of them, many suffering from war wounds or gassing, lived out their days, if they were fortunate in their newly built Soldier's Houses, supported where necessary by the British Legion. As Micheál Ó hUanacháin has written in *The Irish Sword, the Journal of the Military History Society of Ireland* in 1983 (vol. XV 159): "When they returned, it was to a changed environment: a growing guerrilla war with Britain, and widely-held belief that they had been wrong to go. Of those who did not taken part in this new Ireland, or who did not subsequently emigrate, most found themselves alienated. Far from the honour that was their due, they were treated with silence, if not contempt. Their answer was an equal silence, and a potentially rich source of social and military history is now dying with the last of them."

The survivors of over 100,000 Irish men and women who had served in the British forces in the Second World War were welcomed home in 1945 in a more positive way. Indeed, during the war British servicemen who landed in southern Ireland were quickly repatriated, while the Irish intelligence and meteorological services co-operated with their British counterparts. Military personnel from Britain enjoyed visits to Ireland during the war years where, despite rationing, they might still find good food and relaxation.

Political circumstances in the 1960s and 1970s led to a sharp deterioration in cross channel relationships, and as Republican activity escalated, outwards signs of any suggested loyalty to the Crown were likely to cause friction. The discontinuance of commemorations at the Islandbridge Memorial Garden, Dublin, and of the sale of Poppies on Remembrance Day, marked a low period in our perception of the dead of the two World Wars.

Indeed, the Military History Society itself (which was established in 1949) did not publish material on Irishmen in the British Army until 1973, having completed a tour of the battlefields of France and Flanders a couple of years earlier.

But fortunately, times have changed. The first public acknowledgement in recent years of the service of men from Kildare in the Crown Forces in the First World War was the presentation of an oratorio, *Still and Distant Voices,* with music by Mairéad O'Flynn and words by John McKenna, in Athy on Remembrance Day 1992. It was followed by a seminar and exhibition, also held in Athy in 1993, to mark the 75th anniversary of the end of the First World War. *The Fallen,* a play by John McKenna, based on the fictional letters exchanged between a girl in Athy and her soldier at the Front then also had its first performance. The Somme Heritage Centre was opened in Newtownards, County Down, in 1994, and there are exhibitions displaying material on the service of local men in the Great War in many heritage centres such as Athy.

Most importantly, a national acknowledgement of the part played by Irish soldiers in the Great War is the Irish Round Tower in the Peace Park at Messine Ridge in Flanders which was built last year by a voluntary combined effort of Irishmen from north and south of the country.

With this account by James Durney of the men from County Kildare who served in both World Wars the veil has finally been lifted on a part of our history which deserves to be told, and which must encourage other writers to research further in this important aspect of our county's story.

Con Costello, Naas.
8 August 1999.

PART I

STORMING OF THE DARDANELLES

We talk of Irish regiments, no wonder why we do,
The Dublins and the Munsters, you've heard about those two;
You can see by many papers how Irish blood it tells
The way those famous regiments fought at the Dardanelles.

On the 25th of April, when we did make a start,
We were singing Tipperary, a song that reached our hearts;
The ships were packed with khaki lads, such spirits they did show
To the cry Are we downhearted? we quickly answered No.

We got then into our small boats, this way we were to land,
Then every Tommy could be seen with a Woodbine in his hand,
There were boys from Tipperary, from Cork and County Clare,
And the boys from County Dublin and the Short Grass, that's Kildare.

The Turks they were prepared for us, as one and all could tell,
For about one thousand yards from land we were met with shot and shell;
There were bodies floating through the sea and hundreds on the sand,
But the Turks they suffered terribly when we fought them on the land.

The wounded moaning mercy, it was an awful sight;
Those who got badly wounded were wishing for the night,
And when night came our stretcher boys had lots of work to start,
Collecting bodies, legs and arms, the sight near broke their heart.

The Turks were then retreating, their numbers lost were large;
Our officers say Dublins! We'll have a bayonet charge.
The charge was done, the Turks they run, our lads in ringing cheers,
I can't forget those Irish boys - the Dublin Fusiliers.

Before I go, I tell you, be proud and give three cheers.
For those brave fighting Irishmen - the Dublin Fusiliers.

Pte. Thomas Doran, 1st Battn., RDF.

Private Thomas Doran, the Harbour, Naas, was wounded in the Dardanelles while serving with 1st Battn. RDF. He was shipped to a hospital in Exeter, where he penned a tribute to the Dublins titled 'Storming of the Dardanelles.'

CHAPTER 1

Call to Arms
- Cill Dara Abú

On August 4, 1914 Great Britain declared war on Germany in response to the invasion of Belgium. All the great powers of Europe were tied up in an 'interlocking pattern of alliances': Austria with Germany; Serbia with Russia and Britain and France with Belgium. On the morning of June 28 1914, the heir to the Austo-Hungarian throne, Archduke Franz Ferdinand and his wife, Sophie, were assassinated in Sarajevo by a young Bosnian student. Austria-Hungary blamed Serbia for the assassination and declared war on Serbia on July 28. Russia, tied to Serbia by treaty, ordered full mobilisation. Germany demanded that Russia cease her mobilisation and that France announce her neutrality. Both the Russians and French failed to comply and Germany declared war on Russia. On August 2 the German army occupied Luxembourg and demanded that the Belgian government permit the free passage of the German army across Belgium into northern France. Belgium rejected the German demand on August 3. On the same day Germany declared war on France and crossed the Belgian frontier. Britain demanded the withdrawal of German troops from Belgian soil by midnight on August 4.

Call to Arms - Cill Dara Abu

The result of the British ultimatum to Germany was awaited by many at the Post Office in Naas on August 4 at midnight. The hour passed and Britain was at war with Germany. Throughout the next two days Naas was the scene of great animation, as a continual stream of reservists, accompanied by friends and relatives, arrived at the Military Depot in accordance with the Mobilisation Order. The mobilisation of the British Army worked smoothly. Test mobilisations on divisional level over the years before 1914 had proved how efficient the arrangements could be. Within twenty-four hours regular Army reservists were kitted and dispatched to the Home Service Battalion.

The basic unit in the British Army is the regiment. The regiments were, and still are, of various types: infantry, cavalry, artillery and engineer. All regiments are divided into a depot and a service arm and are usually based on a county or city with the depot in the county town. The depot acted as regimental headquarters and recruited and trained men for service. The first battalion of a regiment was often stationed overseas while the second remained at home in the depot. During the two world wars the numbers of recruits increased many times and up to ten extra battalions were formed for each regiment. A battalion was composed of ten to twelve companies, each of which had one hundred men. In theory this would leave battalion strength at around 1,000 men, while in practice the average strength of a battalion was between 600 and 800 men. Cavalry regiments were slightly different in composition and consisted of between six and eight troops of fifty men each.

The most regular destination for Kildare soldiers were the battalions of the Royal Dublin Fusiliers. The 1st and 2nd Battalions of the Royal Dublin Fusiliers had their roots in India where they were originally formed as regiments of the East India Company - where they earned their nicknames, 'the Blue Caps' and 'the Old Toughs.' The two regiments combined in 1881 to form the Royal Dublin Fusiliers.

Call to Arms - Cill Dara Abu

Both Battalions fought in the South African War and as part of Major-General Hart's Irish Brigade in subsequent engagements. Queen Victoria was so impressed with the Irish Brigade's fighting qualities she decreed that henceforth all Irish regiments should wear the shamrock in their head-dress on St. Patrick's Day, March 17, and there was to be formed an Irish Regiment of Footguards to be designated 'The Irish Guards.'

On August 6 280 reservists of the Royal Dublin Fusiliers were met at their Naas depot by the local band of the Irish Volunteers, which played them with Irish airs to the railway station. The *Kildare Observer* had this to say, "When the hour for departure came the gates of the barracks were surrounded by a big crowd of friends and relatives of the departing soldiers, which was considerably augmented when the band of the local Volunteer corps arrived accompanied by a green banner with the inscriptions 'Nas na Riogh' (Naas of the Kings) and 'Nas Abu'. The platform and bridges (of the railway station) were densely crowded with spectators, and as the train steamed out, amid the strains of 'Auld Lang Syne', played by the Volunteer Band and the explosion of fog signals, there was a remarkable demonstration on the part of the spectators who cheered the men vociferously, hats, handkerchiefs and umbrellas being wildly waved. The cheers, needless to say, were heartily returned by the departing soldiers, who, in a few minutes were beyond earshot, and on their way to their destination."

In Athy the Post office was open all night on that Tuesday for the transmission of messages from the army authorities to the men of the reserve in the district. More affecting scenes were witnessed at the railway station the following day when the first batch of the reserve departed on the mid-day train. The men from Athy went to various destinations to join their respective regiments. In addition to the reserve men, Athy also sent men to join the South Irish Horse at

Call to Arms - Cill Dara Abu

Limerick, the officer's cadet corps attached to the universities and the medical and veterinary branches of the army.

The period of service was that ex-soldiers of the Regular Army of special reserve, aged from 19 to 42, could enlist for one year or the period of the war, while other men, from 19 to 30 years of age, could enlist for three years or the period of the war. Soldiers and Sailors Families Associations were set up to alleviate hardship caused by the absence of the bread-winner in most households. Donations were from the public. One of the first donations was from the Duke of Leinster, who presented £1,000 to the fund. All wives of men up for active service were entitled to separation allowances of 1s.1d. a day (1s.7d. in London), together with 2d. a day for each child and 3s.6d. from compulsory allotment out of their husbands pay if they were serving abroad. Those in receipt of separation allowances were not entitled to assistance from the SSFA. Mothers, widows and orphans could apply to the SSFA for assistance. Mrs. Lewis of Back Lane, Naas, had three sons on active service - Patrick and Michael in the special reserve of the RDF and Thomas in the Royal Horse Artillery. Prior to their departure she had received 30s. a week from her sons and with their departure she had to depend on funds from the SSFA.

Kildare as a county with many garrison towns - Naas, Newbridge, Kildare and the Curragh, provided many recruits for the British Army. Most of them were from the poorer homes of the county and many were the sons of former soldiers. The life of a soldier provided them with food and shelter, an opportunity for adventure and a reasonable steady income. Britain had long realised that in the impoverished counties of Ireland there was a military reservoir upon which they could readily draw whenever the need arose. The Irish soldier was reckless, brave and could readily adapt to hardship. When treated fairly he accepted discipline readily and was always dependable in battle. Despite all of England's wrongs inflicted on the Irish, the loyal-

Call to Arms - Cill Dara Abu

Photo: J. CASHMAN.

The Barracks, Newbridge, Co. Kildare.

ty of the Irish regiments was unquestionable and their battle honours stretched from the far corners of the earth. Irish regiments were officered mainly by the Anglo-Irish ascendancy and the rank and file were predominantly Catholic working class or poor.

When the British Expeditionary Force sailed for France, all Irish regiments were represented, either by their first or second battalions. Others, like the 1st Royal Dublin Fusiliers and the 1st Connaught Rangers, stationed in India, quickly arrived home. On the outbreak of war, the Special reserve battalions of the Irish regiments were called up. All their officers and men were sent to France in drafts as replacements for the enormous casualties suffered by the regular battalions. New Army divisions were also formed among them three Irish divisions, the 10th, 16th and 36th (Ulster) Division. The recruits for these divisions found they could not be supplied with uniforms, so great was their numbers. They drilled in civilian clothes until their uniforms

forms arrived and used broom-handles as rifles. The new recruits drilled on the barrack squares of the Curragh, Naas, Newbridge and Kildare and marched along the quiet lanes of the 'short grass.' On the windswept plain of the Curragh they dug trenches until every muscle ached and they marched to the Hill of Allen with full kit and equipment. These arduous trials and tribulations were soon to be regarded as a picnic compared to the hardships of Flanders, Gallipoli and Serbia.

The 10th Division, as the first Irish division, had a decided advantage over the other two. The first flood of recruits went directly to the 10th, while recruiting for the 16th was slower because the regular battalions needed constant replacements, especially following First and Second Ypres, the Gallipoli landings and other battles of 1915. The 16th Division did not leave for France until February 1916, while the 10th was up to full strength in April 1915. (36th Division was recruited mainly from Ulster and was initially recruited from the Ulster Volunteer Force.) The infantry of the 10th was comprised of service battalions of all Irish line regiments and included 6th and 7th Battalions, RDF, which as usual attracted many local recruits. The 16th Division also had two battalions of the 'ould Toughs' the 8th and 9th Battn's, RDF.

The start of the war in August brought a sudden end to the Home Rule crisis. John Redmond, the Nationalist leader and Edward Carson, the Unionist leader, pledged their support to Britain's war effort. Home Rule was suspended for the duration of the war and John Redmond informed the men of the National Volunteers that they were fighting the war to achieve their aims. Britain, they were told, would look favourably upon Ireland after it had showed its loyalty to her in her hour of need.

While the Great War was still in its infancy the county of Kildare saw great change as the country mobilised in response to the German

Call to Arms - Cill Dara Abu

threat. The price of most of the necessities of life were raised in Naas on the first two days of the war to a considerable extent, especially sugar, which made 41/2 per lb; flour was up 25.6d. per cwt; the ordinary loaf was up one farthing; best coal was quoted at 30s. and 32s. 6d. per ton. At the same time the military authorities took over Sheridans Concert Hall at Newbridge, and the premises of Curragh Stand House for the purposes of occupying them with troops during the mobilisation. The headquarters Depot for Irish remounts was established at the offices of the Stand House as hundreds of horses arrived daily from the region for the Cavalry, Artillery and Transport units.

At a meeting of Kildare County Council, a few days after the declaration of war, the following resolution was proposed by Mr. Bergin and seconded by Mr. Phelan, and adopted:- "That in view of the present grave crisis, whereby our country is threatened with calamity, we, the Kildare Co. Council, endorse the action of Mr. John Redmond, pledging the support of the National Volunteers to defend our shores against invasion, and hereby undertake in the event of our office staff taking up arms to keep their respective offices open until their return, and our secretary is hereby directed to make the necessary arrangements for the purpose of carrying out this resolution into effect."

With these loyal sentiments echoing from the chambers of the local council Kildare men once again took up arms to defend Britain. The two great centres for recruitment in Kildare were the towns of Naas and Athy. During the war more than 2,000 men from Athy and district joined the British Army. Many were former soldiers, others joined to escape the poverty of Irish life or were caught up in the excitement of the time. Athy had a long tradition of service in the British Army and the life of the town and its people was, by history, and latterly by economic necessity, closely linked to service in the Crown forces. Both the Leinster Regiment, based in Maryboro

Barracks in Dublin, and the Dublin Fusiliers, based in Naas, drew many recruits from the South Kildare area. In August 1914 a recruitment office was opened in Leinster Street. Initially recruiting was very heavy and while it eased off considerably in 1915, the *Leinster Leader* of June 3 reported that: 'the last official figures obtainable about recruiting in Athy showed that 1,600 men from it and its environs had joined the colours.' Athy responded better than any other town outside Ulster to Britain's call.

A nun from the local Convent of Mercy had noted that: "All the men of our town who belonged to the militia or reserved forces were summoned to the front. Every other day they came to the convent to beg for Sacred Heart scapulars, Agnus Deis, etc., to take away with them. Few of these poor fellows ever saw their homes again."

It was not long before the news of the first deaths reached Athy. Patrick Heydon, a private in the Irish Guards, was the first Athy man killed during the war. He died at Mons, in France on September 4, 1914 when the Great War was just one week old. He was followed by Eddie Stafford three weeks later on September 24. By the time the war ended, four long and bloody years later, 102 men from Athy town and 82 from the surrounding countryside had lost their lives.

Naas being a garrison town with a barracks, had various British regiments stationed in the town through the years. Many local men joined these regiments and served in various parts of the world prior to 1914, including the Boer War in South Africa. The regular unit stationed in Naas (the barracks was completed in 1813) was the 3rd Battalion of the Royal Dublin Fusiliers. Prior to and especially during 1914-18 this regiment enlisted many men from Naas and the surrounding area. Most of those who enlisted came from the poorest streets of the town at the time such as Loch Bui, Back Lane and the

Call to Arms - Cill Dara Abu

Photo: LAWERENCE COLLECTION.

Troops drilling on the square at Naas barracks.

Rathasker Road cottages. It was not unusual for all of the men in a household - perhaps a father and son, or three or four brothers to join up. By June 1917 some 22,611 volunteers had enlisted at the depot in Naas. It was the recruiting centre for the area which included counties Dublin, Wicklow, Carlow and Kildare. Recruits came from as far away as England and Scotland to join the famed Dublin Fusiliers. A Frenchman from Paris even arrived at the barracks and said he was attracted by the 'fame of the Dublins' and wanted to join them!

One day when a reporter from the *Leinster Leader* visited Naas barracks he saw 'squatting about in all directions, the future defenders of the British Empire, waiting to go through the ordeal of fitting khaki uniforms. The congestion is so great that many things appertaining to the comfort of the recruits have to remain unattended to but the poor fellows grin and bear it. You would pity one poor Irish lad as he lay stretched out on the grass humming to himself a few lines of Kickham's ballad, the Irish Youth:

"*Dear countryman, take heed of what I say.*
If you ever join the British ranks, you'll surely rue the day".'

These recruits were welcomed as 'a great boon to the town, the traders of which are sure to benefit by having such a large number of men located in their midst.' The price of commodities in the shops in the county had risen in price 'due to the war.' Trade in Kildare had been greatly enhanced by the increased numbers of men passing through the Curragh and the barracks at Naas, Newbridge and Kildare. At one time there were 30,000 men on the Curragh, and on another occasion, 14,000. In January 1915 2,000 Connaught Rangers and Royal Irish Rifles were stationed in Naas at the barracks and in the jail awaiting transport to the front.

The women of the county were not idle either. They formed groups to collect comforts for the troops. In Athy, Lady Weldon arranged for the entertainment of the men, while in Naas flag days and dances were held to raise funds for gifts to be sent to the prisoners of war in Germany. Miss Evelyn Moore, of Killashee, rallied volunteers to hospital work in the war zone. Baroness de Robeck sought funds for sending hot water bottles and cigarettes to the wounded soldiers in France. Various committees were set up throughout the county to raise funds for many purposes, especially prisoner of war comforts. Such things as the hot bag and cigarette fund, prisoner of war comforts committee, hospital supplies committee, literature for prisoners committee, were run all throughout the war years. In North Kildare an egg committee was set up and schoolchildren were asked to bring in one egg a week for prisoner of war comfort. The children inscribed their names on the egg and these were sent to Germany. Dances, concerts, fetes, field days, golf and tennis tournaments were also run to raise funds.

CHAPTER 2

First Blood
Mons

In the latter half of August 1914 the British Expeditionary Force detrained in the Maubeuge area and marched towards Mons. As they marched along the roads of northern France that glorious summer they sang the most popular song of the war, "It's a long way from Tipperary." Nearly half of the men of the BEF were recalled reservists. Some had been out of uniform for seven years and most were physically unfit. In the rushed mobilisation and departure for the front, there had been no time for training. Unaccustomed to route marches, many suffered from foot blisters and shoulder sores from carrying equipment. Some were carrying weapons for the first time in years. But there were worse shocks in store. The opening months of the war brought scenes of carnage which had never been witnessed before. The Germans had planned for the capture of Paris since 1906. The Schlieffen Plan, named after Count von Schlieffen, called for a sweep into northern France through Belgium and Luxembourg and defeat of France in six weeks. The French clashed with the Germans in the forests of the Ardennes and were soundly defeated with tremendous losses. As the French fell back the major weight of the German wheel-

First Blood - Mons

ing armies fell on the BEF at Mons and another French force at Charleroi.

On August 22 4th Royal Irish Dragoon Guards skirmished with German Uhlans as the BEF moved towards Mons. It was the first contact between the British and German forces. A full retreat by the Belgian Army left the French no choice but to do likewise, which in turn left the British right flank open to attack. Now the British advance stopped and the British II Corps were ordered to take up positions

Photo: M. WALSH.

John Marsh, Sallins, pictured at Aldershot, Aug. 1914.

First Blood – Mons

along the Mons-Conde Canal. Long columns of German troops were reported heading at all angles to the British front. The British, in their hastily dug trenches with machine guns and artillery, were ready. On August 23 masses of German infantry hit the British line. The British were expert marksmen and the young German conscripts paid a heavy price. The 'mad minute' of at least fifteen aimed rounds a minute took a heavy toll on the attacking Germans. But the withdrawal of the French from Charleroi and the Ardennes left the British right flank open to a German envelopment and a general retreat was ordered the following day. The retreat did not end until September 5 at the river Marne, the last major water obstacle on the route to Paris. Here, the Allies counterattacked pushing the Germans back to the Aisne. British reinforcements landed at Ostend in late September and together with the BEF, transferred from the Aisne to La Bassée by rail on October 10 began to push forward. The Allies and the Germans now turned their attention to the Channel ports. In a 'race to the sea,' the two sides tried to outflank one another. The two forces clashed again at the little Belgian city of Ypres (the British pronounced it 'Wipers'). In two battles around this city the Germans lost, in dead and wounded, 135,000 men.

Among the dead of the first casualty list announced in September were many well known officers linked with County Kildare. Major Hubert Crichton of the Irish Guards was killed in the retreat from Mons. From Mullaboden, Ballymore-Eustace, Crichton joined the Guards in 1896 and was with the Nile Expedition of 1898 and at the subsequent battle of Khartoum, receiving the Egyptian medal with clasp. He received the Queen's medal with clasp in the South African War. Also killed was Captain C. F. Blacker of Johnstown, Naas. Captain Blacker, 2nd Connaught Rangers, was wounded in the leg and body at the battle of Mons, but died several days later of pneumonia. His remains were brought back to Ireland and he was buried at Maudlins, Naas.

First Blood - Mons

Lieutenant Thomas de Burgh, the youngest son of Colonel de Burgh, of Oldtown, Naas, was reported missing on September 16, after a reconnaissance at Conde Bridge on the River Aisne. He was believed to have been hit by a shell and his body was never recovered. Born in 1888, he was educated at Wellington College and Sandhurst, and received his commission in 1910. Lieut. de Burgh was a fine horseman and an all-round sportsman. He was one of four brothers on active service and was serving with 31st Lancers, Indian Army, who were attached at the outbreak of war to the 5th Royal Irish Lancers. His name appeared in the October list of casualties along with that of Andrew McGarr, a 41 year old native of Naas, who enlisted in Glasgow, and died at the Curragh from an attack of pneumonia. Lieut. de Burgh was officially reported as killed in action a year later.

On October 12 a reporter from the *Kildare Observer* met 45 'Dublins' when they arrived in Naas from the front. The *Kildare Observer* newspaper was published at 56 South Main Street and followed a strong Redmond and Anglo-Irish policy. It carried weekly reports of Co. Kildare soldiers at war under the heading *"War Notes"* or *"Roll of Honour"*. Recruiting meetings were reported at length and the poet Tom Kettle wrote a long article in the *Observer* encouraging men to join up. These first 'Dubs' to be interviewed were a truly cosmopolitan crowd. They were mostly Irish, though one was from Stirling in Scotland and one was from Liverpool. Among them were Private Treacy from Naas and Private John Lawler of Athy, who had a rather humourous tale to tell. This party of Dublins had become detached from their comrades. "At Le Courtois village, a party of Germans pounced upon us and opened fire. There were only two of us there, but I suppose they didn't know that. We returned the compliments and fired like devils, as we made up our minds to die game. Joe Salinger, of Carlow, was my comrade, and between us we shot eight Germans. Don't forget to say that. Poor Joe got a bullet in the knee and was taken to hospital, but we polished the beggars off. We

First Blood – Mons

were both nearly satisfied to die then as we had eight of them to our credit between us. But what do you think happened? We were fighting them near the hospital and had finished our work when a full corporal rushed up to me, caught me by the back of the neck and asked me did I want to get the hospital destroyed."

On August 26 Pte. Michael White from Rathasker Road, Naas was in the firing line at Cambrai in the retreat from Mons. Pte. White of A Company, 2nd RDF, was in action for three days before been wounded by two German bullets. When his wounds were healed he was given fourteen days furlough, whereupon he returned to Naas and gave this account to a *Kildare Observer* reporter. "I was one of four platoons of the 'Dublins' sent to hold the hills at Cambrai at all costs, but ten times our number could not have performed the task, as we found out when we saw the numbers against us. I was in the fourth platoon under Lieut. Mackey, who was afterwards captured by the Germans and is now a prisoner, I believe. I tasted the lead of the Germans twice. The first wound I believe was here (third finger of his right hand). I paid no heed to that. It was nothing, and I got back into the ranks and fired away after I got a bandage tied around it to keep the blood from bothering me. We were retiring all this time, and I asked Captain Clarke where I could get my hand bound up when the blood was troubling me. He told me to go back to the village - Cambrai - and I would find No. 2 Red Cross Hospital there.

"I had got my finger bandaged when a German aeroplane buzzed right over the Church, which had been turned into a temporary hospital. The people in the aeroplane dropped a black disc suspended by a cord over the church for the purpose, I suppose, of giving the range to the artillery. A few minutes later the steeple of the church came tumbling down and some French doctors and nuns were killed amongst others. This is not hearsay, as I saw it with my own eyes. We - some wounded - were told to clear out, as the place was going to

First Blood - Mons

be shelled and we lost no time in going, those of us who could look after ourselves ... I rejoined my comrades, who were at this time retreating and some four or five hours later, while we were fighting on our retreat some miles from Cambrai I got another bullet - this time in the groin that knocked me over, and I was sent to the field hospital at Rouen. That night we had to clear off from there and got on board a ship which came through the Seine. We disembarked at Southampton, and a lot of us were sent to Plymouth Hospital, which was in charge of civilians and territorials."

Sergeant-Major Nicholas Byrne of Stephenstown, Naas, was with 1st Irish Guards in Flanders at the beginning of the German onslaught. On August 28 1914 he wrote one of many letters to his step-father, Mr Byrtle Byrne, detailing his experiences. The Irish Guards were assigned to the 4th Brigade, which was composed of four Guards battalions. Retiring to the village of Landrecies, the force of 4,500 men were quickly surrounded by a far superior force of Germans, estimated to be about 20,000. The Brigade fought their way out of the trap.

"We defended the town so gallantly that the Germans were not able to break through, but were forced back. Our losses were about 14 killed and about 80 wounded. I got lost with a pack of animals and was very near walking into the German ranks. At daybreak I was at a place where the biggest attack was made at our lines and I could see nothing but piles of dead Germans and some of their wounded had not been taken away. All the troops had gone except the few men I had with me, so I decided to go back again into town, which was deserted. We were the last out of town at 6.30 a.m. At 7 o'clock the Germans shelled the town to bits. I happened to hit on the right road and caught the brigade up about 8 o'clock. During the last eight days we have marched over 160 miles, and in six of these days I could only manage 14 hours' sleep."

First Blood – Mons

On September 2 he wrote, "It was our duty to hold the enemy in check as long as possible to allow the remainder of our army to retire in safety. We had a terrific tussle with them (the Germans) in a tremendous big wood, and although we mowed the Germans down as they came up to us, they kept on sending fresh men against us. They retired at half-past two in the afternoon after nearly five hours hard fighting. Their losses must have been enormous, but unfortunately we have paid dearly for our success. Col. Crichton's son (Major Crichton of Naas) was killed early in the fight.

"… I hope you will excuse pencil, as pen and ink are as scarce as a bottle of Guinness. Tim Kelly, of Mullacash, is still safe and sound. You can tell his people. Jack Cummons did not come out with us, as he was not in London at the time. I lost yesterday one of the best friends I ever had. He was a Company Sergt.-Major the same as myself and we have been together for the last eleven years at Caterham and elsewhere. He was Nicholas's (his son) godfather and I shall never forget his last words as he was struck twice in succession with bullets from a German machine gun, 'Goodbye, Byrne, old man I'm done!' He said no more."

The following month Byrne wrote, "Mark Hickey joined us with the last draft. They arrived here from the base at 4 a.m. last Thursday. I took a patrol out to look for German snipers immediately after daybreak (6 a.m.). It fell to the lot of some of the new draft to come out with me. We were fired on by these snipers and one poor fellow who arrived with the draft that morning was killed. We afterwards killed an under-officer (who was in charge) and four snipers, who had been firing at us all the night before. Jack Cummins is still at the base and will not join us for about another month, so you can tell Mr. Cummins not to worry about Jack for the present, at least."

The Kildare soldiers' allegiance to their Catholic faith is witnessed

First Blood - Mons

by another letter written when the Guards were relieved after five weeks in action. "The following day, Friday, was a rest day, the first one we have had for nearly two months. We had a good clean-up in the morning, and in the evening I took 93 men of my company down to confession in the town. We were to go to Communion yesterday morning at 7 p.m., but unfortunately we had to move off at the time and we could not go then. A few hours march brought us to a little village here, where we spent last night. This morning, being Sunday, we all took the opportunity of going to Communion. It seems very strange for us to be able to go to Mass on Sunday. Previously we generally had a big fight on Sunday. In fact, Sunday and Tuesday were our 'scrapping days' up to now."

John Cummins of Newlands, Naas was also with the Irish Guards in the first months of the war and was wounded at Ypres. He joined the Irish Guards in 1909 and having completed his three years service he was placed on the reserve of the 1st Battalion. In August 1914 he was called up for active service and on September 9 he left with his regiment for the front. Pte. Cummins was at the British base in St. Nazaire for three weeks until they went into the line at the Marne. He fought at Landericies, Soissons, Cambrai and Ypres before been wounded twice on the same day. He was wounded first in the shoulder by a shell fragment and continued to hold his position until another shell fragment struck his left hand almost severing two of his fingers. He described the fighting around Armentieres and his feelings towards his enemies.

"The slaughter amongst them (the Germans) was terrible. You simply could not miss them. All you had to do was level your rifle and fire and you might be sure you'd get someone. I could not tell you how many of them we buried at Armentieres - thousands of them, there must have been, poor devils, half buried in the mud and dirt after our

First Blood – Mons

shells. As far as I could see, the Germans hardly ever buried their dead.

"Anything you could say about them as brutes won't be half enough … In one place eleven of us who had been sniped at for a couple of hours by some German snipers, who were in a house, charged the place and found five German soldiers, one of them an officer. They had two poor women stripped naked, and when we went in on them I tell you we didn't leave them a chance of doing much in this world again. We shot every damn one of them. The officer refused to give up his sword when we entered. He was thrown across the room by a kick from one of our fellows and shot with the others.

"When some of us who had been wounded at Ypres were retiring from the firing line to the field hospital I saw four stretcher bearers carrying a wounded officer. A shell burst amongst them; three of the poor fellows were blown to atoms and the officer's legs were blown off. You get accustomed to these sights out there and take them as they come. The best friend I ever had was fighting beside me when a shell struck him in the stomach and blew him to bits.

"I often thought it strange out there to see little Belgian children walking among and over the dead bodies and picking up cartridge cases and odds and ends for 'plays' in their little dresses. They were too young to know what it was all about and soon got over the first fright on seeing a dead man. Once when three of us went for ammunition there was three children on the road, we went over and found their mother dead - shot. The eldest of the children was not more than four years. We took them away with us, but such a row as they made when we parted them from their mother. We brought them to a convent, and the nuns and priests went on their knees to us and blessed us.

First Blood - Mons

"Yes you get accustomed to deaths and bullets and blood and bombs out there. I remember one sight I saw in a farmyard where several of us went. It had been shelled by our guns and the place was full of dead Germans. Some were only wounded and we dressed them up as best we could. I heard pigs kicking up an awful shindy and went to the pig house. There were eleven pigs in it and they were mad with hunger. I opened the door and let the beasts out. When they started eating the bodies of dead Germans we drove them off with some trouble and into a field.

"I was a prisoner once for eleven hours. The Germans made us carry the packs of dead Germans, and I saw one poor devil, a Scotchman of the Black Watch Highlanders, with six or seven packs on him. We escaped that night, eleven of us through the guards, hid ourselves in a wood covering ourselves with leaves and things, and later worked around the wood and back to our own lines."

After been wounded John Cummins was moved to Boulogne and from there to England. He was given leave until December 21 when he returned to his regiment.

The commander of the 1st Guards Brigade was Kildare man Brigadier-General Charles FitzClarence nicknamed 'The Demon.' Born in 1865 in Bishopscourt, near Kill, he was a veteran of Sudan, having accompanied Kitchener on the Khartoum campaign. In the Boer war he won a Victoria Cross for bravery and had been given no less than three recommendations for the decoration. When the regiment of Irish Guards was formed in 1900 he transferred to it becoming battalion and then regimental commander of the Guards. As a brigadier-general he led the 1st Guards Brigade with the Expeditionary Force in France, and there, on November 11 1914, moving along a country road, in darkness, at the head of his men, he was killed.

First Blood – Mons

In late October the German advance was checked at the city of Ypres. When the British I Corps arrived to relieve the hard pressed IV Corps they went on the offensive. From late October to the end of the year the area around Ypres saw scenes of terrific carnage and slaughter. Pte. Edward Brannigan, 2nd Battalion, Kings Royal Rifles was involved in the fighting around Ypres. Pte. Brannigan formerly lived in Newbridge and moved, with his wife, to New Row, Naas in 1913. His father, who also lived in New Row, served 22 years in the British Army. He had three brothers in the service, two of them in the Dublin Fusiliers and one in the Irish Guards.

Pte. Brannigan left with his regiment for the front in August and was in action during the retreat from Mons. His regiment was involved in numerous battles, culminating, as far as Pte. Brannigan was concerned, in the battle at Ypres on October 31. "I got mixed up with the North Lancashires. They were fighting on the right of the Kings Royal Rifles. We were forced to retreat by enormously superior numbers. Passing across the field in the retreat I put up my hand to pull down a bit of a tree in order to make a gap to get through. I saw hundreds of German soldiers, within a hundred yards of me, and the next moment my arm dropped limp by my side. (A bullet entered his left arm above the elbow making its exit at the other side) I was knocked over but I managed to scramble to my feet, discarded my kit and rifle, which was now no good to me, and ran with the others. When I came to the road I followed it to the hospital, where I was treated, being afterwards sent to Boulogne, from that to Harve, and thence home. I saw a good deal of fighting during my two months at the front, and was in four bayonet charges. The Germans, I can tell you from experience, don't like the British bayonet. When it comes to a bayonet charge the officers drive the Germans on from behind, but when we are coming close to them they drop their rifles and surrender or, if they get a chance away from their officers, they come to our lines and give themselves up."

First Blood - Mons

Bombardier W. Greer of Donadea was wounded at both Mons and Ypres and was invalided home after the latter battle. Bombardier Greer, Royal Garrison Artillery, was a veteran of the South African War and held the Tibetan War medal. He received broken ribs from a shell splinter in the retreat from Mons and on May 8 suffered wounds to his leg, shoulder and arm. "Our artillery had been four days bombarding the German lines beyond Ypres, when about 4 o'clock in the morning, they found our range, and my detachment was knocked out by a German shell. The whole detachment, except three, were either killed or wounded, and out of our battery we lost something more than 30 men. Our sergeant was blown to bits and our young officer got riddled about the legs. Gunner Jim Murphy, of Maynooth, who was one of the lucky ones in our detachment, bandaged up my leg. Then the Germans, finding they had got us, I suppose, started shelling our dug-outs, evidently thinking the wounded would crawl there, but we kept in the open, and although shells were dropping on all sides, we escaped without a further scratch. I was removed to hospital soon after."

Peter Lawler from Halverstown, Naas, took part in one of the only victories of the first year of the war. Peter Lawler had emigrated to New Zealand in 1910 as an electrical engineer. The day after the declaration of war he joined the Australian marines in Sydney. He was sent to German New Guinea and fought against German troops and their native 'conscripts.' He spent around six months on this campaign, seeing action at Rabaul, Mandang, Kikta Island in the Solomons and New Ireland. These were important German coaling stations and with their loss the German fleet had to go as far away as Chile for coal supplies. Peter Lawler was "the only Irishman amongst the force, as far as I know I believe I am the only one that has yet reached England after the New Guinea expedition. We were a small force, but we did some useful work and many a poor fellow who left Sydney with me gave up his life in his doing. I escaped without a

First Blood – Mons

scratch, and was also extremely lucky in escaping the fever which played havoc with our men."

Conditions in the front-line trenches worsened as winter descended. There was no rest in the front-line and little out of it either. Casualties piled up from the constant bombing, sniping, patrols and night-raids. Illness took its toll on the soldiers, too. The trenches were generally shallow and with built-up parapets of unbagged soil, which usually caved in during heavy rain. Planks, brushwood and straw were thrown in the bottom of the trenches to make a secure flooring, but these, too, sank, making life a constant misery for the troops occupying them. A tour of duty was forty-eight hours and most soldiers stood motionless in water, sometimes up to their knees, for two days. Men slept, if they could, standing upright leaning against the back of a trench. Latrines were non-existent and for those with gastric complaints, from the food and conditions, it was a nightmare. No fires were allowed, except for cooking and food was generally cold and unappetising - bully beef and biscuits and sometimes a bit of cheese, bacon and jam.

Pte. John Morrin of Friary Road, Naas, was with the 8th Hussars in that first winter in the trenches and wrote to his mother, Mrs. Mary Morrin, on St. Stephen's Day 1914. The 8th Hussars had arrived from India and were attached to the Indian Expeditionary Force. "Indian troops find it more severe," he wrote, "than any of the others and I must say the British troops are having a hard time in the trenches, but we are not badly off - plenty of food and woollen clothes. The people in England are sending plenty of presents, so you see we are not too badly off ... The cavalry cannot do anything at present, as the Germans will not come out of the trenches, but I assure you when we get them out we will not spare them, for you don't call this struggle a war. It is more of a slaughter house. You may have seen where the poor old Dublins lost heavily, but we will avenge their losses very

First Blood - Mons

soon. The weather here is not as cold as it has been, but is always raining now and the mud is up to your knees, as it is nearly as bad as the cold. I would have been home now if the war had not broken out, but with the help of God, if I pull through, I shall be home to see you all when the war is finished, and I think that will be about March or April."

Shortly after Christmas the regiment was informed that forty men would get home leave. The troops drew lots for the places and John Morrin was one of the lucky ones who got away. He spoke to the *Kildare Observer* while he was home in Naas. "We left India in September with the first Indian Expeditionary Force, and proceeded direct to the front. We reached the base in October, but owing to the jaded conditions of our horses after their long voyage it was the end of November before we got into action at La Bassée, where, like all the cavalry regiments engaged in the present war, we were put to infantry work in the trenches. It was new to us as cavalry men, but after a time we grew accustomed to it; but still there are few of us who would prefer to get to the activity of our cavalry work. Trench work was a novelty to us, but the nature of the country and the character of the fighting has left little chance for cavalry to show what it can do, or has been trained to. The only time there was a chance for cavalry up to the present was in the fighting at Mons and the retreat, but this had all taken place long before we arrived, and since we got into the field there has been no real cavalry work at all.

"We were bracketed with the Highland Light Infantry and the Dragoon Guards, and have been fighting in the trenches at La Bassée with the French holding the ground on our right and the British army - we are of the Indian army - on our left. I have been fortunate, so far, having received no wounds and not having been very badly affected by frost bite; at least, not so badly as many of the others, though I suffered for a good while after my arrival in France with frost-bite of the

First Blood – Mons

toes. Our regiment has been very lucky throughout the campaign so far, as we have only lost 20 men and 2 officers - one a major whose leg was shattered by a shell, and the other a lieut., who was shot in the hand and of whose recovery I believe there is little hope.

"The Dragoon Guards lost a whole squadron - 130 men - a short time ago in a night attack, and their Colonel was killed, while the Highland Light Infantry lost about 700 men out of a thousand. They had forced the enemy out of a trench, which they captured, only, however, to find it had been mined before it was evacuated, and no sooner had the H.L.I. taken it than there was a tremendous explosion with the result I have mentioned. These Germans are undoubtedly clever fighters. We are relieved about every 48 hours in the trenches, but we are pretty safe in the trenches in which we are well sheltered. They are dug about 12 ft. deep. From the bottom on one side an embankment is raised about 4 ft., and after that we burrow into the earth and make loopholes from which to fire through the clay which is thrown up on either side when the trench is being dug. We are, therefore, protected on top from shells, though occasionally the force of an explosion destroys this covering.

"When we first arrived from India there was snow in France and the change was terribly hard on our fellows, but now we are acclimatised. We are well looked after in the matter of food, and there is no scarcity of warm clothing and tobacco and cigarettes sent to us by the people at home. We have not a thing to grumble at in that respect."

Asked about his return to the front Pte. Morrin answered truthfully. "I suppose I should hardly say I am anxious to go, but duty must be done."

Pte. James Rogers, 3rd Battn. RDF, from Millbrook, Naas and wounded at St. Julien, was only too delighted to get back into the fray.

First Blood - Mons

"I arrived in France on the 10th December last and we were at once sent to the trenches, where we had a pretty rough time, I can tell you. There was plenty of snow, which made our life anything but a pleasant one, particularly as we were frequently nearly waist deep in water. Our first really lively time came at St. Julien, where we got a bad cutting up. We got orders to take the town - St. Julien - and we did it, only to find that we were too far advanced from the main body, and so we had to fall back a bit and occupy a position outside the village. We got the order from the Warwicks to retire. We had then only six officers and about fifty men. We got a sort of cover in a ditch and we

Photo: ATHY HERITAGE CENTRE.

Michael Hayden, Athy (left) and The Prince of Wales.

First Blood – Mons

held it, repulsing the enemy several times. When they could not get us out of it they started to shell us, and we had no cover from shells. We were ordered to move to a house which we had taken that morning, and which was only a short distance away. While getting into the house Col. Lovebrand was wounded in the hip. That was the first wound and it knocked him up, though he tried to hang on for a while. He had to give up, however, and told Major Banks to take charge. The enemy made no attack on the house when we reached it, and we started to prepare for what we expected would come very soon. We knocked a portion of the side of the house to allow us to use two machine guns we had pulled with us. Soon they came for us, and I can tell you we fairly cut the ears off them with two machine guns when they did come. We repulsed them, and they left us alone for the rest of the day.

"Next day they started to fire what we call "plug" shells at us - they are used for breaking in a house. They blew away the barn in the yard, which had prevented them from getting at the house before that. When they got the barn away they started at the house with the plug shells and knocked away one of the gables. Then they started to try and gas us out of the house, but did not succeed.

"The following day the Northumberland Fusiliers came to relieve us. They lost heavily in trying to reach us, as the approach to the house was terribly exposed. However, they drove the Germans back, and we left the house and started to dig ourselves in. We entrenched and remained near the farmhouse for six or seven days until we were relieved.

"When the Northumberlands were coming up the Germans were hammering away at them. In the confusion some of them mistook us for Germans, and the first one to get shot was Major Banks, who was shot through the stomach by mistake. That night when things had

First Blood - Mons

become quiet I and another chap came out to look about us. We came across one fine looking German who had been killed in attacking us. We found on him a photograph of his wife and family. That photograph was taken in London. It had the name of a London photographer at the bottom.

"We were next moved to reinforce the Cheshires in the trenches. There we remained for about ten days, after we were shifted to St. John. That was on Whit Monday and here the toughest time began. About 5 o'clock we were saluted with gas from the Germans. The first thing I have any clear recollection of in the excitement was a shout of 'The gas! The gas!" and it was upon us. A lot of our fellows got badly choked by it, but I was not much affected by it all. After giving up the gas they began to shell us with high explosives. Part of our fellows on our right had retired, thus leaving our right flank exposed. Most of our officers had been knocked over by the gas and shells and either killed or wounded. A Scottish regiment came up to reinforce us about 8 o'clock, but they were gassed and had to retire. All our officers and non-commissioned officers had been knocked over except Lieut. Shanks, who was in charge of what was left of us. We held the position until about 11 o'clock, where there were only six or seven of us left. The remainder had all been killed or wounded. When the "Jocks" retired it was a matter of looking out for ourselves. Our right and left flanks were gone. We were told that reinforcements were coming up to us, and I said to the few that was left that we should try and hold on until they arrived. A little later four of the six left stole away to look out for themselves, and they got away. There were only two of us left, myself and a fellow named Andrews, a Dublin chap. We thought we had better try to make a rush to get back to headquarters. The very minute we got out of the trench they turned a machine gun on us, but we managed to cover a it of ground unhurt, and got to about 100 yards behind the reserve trenches, which were unoccupied at this time. The bullets were flying all about us. They tore through my coat

First Blood – Mons

and shirt just under the left arm. I had this (a tin Queen Mary Christmas present box) in the pocket on the left side of my tunic, and that must have saved my life. It was full of fags at the time. A bullet struck it, and going through the cover, glanced off the bottom of the box. The bullets kept on flying and whistling around us, and then I found myself hit in the left arm. I felt the blood running down my sleeve, but in the excitement I did not mind much. Just then Andrews got shot in the wrist and I went to bandage him. We lay down in a ditch, which gave us a bit of cover and every time we tried to get up the machine gun opened fire on us. We thought our best chance was to lie there for a while. We lay down in the ditch for a while, but the other fellow could not "stick" it any longer, and said he would have to go to headquarters. He stood up and made a run for it ... I waited, lying down, until he had time to get clear (and I found he got safely to headquarters) and then I made a bolt for it. I saw there was a little more cover in a ditch on the other side of the road and thought I would make for that side. They cut the ground from under my feet as I crossed the road, but I got into the drain alright, and crept back to headquarters. The first men I saw when I got there were Captain Leahy and Captain Magan.

"We had sent word down for reinforcements and a message came back from Col. Lovebrand to hold on a little longer, that the reinforcements were coming. The Colonel was in a "dug-out" near headquarters. The "Jocks" told us the Warwicks were coming to our aid, and to try and hold out. That was the last message we had from Colonel Loveband, and it was at about 8 o'clock in the morning, as I came back to headquarters past the "dug-out" I saw a man lying near the trench. I thought I knew the boots - a sort of highlaced boots. I went over and found there was a coat over the man's face. I lifted it off and saw it was the body of Colonel Loveband. He had, as far as I could make out, been shot through the lip, just at the bottom of the nose. I looked at the wound and saw the bullet had gone through the back of

First Blood - Mons

his head. He was evidently anxious about us - to see how we were getting on without the reinforcements and wanted to have a look. He came out of the trench and was evidently got by a sniper. His face when I saw him dead seemed as if he was laughing - a sort of smile on his features."

Pte. Rogers was brought back to hospital. He had also witnessed the deaths of other Kildare men in the Dublins. "There was Mick Keogh, of Kill. He was killed going into action at St. Julien. Sergt. Halloran, who was in the Depot, had his two legs blown off by a shell at St. Julien. Michael Lewis, of Naas, was wounded in the leg twice, but when he heard the cheers of our fellows nothing would do him but to put his head out of the trench. I checked him for this, but he would do it and he was killed. I helped bury himself and Mick Keogh that night." Despite the deaths of his comrades and the hardships endured Pte. Rogers was anxious to get back to his unit when his wound healed.

War seemed to suit men like Pte. Rogers, and one of the most heroic of Kildare soldiers Kilcullen man, William Cooke. He went to the front in August with the 2nd Dublins and was promoted from Private to Sergeant. He was a brave and fearless fighter, a shining example to officers and men alike. On one occasion he went out at night, and having reconnoitred the enemy's trench found his way back barred by a party of Germans. He lay still for some time and waited for the next flare shell to locate the enemy, and then poured in shot after shot at them, taking them completely by surprise. He had fifty rounds of ammunition and after about the twenty-fifth shot his rifle jammed. Without hesitation he shouted, "Come on, Dublins. We have them now," to give the Germans the impression that he had more men with him. The Germans broke off the engagement and Sgt. Cooke was able to return in safety to his own lines, where he received an ovation from his comrades.

CHAPTER 3

Gallipoli

In early 1915 the First Lord of the Admiralty, Winston Churchill, conceived a brilliant plan to knock Turkey out of the war and force Germany to a negotiated settlement. The plan was to force the Dardanelles straits, bombard Constantinople and put Turkey out of the war, secure a short sea-route to Russia and open another front against Germany and Austria-Hungary. The plan was doomed for failure from the start. On February 19 1915 Anglo-French forces attacked and silenced the outer forts of the Dardanelles and landed a force of Marines on the Gallipoli peninsula, only to withdraw them several hours later. Complete strategic and tactical surprise was achieved but the operation was not followed up and only served to alert the Turks. The following month the Navy again attacked and silenced the forts commanding the Narrows and once again withdrew. Naval commanders claimed that the Dardanelles could not be forced without the help of land forces. The British began planning an amphibious assault on the peninsula but by know the Turks were well prepared and their defences were reinforced and skillfully strengthened with German help.

Gallipoli

General Sir Ian Hamilton, Commander of the Mediterranean Expeditionary Force, gathered his hastily assembled staff and began planning the amphibious assault. His forces consisted of the 29th Division, the Royal Navy Division, a French division and an Australian and New Zealand Army Corps (Anzac). The main landings were at Ari Burnu while the 29th Division with elements of the RN Division were to land further south at Cape Helles. Among the 29th Division were 3,000 Irishmen of the three Irish battalions - the Dublins, Munsters and Inniskillings. These were all experienced regular soldiers who had been in the British army for years. With the Dublins were many Kildare men who would shortly fight and die on the "Peninsula of Death."

An old collier, *River Clyde*, was converted into an assault ship and was to be used as a modern Trojan Horse. This ex-coal boat was to be filled with Irish troops and run aground at a place marked V beach. Holes were cut into her sides and from these the men could emerge on to a gangway supported by ropes which ran along the sides towards the bow of the vessel. The gangways would then lead down to two barges which were to form a short pier between ship and shore. The troops would arrive dry-shod to fight the Turks. That was the plan. What happened was a horrific disaster in a disastrous campaign.

The *River Clyde* was transformed into a fortress. Armoured cars were sandbagged on the deck and in the bows, their machine guns ready to give close fire-support. Into the holds were packed four companies of 1st Munsters, two companies of 1st Hampshires, one company 1st Dublins and signal and ambulance elements. In addition to the assault ship, four picket boats would tow twelve cutters with three companies of the 1st Dublins to the beach. In all there were about 3,000 troops. These regiments had a history of courage and valour stretching back many years with dozens of battle-honours. They were shortly to add another.

Gallipoli

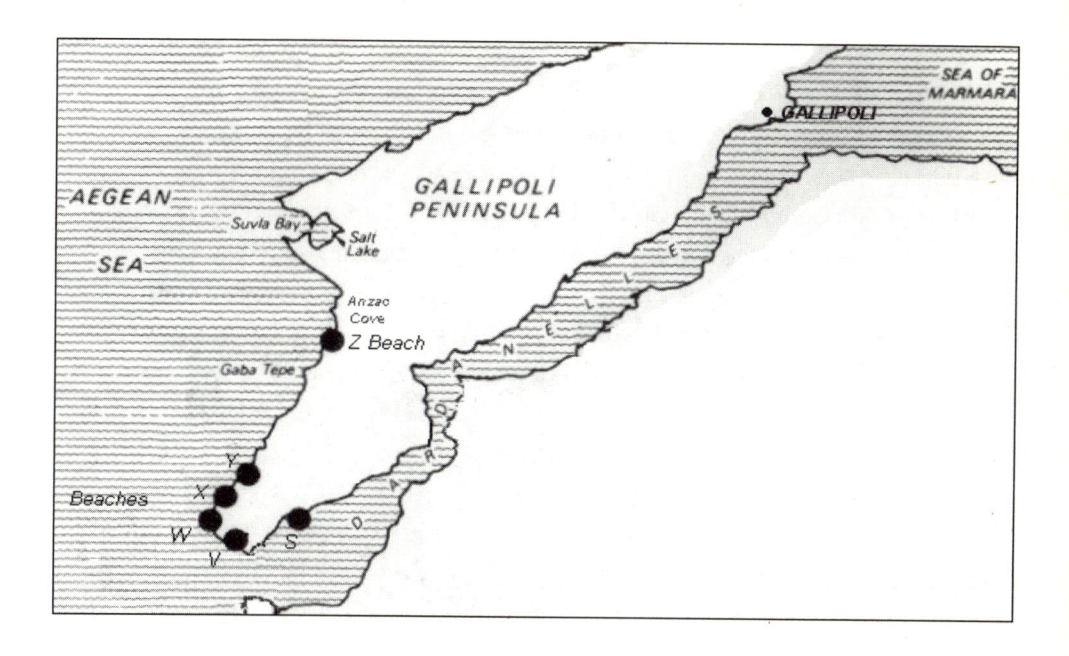

Overlooking V beach was the ancient fortress of Sedd-el-Bahr. The beach was a strip of sand 300 yards in length and about 20 yards wide. Sloping sand dunes formed a half circle around the beach. On the right is the tiny village of Sedd-el-Bahr and an old castle. To the left are steep fifty-foot high cliffs and behind them a fort. Lines of deep trenches ran just under the crest and three rows of strong barbed-wire entanglements reached the waters edge. As one of the most obvious landing places the Turks had not been idle and had prepared strong defensive positions with good fields of fire.

At 0500 the naval bombardment started and continued until the *River Clyde* and the pinnaces were within a mile of the beach. The collier and the pinnaces touched the beach simultaneously at 0625. Then began the horror of V beach. A blizzard of deadly fire swept lighters and the naval party attempting to form the landing bridge. It was a terrible massacre. The Dublins, packed tightly into the cutters, never had a chance. Within minutes almost all were killed or wounded. The navy oarsmen were all hit and the boats drifted helplessly into the unrelenting Turkish fire. Down in the holds the Munsters and the rest of the Dublins could hear the vicious tattoo of bullets against the steel sides. The hinged sides were flung back and they too charged out into the storm of death. Caught in rifle and machine gun fire from the front and both flanks the troops were slaughtered. By now the beach was a harrowing sight. So great was the slaughter that the sea was stained red with blood. Bodies lay four and five deep on the two barges, while the lighters drifted idly, manned only by the dead. All around the ship bodies drifted with the current.

Air Commodore Samson was flying over Sedd-el-Bahr at this time and looking down saw that the calm blue sea was 'absolutely red with blood' for a distance of fifty yards from the shore, 'a horrible sight to see.' Red ripples washed up on the beach, and everywhere the calm surface of the water was whipped up into ghastly discoloured foam by thousands of falling bullets. The expedition commander, General Ian Hamilton, a sensitive writer, was stricken by the horror. He described the sight as 'monstrous; too cold-blooded; like looking at gladiators from the dress-circle.'

From this carnage fourteen Dublins had reached the beach to join about twenty-five Munsters from three companies ordered ashore. They got to the shelter of a little bank on the far side of the beach, and there they huddled while the storm of bullets passed over their heads. Two platoons of Dublins had luckily landed at Camber Beach, just north-east of Sedd-el-Bahr castle, from where they could threaten the Turkish left flank. These few hard-pressed troops remained stranded on the beach until nightfall when the last Munster company and the rest of the troops on board the *River Clyde*, including the company of Dublins, came ashore. The sad task of clearing the gangways and beaches began with the Turkish snipers causing some interference. Gradually, all the wounded were taken to safety and the Turkish resis-

Gallipoli

tance on the stricken beach was beaten down and the landing consolidated. The two Irish battalions had been so decimated they were formed into a single, composite battalion, affectionately known as "The Dubsters." A week later the severity of the casualty rate was evident from the ration return of the Dublins: only 1 officer and 344 other ranks remained out of an original strength of 25 officers and 975 other ranks!

Private Michael Kavanagh, 1st RDF, from Corbans Lane, Naas, was killed on that first day on Gallipoli. So too, was Lance-Corporal Michael Heffernan, 1st RDF, from Eadestown. Twenty-one year old Private Joseph Bermingham, 1st RDF, from Dublin Road, Naas was one of scores wounded on that fateful day. He was transferred to a hospital in Malta where he died from his injuries. Private Thomas Doran, also from the 1st Battn., from the Harbour, Naas, was also wounded and was sent to Exeter Hospital in England to recover. Also wounded were Private Coughlin, Rathasker Road and Private Christopher Pierce, Corbans Lane, Naas.

The SS River Clyde at V Beach during the Gallipoli landings, April 1915.

Gallipoli

Meanwhile the other four landings at Cape Helles had went ahead with much better success. At the fifth landing place, a point called Y beach, about four miles up the coast on the western side of the peninsula, 2,000 men came ashore and climbed up the cliffs without a single shot being fired at them. At the top there was no sign of the enemy at all. While their senior officers strolled about through the scrub inspecting the position the men sat down and brewed themselves a cup of tea. Unknown to them their comrades were being massacred less than an hour's march away. They heard the distant sounds of battle through the clear sunlit air, but without orders they made no move in that direction. Had they but known it these troops at Y beach were equal in numbers to the whole of the Turkish forces in the tip of the peninsula that morning. They could have marched at will and encircled the entire enemy position. By midday they might have cleared the way to Achi Baba and turned a massacre into a brilliant victory. Instead the initiative was lost and with it any hope for a British victory.

An Athy officer in the Naval Service, Dr. P. Burrows Kelly, who took part in the defence of Antwerp and subsequently proceeded to the Dardanelles wrote home describing the landing on V beach. Dr. Kelly was the son of Gilbert Kelly of Athy, Clerk of the Crown and Peace for Queen's County.

"We little expected what we were in for," he said, "as opinion was divided, some saying it was certain death, others saying not a shot would be fired, as nothing could live in the terrible fire of the navy. Anyway, when about 40 yards from the shore, they opened up on us, and such a din of pom-poms and bullets I never want to be in again. The commander went right on and beached us beautifully high and dry. Its this din the guns were playing on the Turks, but could not get the sharpshooters. What followed was a terrible sight. Our men were

Gallipoli

simply butchered, and the water was red with blood and the air boiling with bullets.

"I was far too excited to have any fear, but I made up my mind my hour had come. I next learned that a large shell had gone right through our after hold without exploding, but it killed several. Shortly after one got in the engine room. That ought to have finished us, but did not. All this time our fellows were dropping on their way to the beach, about two to every three. While arranging about a volunteer to assist me in rescuing a poor fellow shot in very narrow water, someone shouted: 'Take cover, you fool.' Almost simultaneously a bullet hit my cap, and one went either side of my head, shaving my ears. As I dropped flat one clipped me on the right shin and another entered my right foot, but came out again.

"I was the first of the staff to go, and was dragged to the chart room. I found I could carry on after being attended to. About 8 a.m. Commander Unwin was carried in, suffering from prolonged immersion and shock and hit badly. I attended him for two hours, and then he got on fresh clothes and returned once more to the beach, though hardly able to walk. All that day I carried on as best I could. At six in the evening there was a lull in the firing, and though we had no food that day we decided to abandon the ship, all the wounded to go back to the ships and everyone else for the shore. The sights on the beach were ghastly, and the day had been a bad one for us."

Several weeks later Dr. Kelly wrote to a friend from Naas, E. L. Gray, again describing the V beach landings and his time in the Dardanelles.

" Dear Gray, seeing the *Kildare Observer* here yesterday reminded me of you, so I decided to write to you, for old times sake. I thought possible you might like some first-hand information.

Gallipoli

" I got out here in March, having spent till then at sea, Antwerp and France. On arrival we were quickly disillusioned as to what was actually happening. Things were about as black as black could be, and nothing but lies been told wholesale. I afterwards volunteered to go as surgeon on '*River Clyde*.' It was a terrible day the 25th April. The immortal 29th Division no longer live to tell the tale, and the Fusilier Brigade - the portion that we took into V Beach - were almost annihilated. I was very lucky. I got hit early in the right leg - nothing much - and then later they pinked me with one in the left foot. I have now a flat foot and no upper teeth, but never felt better in my life. Like all others who have been through the real thing, I want to see the war finished, but only on condition that things are satisfactorily settled, otherwise there can be no peace. The Royal Munsters and Royal Dublins must for ever be immortal after the taking of that V Beach. Our old ship, the '*River Clyde*', is still where we put her on April 25th. I see her every other day. After the landing I was left in Gallipoli till 15th June, and had given up all hope of ever leaving the ruddy place, when suddenly a signal came through that I was to proceed to Madras at once. Life in Gallipoli was extraordinary; heat insufferable, flu's unbearable, and a hellish morning, afternoon and evening 'hate' from a gun called 'Slipper Sian'. He fired from about _____ common, lyddite, shrapnel and high explosive at you. Nobody ever got near to knocking 'Slippery' out.

"The officers and crew of the '*Clyde*', about seventeen all told, as Commander Unwin (Commander Unwin was one of the first ashore from the *River Clyde* and had done everything possible to ensure the landing was a success.) has gone, were on the spot at the tragedy of HMS '*Goliath*' and later when the '*Majestic*' sank like a stone. Both were hopeless dawns. Amongst others and I who saw a lot out here was Major Hutchinson, Munster Fusiliers. He played cricket for Curragh Brigade, Co. Kildare, about '94-'95-'96, with our present

Gallipoli

V Beach, Gallipoli, where the Dublin and Munster Fusiliers were slaughtered.

Admiral de Robeck in the same team. Major Hutchinson came in on the '*River Clyde*' with us. I think he has left to go to France.

"I am afraid all this will bore you very much, but one hears so many tales you get accustomed to boredom. The Turks have played the game, are exceedingly brave, and man for man are our equals, especially since the 29th Division are really no more. I would give words to be home in County Kildare again, and I feel justly proud of the old county now. It has been a great honour to be here serving under Admiral de Robeck. There are a tremendous number of Kildare men serving in the Navy. This ship is a minesweeper, but at present not doing any sweeping. I suppose it will come again later, and then I suppose it's good-bye for ever. There are five naval and two military V.G.'s for the '*Clyde*' - our beach (V) - two naval DSO's and five conspicuous gallantry medals. I need hardly say I am rather lucky and having been will naturally be glad to know what I got one of those DSO's, but I fear it was most undeserved. However, my mother will be delighted and many others in the 'Short Grass', and that's the main thing. I wonder if I'll live to meet you again in the old ground at Naas. Chin Chins, and remember me to all, especially Dr. Murphy."

Gallipoli

On April 26, the day after the landings, the remains of the three regiments at V beach assaulted the heights and under murderous fire captured three lines of trenches, a fortified village and a fort. By April 28 the Allied line stretched across the southern tip of the Peninsula from the Aegean to the Dardanelles. On the night of the April 28/29 the Turks attacked in force inflicting another 2,000 casualties on the 29th Division. A limited advance was made on May 6-8, but, the Turks were heavily reinforced and retained the heights. German submarines worked down the Dardanelles and caused a panic by torpedoing warships and supply vessels, but the situation was saved by moving some of the larger ships to Mudros, 40 miles away, and by constructing anti-submarine defences off the beaches. However, the withdrawal of the warships left the army short of heavy artillery support.

A father and son from Naas were fighting with the 1st RDF on the Peninsula. Nineteen year old Rodney Ahearn, born in Newbridge, joined the army just after the outbreak of the war and went to his father's old regiment, the 1st Dublins. His father, Cork born, Richard Ahearn, was a popular member of the Royal Dublin Fusiliers and was a veteran of the Boer War. Richard Ahearn had left the army and was working in Newbridge Post Office, but immediately volunteered for active service when the war began. He rejoined his old comrades in the 1st Dublins. He was very anxious to meet his son, and although both were in Alexandria, in Egypt, for some hours at the same time, in their different companies, they did not meet. Both were also in the fighting line at the same time, but again, they did not meet. Drummer Rodney Ahearn was wounded in the foot on June 18 and was sent to a convalescent hospital in Port Said, from where he wrote to his mother, who now resided in Newbridge. "So I think I have escaped very lucky, as I think I am one of the last of the old 1st battalion to leave the trenches. It is terrible the cutting up the battalion has got - in fact, the whole division. Each time there has been anything on the mat we have been there, so I think it is very near time that they gave us a rest,

Gallipoli

but there is no such thing. There is no rest or playing football, as there is on the other side. It is a break to get away for a few days after being two months "on the go" day and night. I have been expecting one every day as I should like to know if my father is on his way out, as I have not heard of him."

Drummer Ahearn made a quick recovery from his first wound and was soon back in the firing line. He was again wounded in the fierce fighting, but this time was not so lucky. His mother received a War Office notification that he had "died from wounds."

While Kildaremen continued fighting with the regular battalions who had gained a foothold on the Gallipoli beachhead more were on their way with the new units joining the battle, among them the first Irish division in the British Army - the 10th (Irish) Division. On August 11 1914 a proclamation was issued asking for an immediate addition of 100,000 men to the Regular Army. Six divisions formed the First New Army, among them the 10th (Irish) Division, raised in Ireland in late August. The infantry of the Division comprised of service battalions of all the Irish line regiments - Leinsters, Connaught Rangers, Irish Rifles, Dublin, Inniskilling, Munster and Irish Fusiliers.

By July it was clear the original Allied plan was not working. The natural strength of the Turkish positions, plus their fortifications made frontal assault impossible. General Hamilton devised new plans for more landings twelve miles north of Anzac Cove at Suvla Bay. The landings would coincide with a breakout from the Anzac beach-head. The sea assaults were to be carried out by four divisions, two of them New Army.

The August landings on Gallipoli were designed to break the deadlock and called for surprise landings at Suvla Bay and an all-out attack on Sari Bair. Two planned subsidiary land attacks, at Helles and

Gallipoli

Anzac, were designed to fix the Turkish reserves. Like the initial landings the plans were brilliant in some respects. Again, like the initial landings, the plans did not work out. The offensive relied too heavily on inexperienced troops attacking easily defended dominating heights and made too small allowances for the harsh terrain, heat fatigue, inadequate transport and water supply and lack of artillery support.

On August 7 the 10th Division, less 29th Brigade, landed at Suvla. As the sun rose, the Turkish batteries opened fire and struck the leading elements of 10th Division. In one boat, eighteen men of 7th Dublins were killed or wounded. It was a foretaste of what was to come. The fighting on Gallipoli was particularly savage. Units were pushed into the firing-line, withdrawn for a few hours' sleep, and then sent back to the battlefield once more. It was an exhausting and deadly routine and casualties were heavy and continuous. There were no safe areas on the peninsula. Troops coming to and from the front line were constantly under shell and sniper fire. Even the wounded waiting to be evacuated were not safe. Sheltered accommodation was scarce and many lay in the sun exposed to shell fire and the never ending heat. Thousands of Irishmen died here in battles for forgotten hills and wells. An untold number, possibly a high proportion of 'missing believed killed,' died of wounds or thirst, alone in the scrub or down deep gullies and ravines. Among the 'missing in action' was Private Murtagh Donohoe from New Row, Naas, serving with B Company, 7th Battn. RDF.

Another Naas man, Sergeant-Major John Campbell, of 2 Jubilee Terrace, described the hellish conditions on Gallipoli in letters to his wife. Campbell had served 21 years with the 1st Battalion, RDF., during which time he was through the Mashonland campaign and three years in the South African War. At the outbreak of war he rejoined his regiment and was made Sergeant-Major of the 6th Battalion, RDF. He

Gallipoli

landed at Suvla Bay with his regiment in reserve. On August 15, Lady Day in Ireland, the 6th Dublins, along with the 6th Munsters, were involved in one of the most spectacular attacks on Gallipoli when in a bayonet charge they cleared the heavily defended northern stretch of Kiretch Tepe Sirt ridge.

"It is three weeks today since we landed," Campbell wrote, "and every day since we have been fighting. The fighting here is very fierce and continuous. However, we are making some headway. There are a great many you know have passed away. However, that is all in a day's work and 'who dies when England lives.' The fact remains, the Battalion has suffered heavily, but although there is never a day passes but that we fill in our own casualties, the spirit of the regiment is still strong and anxious to fight until a decision is reached.

"Don't listen to any carpers about sickness - there is none to speak of, and a better lot of NCO's and men I have never come in contact with. They are all anxious and willing to do anything to help me, or to forward the Battalion in the fight. Of course, when I speak of the Battalion I want you to realise that the other Battalions of the Brigade have taken 'their medicine' as well as us, and there is nobody idle here. You know there is no place like the field for making men show the best that is in him, and no matter what the greatest respect and admiration for the fighting qualities of the Turks, I could dilate on the landing under shell fire, and mad rushes uphill to take trenches with shells bursting all around us.

" The news should be coming through of the fighting we have been doing, and no doubt the names of casualties. All the Roman Catholics have got Absolution and Holy Communion from Father Murphy. I was amongst the number, and that should please you."

Father Murphy, chaplain of the 7th Dublins, had said mass and

Gallipoli

gave general absolution in the open air on August 15 before the attack on Kiretch Tepe Sirt. Canon Maclean also celebrated Holy Communion for Protestants in a marquee.

Corporal Ronald Semmence, 6th Battn. RDF, was wounded after the landing at Suvla Bay. Twenty-one year old Semmence joined the Dubs from the clerical staff of the County Kildare Insurance Society and had previously worked for the *Kildare Observer*. He lived at Greenmount Cottages, Naas, with his parents. Semmence landed with his battalion and immediately came under shell fire. "I confess I felt rather queer and nervous. When the shrapnel first began to whiz over our heads, and used to duck my head instinctively when I heard it coming along." The 6th RDF spent the next two days in support, bringing up stores and ammunition. On the Monday after the landing the battalion went into the line and Corporal Semmence saw action on and off until he was wounded and evacuated to Cairo. He takes up the narrative for his last day on the peninsula.

"While I was taking back a fellow named Barrett a shell whizzed by my head. That fairly brought me to my senses. I brought my man back some distance and told him I would have to leave him, but he seemed terrified. He was wounded, and I could appreciate his fear some time afterwards when I was hit myself. My real nervousness commenced then for fear I would get hit a second time. Barrett asked me to bring him back to the first dressing station, which I did. Here I met Jim Robinson (another Naas man, who was wounded two weeks later). Robinson brought down a chap named Rothwell, who is now in Naas barracks.

"The Dublins retired and took up a position on the right of the Queen's and entrenched. I then joined my own battalion, but there were only 20 or 30 of us altogether. The others had got mixed with other regiments in retreat, but many of them had fallen in the fight, as

Gallipoli

you will realise from the fact that of our total strength of about 700, we lost 300 that day. We were joined afterwards by A Company of the Dublins who, I heard, had done good work in charging the hill. Captain Preston, who was afterwards killed was recommended for his bravery in leading them.

Photo: P. GOREY.

Pte. Paddy Gorey, RDF, from Lullymore, Rathangan, a veteran of Gallipoli.

Gallipoli

"For the greater part of the evening firing was kept up at intervals, but there was no counter-attack, and we occupied the same trench the whole of the next day. On our right there was considerable excitement, and we learned that the Gurkhas were in action. Our attention was attracted during the evening by the bugles blowing 'Cease fire and come for orders', but we were told to take no notice of it, as the call came from the Turks. There was an unending stream of fellows from all battalions making their way about this time to a small trickle of water, and to see the crowds waiting for their turn to get at the little trickle, for sorely needed water, reminded one of 'early doors' at some big play. Turks directed their fire towards this and another well further on, and many a poor fellow lost his life in trying to get water to quench his thirst. That evening we left these trenches and took up position more to the right in front of 7th Battalion, who were in support of us. While here I heard a familiar voice wih a Northern accent in the trench of the 7th and found it was 'Fatty' Clements (a Private in the 7th, who volunteered from the Naas branch of the Ulster Bank). We held on to the trench for a couple of days. A Sergeant and I spent a most enjoyable time sniping. About a thousand yards away there was a Turk who offered a most tempting target. He coolly walked out into the open and surveyed his surroundings. He took not the slightest notice of our bullets, some of which struck the ground quite close to him, as the man with the glass told us. Walking back to where he came from he was joined by another, and the two walked off. We did our best to 'pot' them, but the range was long and we failed. While we were engaged at this 'sport', taking the range in turn, a chap named Myles, when putting his head up to take his range, got a bullet through the brain.

"In this trench from which we were firing there was a most horrible smell owing to the Turks having buried their dead close by. Word came up that we were to be relieved for a welcome 48 hours' rest. We

Gallipoli

were fairly beaten up, and back we started by the Salt Lake with the 7th Battalion. We seemed to have lost our direction, however, going back to the base, and there was little chance of our getting there before dawn. Lots of the fellows were so dead fagged that they were unable to continue, and threw themselves down to rest. We eventually got to the base and had a welcome 'dip' - the first since we landed. We had to come back again then to wake the fellows up that had fallen behind or missed their way. I was one of the NCO's who went back, and I actually found one fellow lying on his back, asleep, with his eyes open. I never saw anything like it, and I honestly believe he was too tired to close his eyes. You may laugh, but the weariness of some of the fellows was something terrible.

"A couple of hours after we had come to rest a telegram arrived from General Sir Bryan Mahon (Commander of the 10th Division) saying we were to fall in immediately and to join the 54th Brigade. In the telegram the General said he recognised the amount of work we had done and thanked us. We took up our position as ordered and remained there until Sunday. All we had to do there was to put our patrols and sentry guards at night. We were instructed on no account to fire should the Turks show themselves, but simply to bayonet them.

"It was on this Sunday we had our first Church service, Father Murphy saying Mass, That day our artillery from the boats started a bombardment and we ordered to fall in and act as flank guards. We advanced along the hill on which we had been posted. The Turks had a trench at the other end of it and kept up a steady fire on us. Our torpedo boats from the sea were bombarding the trench. These Turks can shoot, I tell you. They are fine marksmen. As we advanced, getting what cover we could, bullets struck patches of earth where some of our fellows stood a second before. About 4 o'clock we were about three-quarters of the way up the hill - the Dublins, Munsters and Inniskillings, with sadly depleted ranks. Captain Preston kept urging

Gallipoli

our fellows on and inspired all who were near him with confidence. As we advanced some hand bombs exploded quite near us, and we knew then we were near the Turkish trench. There was a shout of 'Charge!' and we raced to the top of the hill. On the other side at the top was a trench occupied by about 20 Turks. Immediately they saw us they threw down their rifles, jumped out of the trench and ran to us shaking hands with us. We took them prisoner and passed them on to the fellows in reserve. From the top of the hill we saw a fine sight where our fellows had dislodged the Turks, who were running away. We only awaited the word to be down in the thick of the fun, but the word did not come, and we started firing at them from the top of the hill. Immediately we took the trench a great cheer broke from the fellows below, and also from the 'Tars' on the torpedo boat. Just then word came along that Captain Preston had been badly wounded with a piece of shell in the stomach.

"I knelt on my right knee and started to fire at the Turks below. I found my range - 200 yards - was short and altered it to 300 yards, which was right. I was taking my third shot at 300 yards when I got a bullet through the knee. I rolled over on my back and was attended to by a Sergeant. Sergeant Major Campbell (Naas), now Lieut. Campbell, had me put on a stretcher and got me carried down to Battalion headquarters. On our way down we passed the 7th Battalion, and my stretcher bearers asking the way down the answer came from 'Fatty' Clements, who was at this time acting as stretcher bearer also. I recognised him and he came over to my stretcher. He noticed what I did not know before - that there was blood on my right leg where the bullet had passed through, having gone through my left knee. This wound he dressed, and we parted. It took four hours for my bearers to take me to where my wounds were properly seen to. I had the first good nights sleep I had for ten days under a blanket.

"Next morning I was brought to a clearing station, and as four of

Gallipoli

us lay outside it on stretchers the Turkish guns were throwing shells close to us. I crept off the stretcher and sheltered behind a boulder until I was taken to the boat for Cairo that afternoon."

An unnamed 'old tough' of Naas, gave this account of the landings at Suvla Bay. "On the evening of 6th August we set sail from an island in the Aegean Sea, after a dreary wait, and heartily sick of the rather uneventful voyage from dear old England (even England was a home after we left the Emerald Isle)."

With the 7th Dublins he was put ashore at Suvla. "Our boat grounded. With a cheer and shout to "Jack" to "send it into 'em'," the boys leaped , lighting ashore on the shingle, loaded with ammunition, three days' rations and packs, and dashed up to cover under the headland which afforded perfect shelter. This headland formed the right hand promontory of Suvla Bay, looking landward from the sea.

"Our platoon was detailed to remove the reserve stores, ammunitions, etc., from the boat and this was accomplished without a single casualty, though the sea all around the boat was whipped white with foam from the descending shrapnel bullets. After a short rest of about half an hour we crossed the headland and advanced along the beach of Suvla Bay. Half way, we divested ourselves of our packs and what a relief too! The sun was getting up and the heat was intense. All the while the enemy kept up a steady and incessant shrapnel fire, but our ships soon located their batteries and silenced them one by one. The wily Turk had something else in store for us, for as we approached the 'Causeway' (a muddy passage through which the overflow of water that covers the salt lake in the rainy season and flows into the sea, but was now soft sand that covers its bed). They hurled a perfect hail of high explosive shells from their big guns which ploughed deep into that muddy swamp. We had to cross the 'causeway'- Providence was

Gallipoli

on our side, for many shells failed to explode. However, we lost many in that mad race across that 30 or 40 yards of mud and swamp.

The 'old tough' was wounded in the fighting on August 8. "It was about two hours before dawn, and across the Salt Lake once more we moved. Almost across, and one of our chaps was careless enough to forget putting his safety catch to the rear and a round went off accidentally and a chap in the front of him got hit. Immediately after this report the bullets came hissing and whistling over our heads and we obtained shelter under the ridge. Here we received our orders; we were to act as support to the … Brigade and attack Chocolate Hill. Amidst a storm of shrapnel, high explosives and bullets we advanced at a double across the bushy and uneven plain, and we were soon in the thick of it. The country we were covering was a wilderness, intersected by numerous gullies here and there a cornfield with crops in stacks, but the greater part was barren rock thick with scrub which our enemies made the most of. All around men fell like corn before a scythe. On we went; I got detached from my battalion among two battalions that were forced to retire. We rallied and recaptured a trench. An officer (wounded) of the Staffords took command; also an NCO of the Royal Irish, who worked like heroes. The officer's trouble did not end with his first wound, and we forced him to go back and be seen to, and send us reinforcements. This he reluctantly did and another officer coming up, took charge. I took charge of a mixed lot and got orders to advance a half-left to check an advance of the enemy that were outflanking us and sending across a destructive enfilade fire. After a few adventures and narrow shaves we got in touch with the enemy and got them on the move over the hill and down to the railway. It was here I "stopped one". I shall ever remember that brave Stafford officer and Irish Fusiliers NCO. I was proud of being Irish then. When I got hit I thought it was all over. My bandage was used on the officer and I was alone, for the Turks had got reinforcements and forced the boys back. But over rushed the bravest man I ever

Gallipoli

met, I beleve he was a Stafford, and rushed up to me with a shout, "Come along, I won't leave you." He fixed me up, but a machine gun got him and "winged" both his legs - the fix was complete. It was now my turn to patch him up while he pumped bullets into the on-coming Turks. He held them back, and we got back yard by yard, blazing away all the while for dear life. He never uttered a groan as I dragged him through the undergrowth. God and nature of the ground saved us. We got back safely, but not before the poor chap got another in the shoulder, which I did not discover till I put him on a stretcher and had him sent down. I never saw him after that nor, I suppose, never shall again, but God bless him! I got down to the beach without much incident."

While the rest of the 10th Division fought at Suvla, the 29th Brigade was landed at Anzac. The 29th Brigade consisted of 5th Connaught Rangers, 6th Leinsters, 6th Irish Rifles and 10th Hampshires. The 29th Brigade were concentrated in the area around Shrapnel Gully and was involved in the battles for Sari Bair and a stronghold known as the Farm. Corporal Patrick Nolan, from Derryoughta, Monasterevan fought with the 5th Connaught Rangers in Gallipoli. He was in the reserve at the outbreak of the war and was called up soon afterwards. He landed at Anzac on August 27, just in time for the Rangers first attack on the Kabak Kuyu wells and Hill 60. It was Private Nolan's first experience of the Dardanelles fighting. The Rangers along with the Australian and New Zealander units attacked Hill 60 in a bayonet charge, described by the tough Aussies as 'the finest they had ever seen.' Of the barely 1,000 men involved in the attack, only 300 escaped unwounded. Nolan said he did not know how he escaped, as his comrades were shot down in scores all around him. Of the 250 Connaught Rangers involved in the action, only less than 100 remained unwounded and almost all of these had some form of gastric complaint. Two days after the charge the Rangers took three snipers prisoners and these turned out to be females.

Gallipoli

These attacks were virtually the end of the offensive operations at Gallipoli. From the end of August onwards the Allies were content to hold their positions. Following the failure of the August offensives the men of the 10th Division, at Suvla and Anzac, settled down to the monotony of line duty and fatigues. Still, no place was safe on the peninsula and the Irishmen continued to take casualties. "Do not assume because it is Sunday the work is knocked off," Sgt-Major Campbell wrote. "Fighting is proceeding briskly as usual, and there is no questioning that the Turk is a brave fighter; however, he has met his master in us. The issue cannot be long in doubt. The battalion is growing smaller and the old faces are disappearing daily, but you will always remember that whatever comes or goes, I at all times showed a good soldierly example."

One veteran whose loss was felt was Sergeant William Cooke, 1st RDF, a native of Kilcullen. The gallant sergeant whose exploits in France and Flanders were published from time to time and whose heroism was the talk of all Irish soldiers was killed in action on the peninsula on October 3. For a single act of gallantry in France at the beginning of 1915, when Sgt. Cooke disposed of ten Germans single-handed, he was awarded the Distinguished Conduct Medal. Sergt. Cooke had perched himself on top of a farmhouse from where he could look down upon the German trenches. In one of them he saw an officer and ten men crawling along. He picked off the men one by one, then hurrying from his position, he ran into the other end of the trench, and levelling his rifle at the astonished Lieutenant, shouted "Hands up!" Sergt. Cooke walked back to his own lines with his shocked prisoner. He was wounded and gassed in May 1915 and sent back home to recuperate. The heroic sergeant jumped at the opportunity to return to the fightng after his wounds healed and he was sent to Gallipoli, as a replacement, as the hot climate was deemed better for his lungs.

Gallipoli

Conditions on the Gallipoli peninsula were harsh. The terrain was dusty, rocky and hard to dig. Thirst was one of the worst enemies. There were not enough ships to supply the huge amount of water needed as the Turks had control of all the wells. A quarter of the fighting men on the Peninsula had to be used as water carriers to and from the beaches at night. By day the men were exposed to the heat and tormented by flies. Slightest movement brought snipers' fire upon them. Whether in or out of the line, nowhere was safe from the Turkish fire. At least on the Western Front when regiments were withdrawn from the line they were out of harms way. There was no such respite on Gallipoli. Even a dip in the cool Aegean was not safe, as the Turks often dropped shells on groups of swimmers. The heat and the food, salty bully beef and hard biscuit, brought on dysentery and enteric fever. Sickness began to take its toll on the troops, who were wore down from constant fighting and lack of decent food and rest.

In September, reinforcements for the battered Irish regiments arrived. Some of them were recovered wounded from the battles in France and these were particularly welcome as they included excellent combat-hardened regular soldiers. On September 17 the 10th Division was ordered to leave the Gallipoli peninsula. Behind them they left thousands of other Irishmen who fought until the evacuation of the expeditionary force in December and January of the following year. The 29th Division was brought round from Helles to Suvla but the British Government had lost faith in the venture and prepared to evacuate. The evacuation went off smoothly, mostly at night. On the night of January 8 1916 the last troops left under cover of a storm. The next morning the Turks found the Allied trenches empty. The ill-fated Gallipoli campaign, which had achieved nothing, was over.

The cost to the Allies was enormous, around 200,000 killed, wounded and missing. The 10th Division lost 2,017 Killed in Action and Died of Wounds while the three regular battalions of the 29th

Division lost another 1,394 Killed in Action, a total of 3,411. When the Mediterranean Expeditionary Force was withdrawn from the Peninsula in January 1916, only 11 men remained of the original 1st Battn., RDF, who had landed on April 25 1915.

The Irishmen in the 10th Division had scarcely time to rest and recuperate when their services were called on again. Bulgaria had entered the war on the side of Germany and with Austria began preparations to invade Serbia. The British and French promptly sent troops, partly drawn from the force at Gallipoli, to Serbia's assistance. The campaign which ensued was to be one of the most pointless and frustrating of the war. Serbia was quickly disposed of by a converging attack and in November the Bulgarians attacked the British and French lines around Kosturino. The fighting in terrible winter conditions was savage. Cpl. Patrick Nolan, of Monasterevan, a veteran of Gallipoli, was with his battalion, 5th Connaught Rangers, in Serbia. On October 6 his regiment, as part of the 10th Division, was ordered to Serbia. They landed at Salonika in Greece and crossed into Serbia taking up positions on a line from Kosturino to the shores of Lake Doiran. The Rangers line was in a rough hill-top country broken by deep gullies, barren rock and with little vegetation. Cold rain and blizzards struck the Balkans and the exposed infantrymen, their health already undermined by the conditions on Gallipoli, deteriorated. Hundreds collapsed from frostbite and exposure. Then, the fierce Bulgarians attacked. The Rangers fought for seven days side by side with the Munsters, Leinsters and Dublins. While there Cpl. Nolan fought continually for nine days without any sleep, with the exception of a few odd moments. There was constant snow and frost throughout the fighting and they suffered very much in consequence.

In describing a retreat amongst the hills in Serbia, Cpl Nolan said that the retreat was fast enough at one stage, when they were hurriedly ordered to retire owing to an attack by overwhelming masses of

Gallipoli

Bulgarians, "but having been reinforced, the Munster and Leinsters were goad to avenge the death of so many of their fellow-chums, and when we got the order to again charge, the dash back to the attack of the Munsters and Leinsters was a spiriting one. There were a few Queen's Co. and Kildare boys in the charge and I can assure you, as far as the boys were concerned, the pace was as hard as we ever saw at the old Vicarstown sports." Cpl. Nolan was wounded twice in the fighting and was recommended for his brave conduct in the Serbian campaign, where he was promoted corporal on the field.

Another local man mentioned for bravery was Private William Scully of Town Hall, Naas, serving with the Army Ordinance Corps. Private Scully was awarded the Gold Medal by the King of Serbia in recognition of his distinguished service during the Serbian campaign. The Gold Medal carried with it a gratuity of £10. Private Scully was the second eldest son of Warrant-Officer Scully, Durham Light Infantry and had two other brothers on active service.

CHAPTER 4

The Green Fields of France

The war dragged on into 1915 with no great change in the situation. All up and down the Western Front the trench system was transformed, of necessity, into a permanent labyrinth as the Allies and the Germans settled into a stalemate which neither side could break. The front line ran from Nieuport in Belgium to Alsace-Lorraine. Some sections of trenches were quite deep and had elaborate living quarters. However, trenches were mostly a little over two metres deep and a little less than two metres wide. The sides were supported by sandbags. A raised section or parapet of sandbags at the front gave an overall depth of about three metres to a trench. (Contrary to belief trenches did not run straight for more than four yards as they were 'traversed' to prevent enfilade and shell fire having much effect.) The lines consisted of three parallel trenches, a front line trench, a centre line trench and a reserve trench all linked by communications trenches. The reserve trench was usually out of enemy range. A 'firestep' was built to allow soldiers to shoot over the top of the trench. At the back a 'dugout' provided a small room-like shelter. The bottom of the trench was usually lined with wooden planks called

The Green Fields of France

'duckboards'. The front of the trenches was protected by rows of barbed wire. The ground between rival trenches was known as 'no-man's land' and was littered with shell-holes and, after a while, rotting bodies of unclaimed dead soldiers.

Troops usually spent eight days in the front line trenches followed by four days in the reserve trenches. They developed 'trench foot' and 'trench fever' from standing in wet and muddy trenches. Lice, mites, flies and rats continually irritated the men. Many suffered from 'shell-shock', and developed stammers and uncontrollable nervous reactions, and even went mad. These men were often harshly treated and sent back into the line. There was very little sympathy from the top brass for men in the front lines. The food was monotonous - a diet of bread, biscuits and tinned corned beef called 'bully beef'. The days passed with regular monotony punctuated by violent bursts of combat, patrolling, raids, artillery barrages and full-scale attacks. Entertainment in the trenches consisted of the usual soldiers pasttimes of cards, storytelling and singing such fatalistic songs as 'Hanging on The Old Barbed Wire.'

'If you want to find the old battalion,
I know where they are, I know where they are,
If you want to find the old battalion,
I know where they are,
They're hanging on the old barbed wire,
I've seen 'em, I've seen 'em,
Hanging on the old barbed wire,
I've seen 'em,
Hanging on the old barbed wire.'

For the first three months of the new year the 2nd Royal Dublin Fusiliers were near the French village of Nieppe, moving up to the front line and back again into reserve with monotonous regularity. The

The Green Fields of France

official history states: "... one reads daily in the war diary of heavy shelling, of intermittent sniping, of reports that the enemy has been heard engaged in mining: but of major operations of any kind there is no mention." On February 16 Private John McCormack, G Company, 2nd RDF, from Monasterevan, was killed in action. He was buried with three other comrades killed in the preceding days. Pte. Christopher Rogers, Dublin, was killed on February 13. The next day Pte. Austin Delaney, also of Dublin, died, followed by Pte. Joseph Brennan, from Edenderry, on the 15th and John McCormack on the 16th. These four men were buried beside each other and after the war were reinterred together in Prowse Point Military Cemetery in Belgium.

In early 1915 the British and French made a number of attempts at breaking through the German lines. They gained a few miles at Neuve-Chapelle, but casualties were very heavy. In the Spring of 1915 the Germans employed a new weapon in an attempt to break the deadlock in the trenches. On April 22 the British and French positions at Ypres were hit by a cloud of xylyl bromide, a tear gas, which threatened devastating results. As the cloud of gas descended on the unsuspecting British and French lines the Germans advanced behind it to capture Ypres. The British and French abandoned their trenches and soon, almost everywhere Allied soldiers were streaming to the rear, tearing at their collars and gasping and choking for breath. Hastily reinforcements were rushed to the front and a crisis was averted. The Germans were beaten back, but trench warfare had now entered a new era. New weapons were arriving on the scene regularly; grenades, trench mortars, flare pistols, flame throwers, barbed wire, periscopes and the steel helmet.

The Allies were unprepared for gas attacks and suffered hundreds of casualties until gas masks were issued to front-line troops. Next to machine gun fire gas proved to be the biggest killer of the war. A letter taken from the *Leinster Leader* dated May 15 1915 describes the

The Green Fields of France

horrors of a gas attack. An unnamed officer of the 2nd Royal Dublin Fusiliers sent back this vivid account of his regiment's part in the fighting in Flanders and mentioned that heroic of Kildare men, Corporal Cooke from Kilcullen.

William Cooke, pictured with his mother and sister.

Photo: T. TRACEY.

The Green Fields of France

"4th May - My birthday, and a very noisy one but I don't know what it is all about as we came out of the trenches early this morning after a pretty severe time - viz., a pitched battle. We were nine days on the ground where we dug but we got a bit of our own back on Sunday. At about 5 p.m. the Germans bombarded us with gun fire and poisonous gas, a thick, yellow-greenish vapour, and then rattled the top of the parapet with machine gun fire. The gas was pretty awful, but in our most important front trench we were able to stick it. All the officers shouted along the line to stick handkerchiefs and rags in water and put them over the mouth and nose. The whole thing came absolutely suddenly, and, as the Germans could not advance for five minutes in fear of their own poisonous gas, we were able to pull ourselves together, although it was pretty awful, and fairly got into one's lungs. When the Germans did advance we were ready for them with machine guns and rifle fire, and they suffered heavily. About midnight they came forward again, and we had great shooting at close range. At first I would not believe that there was an attack, but a flare went up, and I saw bodies within twenty or thirty yards of us. We considered that where they were dead men there must be live ones, so we blazed away. We counted nine bodies just in front, and brought in two wounded who were yelling on the ground: how many there were further off we could not tell.

"There is one man with us - one Corporal Cook(e), from Kilcullen - an absolute marvel when any fighting is on: he is all over the place, and will patrol anywhere. During the fight on Sunday he made off to an old building, and got upstairs and reported movements of Germans - and got about 12 himself. They advanced in file up a ditch straight at him; so he took the furthest first, and did for about the lot in turn. Then he came running back to me more or less in the open, and it was the only time I have seen him excited. He was beaming all over, and described the affair and said: 'I fairly cut the legs off them.' Then back with him, and in about 15 minutes he returned with a

The Green Fields of France

German officer as prisoner. He spotted him from upstairs hiding in a ditch, came down and got round to the back of him, and gave the 'Hands up!' I took his bayonet from him, which I am sending to_____, with three helmets. If you do not want them all, you could send it to Kilcullen. The men got a lot of things - one man an Iron Cross.

"It was a hot shop out there. We had one death from gas - chiefly, I think, because some men lie down when anything goes wrong. The gas is far worse near the ground, and, if you stand up, you get a bit of fresh air over the parapet. Sergeant Burke is all right - pretty lucky, I fancy, as his company suffered a good bit. Our casualties throughout the whole nine days are, I think, eight officers killed and ten officers wounded, or about 100 N.C. officers and men, or more. We treat our prisoners very well; brutes as the Germans are, one is sorry for them. In a way they are only sheep - the bosses are the ones to get hold of. Horrible as it may sound, one could not help laughing at a description Cook(e) gave of his patrolling. He has a sort of stammer, and he said - 'you see, when I am out in front and I have any signs of the Germans, I take cover behind a body. But these young fellows won't do it - say it makes them sick'."

Sergeant Cooke was awarded the Distinguished Conduct Medal for the capture of the German patrol and relating the incident he said that at St. Julien the enemy commenced to 'gas' them, and he said to his officers they would surely attack under cover of the cloud of gas, some 20 feet high, which was approaching them. He then crept out to the farmhouse for the purpose of watching the enemies movements, and from the roof saw about a dozen Germans advancing up the laneway towards the houses. He opened fire, taking first the furthermost man, and succeeded in 'bagging' the lot. "They came in force," he said, " and I got a young chap named Maloney to get the machine

The Green Fields of France

gun into the lower part of the house. I remained on the roof directing the fire and the gun simply mowed them down. On leaving the roof I observed a German officer crouching beside a ditch, and advancing on him with my rifle presented, I took him completely by surprise, and he surrendered and I brought him back to our lines." Sgt. Cooke was wounded on the side of the head by a bullet on May 10 and was also affected by gas poisoning. William Cooke also won the Medal of St. George, 2nd Class. His brother, Corporal John Cooke was serving with the 2nd Battn., Irish Guards. (Cpl. John Cooke died of wounds on July 31 1917. He was aged 30 and holder of the 1914 Star.)

Death by gassing was an unpleasant experience and could take days, and sometimes weeks before a victim would succumb. Private Edward Moran, of Kilcock, died on May 22, five days after he was picked up on the battlefield in France. A victim of asphyxiating gas, it took the young private five torturous days to die. Several more of his countymen became casualties during the Spring fighting.

Sergeant P. Dempsey, of Celbridge, serving with the Royal Dublin Fusiliers, was killed in April in the fighting around Ypres. Sergeant Dempsey had only recently gained promotion on the battlefield. Three brothers from Monasterevan were invalided home after the Spring battles. Privates Jack, Martin and Joseph Kelly of Mary's Lane, Monasterevan, all of the Connaught Rangers, returned home wounded. A fourth brother, Thomas, serving with the Leinster Regiment had also been wounded, while a fifth brother, Michael, serving with the R.G.A., was still at the front. Joseph Kelly had a miraculous escape from death by the bullet which invalided him. It entered his shoulder, passing behind his ear where it was deflected by a bone and exited through his eye. Private James Brown, Irish Guards, was not so fortunate. The twenty year old from Basin Street, Naas, had only been a short time at the front when he was mortally wounded. Sergeant W. J.

The Green Fields of France

Masterson, also of Naas, was killed at Ypres while leading his platoon on a charge. Sergt. Masterson, 1st Blackwatch, had been wounded the previous November and had returned to the front in January. Lieutenant N. C. Hannon, one of four brothers from Athy in the service, was killed on April 16 in fierce fighting at Festubert. Lieut. Hannon was only 20 years of age and was at the front for three months, having taken part in several engagements with his battalion, 7th King's Liverpool Regiment. He was the youngest son of Mr. John A. Hannon, Ardreigh House, Athy. He had a brilliant college career, having entered Trinity from High School, Dublin, in June 1913, and in the following October obtained a school exibition in classical honours. He joined the Officers' Training Corps, from which he received a commission in the Liverpool Regiment in August. A brother of his, Lieut. J.C. Hannon, was in the 3rd Battalion of the same regiment.

Private E. Lynch, D Company, King's Liverpool Regt., wrote home,- "It is my duty to write and inform you of Lieut. Hannon's death. I was his servant, and a better and kinder master one could not wish for. He entrusted me with the enclosed letters with instructions to send them to you if anything happened. He went into the charge full of dash and vigour, but alas! He never reached the German lines. He was shot in the stomach and died crying to his men "Go on and win." He was a hero, and was loved and respected by all his men. All assisted at his burial. He is interred behind the firing line, and his grave is marked with a cross. With deepest sympathy for your great loss."

Andrew Delaney of Crookstown died on May 31 from that most evil weapon of the war - poison gas. Pte. Delaney had enlisted in Naas at the age of twenty, joining the Dublin Fusiliers just in time for the Boer War in South Africa. He later served in the East Indies and Aden and after his discharge he continued on the reserve until he was called up at the outbreak of war. As a member of the Royal Army Medical Corps he was gassed during the Spring battles. He was shipped back

The Green Fields of France

from France to a military hospital in Netley, England. He hardly realised that death was but hours away when on May 28 he penned this poignant postcard to his wife:

Victoria Hospital,
Netley.

Mrs. A. Delaney, Ballitore.

Dear wife,
I have arrived safe here in England and feel not as bad as I was. Write me a note as soon as you get this. Send nothing,

Your loving husband,
Andrew.

But the postcard which would have brought relief to Mrs. Delaney, waiting like so many soldier's wives, was overtaken by a grimmer message:

Telegram: 31 May 1915.
From: Officer Commanding, Netley Military Hospital.
To: Mrs A. Delaney, Ballitore.
Regret No. 2922 Private Andrew Delaney died here today from acute bronchitis due to gas poisoning.

Andrew Delaney was brought back to Crookstown to be buried. His death did nothing to slow down recruiting in Kildare and did not deter the young men of the area from answering Kitchener's call. Throughout 1915 the Co. Kildare Recruiting Committee was busy holding meetings with the object of securing recruits for the army. The

The Green Fields of France

Kildare Observer reported that over 400 men had gone into the ranks from Athy. In Robertstown, according to the October edition, fifty-four men had joined up. The village with a population of 2,400 had given more men to the colours than any other rural district of its size and population, the paper claimed. By June 1916 Celbridge reported 203 men serving while the previous April a report gave the names of 197 men who had enlisted from Naas and a week later another 40 names were added. (This was apart from those who had joined before the war started or were already serving). Below are extracts from the *Observer*.

NAAS ROLL OF HONOUR

In addition to the list of 197 Naas men whose names appeared in our last issue as having joined the colours since the outbreak of war, we have received the following which were omitted and have forwarded them to the Controller of Recruitment for the county;

B - Baldry, F., RDF; Butler, James, Machine Gun Corps; Bermingham, Joseph, RDF (killed); Byrne, Laurence, East Lancs; Byrne, Thomas, ASC; Boyhan, 2nd Lieut. T.F., RIR; Brooks, J., RFA; Burke, James, RFG; Bermingham, Patrick, RDF.

C - Chanler, John, Canadians.

H - Hale, -, Royal Flying Corps; Hanlon, Denis, RDF; Harris, Samuel, RDF; Harrington, T., Irish Guards; Hickey, Patrick, Irish Guards.

K - Kelly, Martin, Connaught Rangers; Keaveny, Patrick, RDF.

L - Legge, Thomas, RHA; Lennon, John, RDF (wounded).

M - Meredith, F.C., Driscoll's Scouts; Marsh, T., RFA; McDermott, R., Inniskilling Fusiliers; Morrin, James, RAMC.

N - Noone, Edward, Irish Guards; Nolan, P., RDF.

R - Rogers, John, Irish Guards; Reilly, Christopher, RDF (dead).

S - Smith, George, ASC.

T - Turpin, 2nd Lieut. H., Royal Irish Rifles.

Kildare Observer, April 1916.

The Green Fields of France

The Observer also had the job of reporting the horrors of the fighting and the cost in human terms.

ROLL OF HONOUR
The following names appeared in the casualty list during the week.

KILLED
Private A. Kavanagh, 16678, RDF (Naas).
Private F. Nolan, 5023, RDF (Athy).
Private A. Farrell, 28996, Machine Gun Corps (Naas).

PRESUMED KILLED
Private Murtha Donoghue, 12556, RDF (Naas).
WOUNDED
Thomas Lewis, 80551, RFA (Naas).
Lce.-Corporal J. Leonard, RDF (Naas).
Private J. Harrington, RDF (Naas).
Lieut. W. J. McVeigh, Munster Fusiliers (Naas).

SHELL SHOCK
Private J. Morrin, 69501, RAMC (Naas)

MISSING
Private M. Morrin, RDF (Naas)

Kildare Observer, August 1916.

far from the short grass

The Green Fields of France

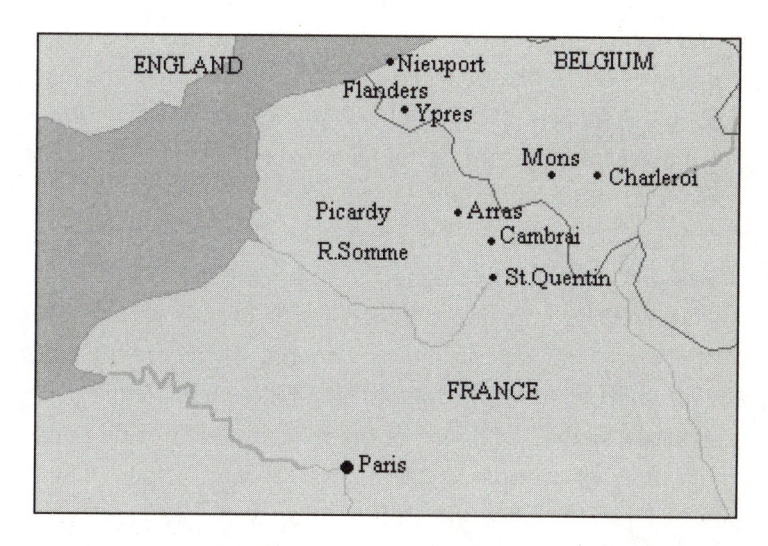

In September 1915 both the British and the French launched full-scale offensives against the German lines. The Germans were ready, however, and the two offensives resulted largely in failure. The French made some gains, but at terrific cost. The British attack at Loos resulted in 8,000 killed and wounded and achieved nothing, except the destruction of the remnants of the old regular army. The following month the Lord Lieutenant of Ireland, Sir John French, announced that 10,000 recruits were needed from Ireland before the end of November, and that thereafter a steady flow of 1,100 a week should be maintained. In 1916 conscription was introduced in Britain. Recruits poured into the army and after two years of war, the British had assembled an army of a size sufficient for them to take over a major stretch of the Allied front. The winter of 1915 marked the introduction of the 16th (Irish) Division to the trenches of the Western Front.

On Easter Monday April 24 1916 the Irish Volunteers and the Irish Citizens Army began an insurrection against British rule in Ireland. The Easter Rebellion lasted a week and ended in defeat, but ultimately sealed the fate of the British presence in Ireland. The serving soldiers

The Green Fields of France

at the front - and even the population as a whole - were horrified at the actions of the rebels. There was little sympathy for the insurrection among the soldiers at the front and the Easter Rebellion would probably have joined the long list of failed insurrection's were it not for the harsh and cruel treatment of the captured leaders by the British authorities. The leaders of the Rebellion were shot in a series of long drawn out executions designed to maximise the effect. The reaction to this brutality and the rounding up of thousands of 'rebels' was almost immediate among the Irish people. It was not the reaction the British were expecting. Instead of stamping out the flame of liberty the executions kindled a flame that burst into a nation-wide conflagration in the years which were to follow. This became apparent in the slow-down of recruiting for the British Army and the questioning of the wholesale slaughter of Irish soldiers at the front. (Enthusaism for the war was never as great in Ireland as it was in Britain as only about 10 per cent of Irishmen of a military age went to war, compared with about 25 per cent in Britain. Even before the Easter Rebellion recruitment had begun to decline. From August - December 1914 43,000 men enlisted; January - August 1915 37,000 men enlisted while from September 1915 - March 1916 12,000 men enlisted. From April - September 1916 recruitment had fallen to 9,000. A year later the figure had almost halved again and the country was not providing enough recruits to replace the casualties in Irish regiments.)

While the Easter Rebellion was taking place at home 570 Irishmen gave their lives on the far-off fields of Flanders. The most serious German gas attack since Second Ypres a year before took place at Hulluch between April 27 and 29 resulting in 1,980 casualties in 16th Division. In Dublin there was one local casualty - on the British side - in the fighting. Captain A. E. Warmington, 10th Royal Irish Regiment, was killed while acting with his battalion near the South Dublin Union on Easter Monday at the commencement of the Rebellion. Capt. Warmington who was the only son of Mr and Mrs Warmington,

The Green Fields of France

Munster and Leinster Bank, Naas, fought through the Boer War and rejoined the colours at the outbreak of the war in 1914. He had only just returned from Flanders.

In the summer of 1916 the British felt they were strong enough to launch an offensive that would end the war. That offensive became known as the Battle of the Somme. The command of the British army had passed to Sir Douglas Haig, a dour Scotsman, who was to become one of the most controversial generals of the war. He appeared to work on the theory that given enough men and materials, a breakthrough would be inevitable.

The British attack - it was a joint offensive - was on a front stretching for 18 miles at the River Somme and opened on the morning of July 1 1916. It was the bloodiest day in the history of the British army. In all, 60,000 British soldiers were hit on that first day and 20,000 were killed. Attacks continued throughout the summer and autumn. The British introduced a new weapon of warfare - the Mark I Tank - a huge success at first, but they were too few and often sank in the mud. Haig and his generals would not give up. The battle lasted for four months with casualties running at about 4,000 a day, finally petering out on November 18 in the midst of freezing winter conditions. About 125 square miles of territory, a strip 20 miles long by six deep, had been wrested from the Germans at a cost of 420,000 British and 194,000 French casualties. German losses were about 360,000. The New Armies created by Lord Kitchener were destroyed. The 16th Irish and the 36th Ulster Division were also decimated in the Somme batles, suffering casualties of 1,167 and 1,944 killed respectively.

Kildare men were to the fro in the Somme offensive. Private J. Kelly, 6th Royal Irish Regiment, one of five brothers in the army, from New Row, Naas received the following on parchment as a record of his gallantry on the battlefield.

The Green Fields of France

Troops going over the top Western Front 1916.

"I have read with much pleasure the reports of your regimental commander and brigadier-commander regarding your gallant conduct and devotion to duty in the field on 19 June 1916 and have ordered your name and deed to be entered into the record of the Irish Division. - W. B. Hickie, Major-General, Commanding 16th Irish Division."

Private Thomas Goucher of Bishopscourt, Straffan, one of three brothers serving in France, was with the 9th Inniskilling Fusiliers, 36th Ulster Division, on the first day of the 'Big Push'.

"We went into the trenches on the night of June 30th," he wrote. "At 5 next morning, July 1st, we got some tea; at 8 o'clock we topped the parapet like men. Over we went through cannons, machine guns, rifle fire, bombs, and everything you could mention, into the German lines. My God, what a sight! It was absolutely Hell all that day - poor fellows blown to pieces, heads here and legs and arms there, some riddled with bullets. I was along with our officer in the German lines. He was wounded in the back and the blood ran down and filled his boots, but he stuck it for 13 hours - from 9 in the morning till ten at night - the Germans bombing us nearly all the time. We had to lie

far from the short grass

The Green Fields of France

down till it got dark; then we tried to crawl in but the officer did not seem to be in luck, for he got shot again in the legs. He then gave me his field glasses to keep and told me to go on myself, as there was no use in the two of us getting done for. We were only twenty yards from the Germans at that time. I had to crawl 300 yards to get to our lines, and, thank God, I got safe, though I had some wonderful escapes. My chums are gone all but two of them, but I tell you we gave it to the Germans hot with bayonet, bullet and boot - anything that was handy. We were up against the Prussian Guard, the pick of the German Army, but I am happy to say the pick of the British Army was against them, for we took about 600 prisoners and got great praise for our gallantry."

Private Andrew Farrell of Kilcullen Road, Naas, was also in action on the Somme, but was killed on July 23. Private Farrell, aged twenty, had only left for the front on May 30. He was an apprentice printer with the *Kildare Observer* but left to work in Scotland. He worked in a munitions factory in Falkirk for six months and then joined the Connaught Rangers on September 19 1915. He afterwards transferred to the Machine Gun Corps and left for the front on May 30. Mrs. Farrell received the following letter:

B. E. Forces, France,
23 July 1916

Dear Madam - It is with the most sincere regret that I have to write and tell you that your son, No. 28996, Private A. Farrell, of my Company, has been killed in action, about 5.30 pm on 23 July 1916. My officers and men, one and all, join me in my desire to convey to you the great loss your son is to not only his parents and relatives, but his King and country, and also to my Company. He was quite one of the best soldiers I had in my Company - brave, steady, always reliable, smart, and in every way a credit to the corps. I am arranging that his body be brought back from the

The Green Fields of France

Photo: ATHY HERITAGE CENTRE.

Lieut. J.V. Holland V.C. winner, at the Battle of the Somme.

trenches and that he will be interred in the cemetery by a Catholic priest with full military honours. He will be greatly missed by both officers and men, but it is gratifying to know that he died the death of a soldier, fighting for a great cause and no man can do more than give his life for his King and country. I may state that he was instantly killed by shell fire and it will be something to know that the end was sudden and painless. Please accept the most sincere sympathies of officers and men of this Company in your great bereavement.

Yours sincerely,
P. Mathisen (Captain)
O.C. 121 MG Company, France, 23 July 1916.

The Green Fields of France

At the end of August the 16th Division was moved into positions around Bray in the Somme valley. Before them stood Guillemont, a village strongpoint in the second line of German defences. Since July six British divisions had gallantly broken themselves against its concrete emplacements and bastions. Now it was the turn of the Irish. On the morning of September 2 the battalions massed in a sector of three shallow, parallel trenches as a massive artillery barrage pounded the German positions. The German counter-barrage began as the leading companies went over the top in perfect lines. Before the Germans had time to get out of their dug-outs and fire their machine-guns the Irish troops were on top of them. The part played by the trench bombers of 7th Leinsters, under the command of Lt. J. V. Holland, of Athy, was crucial to the victory. Lt. Holland's exploits won his division its first Victoria Cross.

John V. Holland, aged 27, was one of eight children from Athy, the eldest son of the local veterinary surgeon. Vincent, as he was known to his friends, had enlisted in the 2nd Life Guards in 1914 after spending some time in Argentina as a railway engineer. The story goes that he had laid a five pound bet with another officer that he would be first over the parapet when the whistle blew. Whether this is true or not, Holland took a calculated gamble and led his men ahead of his own artillery's barrage, thus ensuring that few Germans would have left the safety of their dug-outs. As a result he caught many groups of enemy soldiers by surprise. The citation of his Victoria Cross read, 'By this very gallant action he undoubtedly broke the spirit of the enemy and thus saved us many casualties when the battalion made a further advance.' But the escapade was a costly one. Of the twenty-six bombers in the Leinster Bombing Platoon, only five were left standing after the battle: all the rest were either killed or wouned. Lt. Holland had a narrow escape when a shrapnel shell burst only yards from him and the steel hail missed him completely. Along with their commanders V.C. the Bombing Platoon also won two DCMs, six MMs and one man, Pte. John Ford, was recommended for a battlefield commission.

Holland personally bombed several dug-outs and forced out the garrison, shooting several Germans with his revolver. A German officer shot one of Holland's men, then raised his arms in surrender, a gesture which, to his credit, Holland accepted. Seven Germans, including the officer, were captured. Sending the prisoners back to the rear, Holland carried on with the battle. Some hours later, he returned. "I found this poor devil lying outside the place I bombed. He cried out 'You English, you English, don't leave me here to die'" Along with a Royal Irish soldier he carried the German, seated on a rifle, back to safety. John V. Holland survived the war and saw further service in World War 11 before emigrating and settling in Tasmania.

Lieutenant J.J. Dempsey, Scottish Rifles (Cameronians) from Drehid, Carbury, was the first officer from North Kildare to win the Military Cross. He was in France since July 1915 and had seen action at Loos in September and was in the Somme battles from the start. He was promoted to Captain and Adjutant of his battalion. Monasterevin man, Lieutenant John Tynan, of the Wiltshire Regiment, was awarded the DSO for capturing a listening post at the front, killing one sentry and capturing another.

The Battle of the Somme continued its bloody course and casualties mounted rapidly. Private Edward Wolfred, Milemill, Kilcullen, was killed in action in August while serving with the RDF. He had joined the army shortly after the outbreak of war and had been wounded at the Dardanelles, and having recovered was sent to France. Two Naas brothers, Privates William and Patrick McCormack, of Abbey Street, were wounded in the Big Push while serving with the Royal Dublin Fusiliers. The brothers were working together as signallers with a cor-

The Green Fields of France

poral and another private when a shell burst, killing one man and wounding the brothers McCormack. The corporal was uninjured. Patrick, who was only eighteen, received eight wounds - two on the right arm, one in the right hand, one in the left hand, one in the left arm, one in the right knee and two in the left knee. William was wounded in the left leg. Both survived their wounds. Another Naas man, Pte. P. Bermingham, of Caragh Road, was evacuated to England suffering from shell-shock. Dozens more Kildaremen were wounded in the following weeks. The Ven. Archdeacon of Kildare received the following from one of them, W. Goucher, of Bishopscourt, Straffan:

No. 8 Stationary Hospital,
B.E.F., Boulogne, France,
September 20th, 1916.

"Dear Archdeacon, - I am in the above hospital, having been wounded on Friday, September 15th, at 6.30 am. I lay out in a shell hole past the German trenches until the morning of the 17th, when I was found and carried in by the stretcher-bearers. I was taken first to an advanced dressing station, had my wounds attended to, and then sent to a casualty clearing station in a town near the front; then I was sent down to this base hospital at Boulogne. Here they have operated on me twice, and I am pleased to say I am going on most famously and am getting better quick. I have been marked up for "Blighty" and I am going over in a hospital ship tomorrow. I have been hit in two places, one in the right thigh and the other in the right forearm. I am quite comfortable and happy, and am not in a great deal of pain. When I get to a hospital in England I will let you have the address and then you can write to me, and perhaps come and see me. I have been well looked after here by the doctors and nurses, and it is a nice hospital."

Despite being in such good form Pte. Goucher was lucky to be

The Green Fields of France

alive. When he was picked up in no man's land, where he had lain for nearly two days, he was at death's door. Within a day he was back on the mend and was, according to the Chaplain of the hospital, 'bright and quite happy.' He was one of the lucky ones. Many more met tragic fates that autumn as the doomed Somme offensive plodded on. Private Gilbert (Bertie) Kelly, a well known sportsman from Athy was killed in action on September 25, while serving with the 1st Battn. Wellington Regt., New Zealand Expeditionary Force. Bertie Kelly was the youngest brother of Surgeon B. Kelly, DCM, and Surgeon T. Kelly, both serving Kildaremen. He had emigrated to New Zealand before finishing college and had joined the colours at the outbreak of war. After training in Egypt he went to the front with his regiment.

As the struggle for Ireland's independence continued the main theme of Irish loyalists was one of disgust at how men serving at the front were let down by those at home. As the war entered its fourth year and the slaughter continued the outcry in Ireland became louder. The far-off fields of Flanders were beginning to take their toll on young Irishmen and the country was not providing enough recruits to replace those becoming casualties. With the massive casualties of Third Ypres and the call for conscription the young men of Ireland began to question the reasons why they were fighting and dying for no foreseeable gain. The generals of the British Army seemed hell-bent on destroying a whole generation rather than admit their tactics of attrition were not winning the war. Verdun and the Somme showed the stupidity of the generals and the incredible waste of human lives. The amazing courage of the ordinary soldier was also revealed and the term 'lions led by donkeys' was never more appropriate. After Passachanaele the outcry in Ireland became a tumultuous protest.

CHAPTER 5

Paths of Glory

At the beginning of 1917 the British Army was stronger than it had ever been, with nearly 60 divisions, 3,000,000 men, in the field, most of them in France. The French with 100 divisions had survived Verdun and won back much of the ground lost there. Both High Commands were confident now of victory and planned yet another great joint offensive. The offensive began on April 16 and for the French it was a disaster comparable to the first day of the Battle of the Somme. By the end of the month the French Army had lost 200,000 men and the five armies that went into the attack were on the verge of full-scale mutiny. Infantry units refused to go up to the front, others refused to attack. Some of these soldiers were court-martialled and officially shot, while others were executed without sentence. Demonstrations against the war were held, red flags were flown and soldiers attacked transports and rear-area troops and unpopular officers. It was more of a strike than a mutiny, but the French High Command was in a panic in case word reached the Germans. The onus of the offensive therefore fell upon the British Army, while the French tried to restore order in their troubled ranks.

Paths of Glory

The British despite the losses of the Somme were still in good spirits, though they were now depending upon conscripts instead of volunteers to fill the gaps in their ranks. The Irish divisions and regiments had received new drafts of replacements, but in the absence of conscription in Ireland, most of them were English and the nature of the Irish units were radically altered. As a preliminary the Second Army

Photo: N. DOWLING.

William Nolan, Ballymore-Eustace, died in captivity 1917.

Paths of Glory

undertook to widen the Ypres salient by the capture of the Messines Ridge. This attack had been meticulously planned and was an enormous success. Nine divisions, including the 36th and 16th, took part in the attack which was the first wholly successful British battle of the war so far. The next phase of the offensive began, the Third Battle of Ypres or Passchendaele, as it came to be called.

The terrain around Ypres favoured the Germans very strongly. Beyond the walled-fortress city the open plain rose in a series of shallow swells toward the distant Passchendaele ridge from which the defenders could observe every movement in the British positions. The ground, moreover, was waterlogged, which a combination of heavy shelling and unseasonable rain had turned into a quagmire. Coupled with the new addition to the German defences, the pill-box, this made the Ypres salient a formidable and deadly opponent. The pill-box faced its first test at Ypres and was responsible for heavy casualties among the attackers, who had to learn the hard way, the art of Pill Box fighting. The battle began on July 31 after a week's bombardment which only softened up the ground more. As the offensive opened so, too, did the heavens. Unseasonable rain continued throughout the campaign which did not end until November 10 with 240,000 British casualties and an advance of six miles. The conditions throughout beggared descripton.

There was not one tree left in the featureless landscape. Mud was thigh deep and the shell holes so deep and full of water that men and animals often drowned in them. The smell of death was prevalent and the hardship of the journey in and out of the line outweighed the value of a few hours rest. Trenches collapsed and dug-outs were flooded constantly. It was literally a hell on earth and few that fought there ever forgot the experience.

Corporal James Garry, from Monasterevan, died of wounds on

Paths of Glory

April 9 1917, in Calais Hospital, while serving with the 2nd Leinsters. The Duchess of Sutherland sent the following letter to his father, Mr. James Garry.

"I am very sorry indeed to tell you that your son died of wounds in hospital yesterday morning at 11 o' clock. He was only in hospital 24 hours. He had gas gangrene in the leg, which was amputated, but it was impossible to save him, and he died whilst still unconscious and without any pain. I am sending you his pocket book, which he had when he came in, as I thought you might like to have it."

On April 28 brothers Alfred and John Goodman, Bishopscourt, Kill, were both killed in action. It was Easter Monday and Alfred had volunteered to carry out a dangerous operation when he was killed while endeavouring to accomplish it. Lieutenant George Baker, from Newbridge, was severely wounded in the arm in the fighting around Ypres. Lieut. Baker served with the Dublin Fusiliers in the South African War and India and was with the Dublins in the famous dash for the beach at Suvla Bay where he was also severely wounded.

Private William Nolan, from Tipperkevin, Ballymore-Eustace, was serving with No.3 Platoon, A Company, 1st Royal Irish Fusiliers, during the summer of 1917. He had only arrived in France in early May having joined up in Monaghen town, where his girlfriend, Mollie, lived. He had formerly been in the RIC and had left the force when all his comrades had enlisted. He was planning to marry when he returned. In one of his last letters to his sister Mary the twenty-three year old private wrote "please do not send any more socks," and on June 10 he wrote her saying, "We have a chaplain here (and) we get a splendid opportunity of fulfilling our religious duties ... I must say there is a great change in me for the better since I came out here." A few days later William Nolan was reported 'missing in action.' The circumstances of his fate were unknown until it was announced he died of

Paths of Glory

wounds on June 27 while a prisoner of war in Germany. More than likely Pte. Nolan had been wounded in action and picked up by German stretcher-bearers and transported to a POW camp in Germany, where he subsequently succumbed to his wounds.

Photo: P. GOREY

Pte. Thomas Bermingham, Kilina Robertstown, killed in action July 31, 1917.

Paths of Glory

Pte. Thomas Bermingham, Kilina, Robertstown, was serving with the 2nd Irish Guards at the Third Battle of Ypres. The Battalion were in the trenches to the east of Boesinghe (Boezinge in modern Flemish). Two of the days objectives were Pilckem and Artillery Wood. They went over the top at 4.23 hrs local time and he was probably killed not long after. Casualties were very heavy and also killed that day were the Battalion C.O. and Fr. Simon Knapp, who although nearly sixty years old, was in the line with the troops. Thomas Bermingham was one of three brothers serving with the colours. Corporal James Bermingham was also serving with the 2nd Irish Guards and was wounded at 3rd Ypres. Sergeant Major Thomas Bermingham served with an artillery regiment in France from 1914 to 1918 and, like his brother James, survived the war.

Photo: P. GOREY

James Bermingham, Kilina, Robertstown, pictured here in his Railwayman's uniform.

far from the short grass

Paths of Glory

Private John Cooke, Kilcullen, was also serving in the Irish Guards and was also killed on the first day of Third Ypres. John Cooke was a brother of William Cooke, a hero of the Dublin Fusiliers, who was killed in the Dardanelles in 1915. He had another brother, Pte. Robert Cooke, who was in France since 1914 with the Durham Light Infantry.

The 48th Brigade of the 16th (Irish) Division consisted of all the battalions of the Dublin Fusiliers now serving in the Great War. The battalions were the 1st, 2nd, 8th, 9th and 10th. It could easily have been called the 'Dublin Brigade.' 16th and 36th Divisions were in support when the offensive opened on July 31. Gains were made, but the attack was not wholly successful. It was to be continued the next day, but that evening the heavens opened and the attack was postponed. The heavy rain continued for a month and combined with shell-cratering created appalling battlefield conditions. The Irish Divisions remained in the trenches, suffering heavy casualties from unrelenting artillery barrages. When the time came for the next attack the divisions were already understrength and exhausted. On August 16 they attacked at Langemarck. Two days later both divisions were withdrawn having suffered 7,816 casualties - 16th Division, 4,231 and 36th Division, 3,585. The battle continued until November 10 and Irish battalions in other divisions fought at Menin Road Ridge, Polygon Wood, Broodseinde, Poelcapplle and Passchendaele, where the two most costly attacks took place. The series of battles are often referred to as Passchendaele. The nightmare in the mud continued until Passchendaele Ridge and village were finally taken. The battle bled the BEF white and drove a deep wedge between government ministers and army commanders. Morale plummeted and dissenting subordinate officers were relieved of command. There was no such choice for the 'Poor Bloody Infantryman.' He stayed in the trenches waiting for a miracle to avert his fate.

Second Lieutenant Maurice Cane, Royal Field Artillery, was killed

Paths of Glory

in action on August 14. He was the only son of Colonel Claude Cane, St. Wolstan's, Celbridge and left behind a wife and young son. Lieut. Cane was killed while firing his guns, having only returned from sick leave a few days earlier, and having only joined his battery on the day he lost his life. He was in British Columbia when war broke out and joined the Canadian Naval Volunteers, serving several months as an able seaman and then a leading seaman. When the German raiders in the Pacific ceased to exist, he took his discharge and came home and was given a commission in his fathers old regiment, the Royal Artillery.

Two days later Naas veteran, 2nd Lieutenant W. H. Clements, was killed in action. On the staff of Ulster Bank, Naas, he joined the 'Pals' of the 7th RDF. Lieut. Clements saw action in the Dardanelles and was awarded the MC. He received his commission earlier in the year. He was reportedly wounded and fell into a shell-hole, where he subsequently drowned, a not uncommon death in the waterlogged landscape of Ypres. Captain Herbert O'Connor, MC, Shropshire Light Infantry, died of wounds on August 17. He was the son of Dr. O'Connor, Celbridge. He had only been in France two months when he won the Military Cross.

On September 8 two brothers from Reban, Athy, Christopher and Patrick Flynn, were killed in action. Private Christopher Flynn, 32, joined the Irish Guards on November 1 1915 while Patrick, 22, joined the 8th Dublin Fusiliers on the same day. Ironically, both died on the same day in separate actions. Patrick, a Lance-Corporal, had fought through several engagements and had been wounded twice.

On September 29 CQMS Lee Byrne, New Row, Naas, was awarded the *Croix de Guerre* for service in the field. He also held the Russian Order, granted in 1916 by the then Czar. Sgt. Byrne was a veteran of the Dardanelles landing, with the Dublins, where he was wounded. After recovering he was sent to France, where he spent a considerable time before been again wounded. After again recovering he was sent home on leave and on his return to the front he was wounded for the third time on July 17 with no less than three pieces of shrapnel in his body. Sgt. Byrne was the eldest son of Michael Byrne, late of the RDF, and had three brothers serving in France.

On November 3 Private William McCormack, Abbey Street, Naas, serving with the Dublins was hospitalised suffering from shell-shock. In a letter to his mother he said he was buried for three hours under earth thrown up by a shell. Pte. McCormack was a veteran of Guillemont and the Somme in the course of which battle he received no less than five wounds.

In a bid to close the year with success the British again went on the offensive on November 20 breaching the formidable Hindenburg Line with tanks and infantry. 380 tanks were used and huge bundles of wood were dropped into the German trenches to allow the tanks to advance over them. The offensive was at first successful but exploitation of the initial break-in at Cambrai faded as the Germans counter-attacked. The weather turned colder and the rain turned to snow. The British poured in more reserves and the meat-grinder swallowed them up. The front stabilised on December 7 and the British offensive petered out. 2nd Lieutenant Thomas J. Hannon, 6th Shropshire Light Infantry, was killed in action on December 8 in the Cambrai fighting. Lieut. Hannon, from Millview House, Athy, had only returned to France from a visit to his mother in London. The twenty year old was a veteran of several previous engagements and was severely wounded the previous August.

On January 22 1918 Sergeant Thomas Goucher, Bishopscourt, Straffan was killed in action near St. Quentin, where his regiment, 9th Inniskillings, had moved after the Battle of Cambrai. Nineteen year old Sgt. Goucher had fought through the Somme offensive and the bat-

Paths of Glory

Cardinal Bourne addressing the Dublin Fusilier Brigade from a horse drawn wagon at Ervillers. October 27 1917.

tles of Third Ypres and Cambrai. His loss was sadly felt in his depleted regiment. There were few of the 'old hands' remaining in the old line regiments, who now had to take over an additional twenty-eight miles of front from the French. The stage was now set for the BEF's gravest period since autumn 1914.

far from the short grass

CHAPTER 6

Guests of the Kaiser

On 17 June 1916 the County Kildare Prisoners of War Committee submitted a list of 43 names of Co. Kildare soldiers held prisoner by the Germans. Twenty-one were Dublin Fusiliers and the balance was distributed over many Irish and English regiments. Most of the prisoners were captured in the opening battles of the war and the majority were taken in the retreat from Mons. A great deal of anxiety prevailed in the country in those first few weeks concerning the fate of soldiers in the BEF who had been listed as missing. News returned of the deaths of some and then letters began arriving from Germany informing the anxious families that many of those missing, were, indeed, prisoners of the Germans.

Mrs. Hickey, Naas, received this letter from her son Private Joseph Hickey, in October 1914.

"Dear Mother,- Just a line hoping to find you all at home in good health, as I am. I am at present along with the rest of the Battalion. We are getting no cigarettes here, so I would be very thankful if you could send me a box of Woodbines and some story book and a cake of bread. We are allowed to receive parcels up to the width of 10lbs, and don't put any stamps on it, as it is allowed to come free of charge. Make up the weight of the parcel or box with the story books. We get no money here, so we can't buy anything. I would like to be with you for Christmas and I hope you enjoy it. Tell father to send me some of his books, as I can't read German and they are the only thing we can get here …

"P.S. - Johnny Doran and Paddy McCann (also of Naas) are here and they are writing along with me for cigarettes and other things."

Private Hickey was nineteen at the time of writing and had joined the Dublin Fusiliers in May 1913. He was wounded in the Battle of Mons and had an older brother serving in the 1st Battn., RDF.

Private Johnny Doran, 2nd Battn., RDF, was also captured at Mons, and wrote to his wife, who lived at Corban's Lane, Naas, on September 11, though the letter was not received until October 24.

"My dear wife, - I suppose you must be in a bad way since you got no letter from me, but it was not my fault. I would have written long ago, but we are only getting the privilege now. When you receive this letter I want you to send me a box of cigarettes, as we can't get any smokes here, as we have no money …

"Tell my mother to send on Paddy (his step-brother) the same as you will send me. Tell her that Paddy and I are prisoner of war together, and Paddy is all right and in good health. Let me know if you have heard anything about T. Higgins, as I did not see him since I came out. I wish to God the war was over until we get home."

Guests of the Kaiser

PHOTO: T. DORAN.

Group photo of Royal Dublin Fusiliers at York Barracks. John Doran is pictured front centre.

Private Doran was on the special reserve after twelve years service in the Dublin Fusiliers and was called up on the outbreak of war.

Mrs. Higgins, Fair Green, Naas, received a postcard from her husband Private Thomas Higgins, 2nd RDF, who was a prisoner at Gefanegen Lager, Doeoeritz, Ubungsplatz in Germany. (Ptes. Hickey, Doran and McCann were all held at Seane Lager, Paderborn.) "Just a few lines to let you know that I am still alive. I got wounded in the hand, but it is nearly all right again now. I was taken prisoner in France and brought here. I am quite safe here and you need not be fretting. I hope you receive the pay I left you all right. Tell little Nelson (his daughter) not to be fretting as I will be home as soon as the war is over. Do not mention the war when writing to me, as I will not get it if you do. If you can send me some cigarettes."

Private Higgins was wounded at the Battle of Mons, and at the

Guests of the Kaiser

time of the outbreak of hostilities had only been five months on the reserve, after his return from India. On Christmas Eve 1915 Pte. Higgins arrived at his home in Naas after a sojourn of 16 months as a wounded prisoner of war in Germany. He was sent back in a draft of 65 men who had been rendered unfit for further military service in consequence of wounds received. His left hand had been amputated from the wrist, the hand having been shattered by shrapnel in the retreat from Mons.

"I have spent 9 years and 3 months in the 'Dublins'" Pte. Higgins said, "and I was on the reserve, and on the outbreak of war was called up and joined my battalion, which was sent from India to France. Landing in France we were sent to the firing line at once, and we were in our first engagement on the 24th August, 1914. My military career ended on the 27th August, when during the retreat from Mons, near Le Cateau, while endeavouring to hold back the German rush, I was struck by shrapnel, which blew my left hand to fragments."

"Having been struck, I ran for about fifty yards in an effort to get away from the enemy and save myself, but collapsed from pain and loss of blood. I fell unconscious on the field and lay there in this condition bleeding profusely for four hours. When I recovered consciousness I found myself with 38 others of my battalion in the hands of the Germans. We were in a school house, which was being used as a sort of hospital, the floor being littered with straw. Around me were German, French and British wounded. From there I was removed with others to Cambrai hospital where, a couple of days later, my hand was amputated by a German and a French doctor. Here I remained for about ten weeks, and it makes me sick when I hear people say the Germans treat their prisoners well. From the first it was quite the reverse. We were treated more like dogs than human beings, and frequently called English swine, and told that only for the English the war would be finished.

Guests of the Kaiser

"They took us from Cambrai hospital for removal to Doberitz. On the way to the railway station we were searched in the Town Hall, and a German officer who spoke English well, told us if we had any dum-dum bullets on us they would shoot us. We told him we never used dum-dum bullets. He said we used our jack-knives to cut off the ears of German wounded as souvenirs and to pick out their eyes. We tried to convince him that was all nonsense, telling him that we used our knives only for opening tins, splicing ropes, etc. They searched us, but, of course, found none of the dum-dum bullets they evidently hoped to find.

"We were then taken to the railway station at Cambrai and put into horse boxes. There were ten British and several French prisoners with me in the one in which I found myself. In this the Germans locked us, and we never saw daylight until the next morning, when they opened the doors of the horse box. The fresh air was welcome, indeed as we were almost suffocated in the dark box. There was a seat in the box which we were told was to be used by the French, but not by the British. However, the French allowed us to use it in turns to rest ourselves. When the box was opened in the morning they handed in the French some bread, but said we were to get none of it. When the box was locked up again, and the Germans could no longer see us, the French gave us some of the bread.

"On the way to Doberitz, the door of the horse box being opened, the German guards tried to stamp on our toes, jostle us, and otherwise make us commit ourselves. At every station after we crossed the frontier, they opened the box to let the civilians see us. In they trooped on top of us - old men, women and children. They called us names - English swine and other things we did not understand, spat on us and some of them even kicked us.

"We reached Doberitz after a weary journey on our horse box. There were no huts erected here at the time, and we were put in tents.

Guests of the Kaiser

I was put into the hospital tent, and we were given some black bread. Then, and almost all the time, until parcels began to arrive from home for us we were half-starved. You can imagine how hungry we were when we used to ransack the swill barrels or refuse buckets like famished dogs in search of anything eatable. Some times we got old skins or other refuse which we washed, boiled and ate. The black bread was awful, sour stuff, but bad as it was we devoured it, so terrible was our hunger.

"Twice a week a doctor would come and look at the wounded in hospital, bandaging our wounds. We had no sleeping accommodation beyond a blanket to lie on with another over us. Owing to the cold we could not possibly take off our clothes.

"All this time huts were in process of erection. When they were finished we were shifted into them. I was two days in the hut when I was sent to Lemberg, which was to be my home during the rest of my stay - extending over 16 months in Germany. I was about six weeks altogether in Doberitz. When we were taken to Lemberg they treated us well for the first week, and we were not at all badly off. We began to feel that the Germans were not so bad fellows after all as our first impressions of them led us to believe. But we were soon to learn the reason for our good treatment. The Irish prisoners were kept by themselves. One day Sir Roger Casement came to us to read some Irish history for us and told us about Ireland's wrongs of the past. Now, he said, is the time to strike a blow for Ireland, and lots of other stuff like that. We were then told that an Irish Brigade was to be formed from amongst the prisoners. We were to be given uniforms of green with shamrocks as collar badges. We were to be equipped and fitted out n every way to fight for Ireland. They took the precaution of meeting an objection that would occur to many of us even supposing we were willing to become traitors to our Empire. They told us: If you join the Irish Brigade and the Germans win this war they will land the Irish

Guests of the Kaiser

Brigade in Ireland to free Ireland, and send some German troops to reinforce you. If the Germans do not win the war we will give you £20 each, send you to America, and guarantee you employment there with German firms. We boohed Sir Roger Casement out of the camp, and he only come once again after that to distribute books about history and wrongs of Ireland - things that happened years ago.

"Some of our fellows were foolish enough to take the bait. In a sense they could hardly be blamed for it. Any man who joined the Irish Brigade was starved into it. Very few, however, went. They were taken to Berlin and dressed in green uniforms, and a couple of them came back and had the neck to walk before us with swords clanking behind them. They knew the reception they'd get from the rest of us, and there were German sentries with them with fixed bayonets to protect them through the camp. These fellows knew they had done wrong, and when they came back before us - the couple who did - they hung down their heads as if ashamed of themselves, as well they might be. These fellows who joined the Irish Brigade write home pretending they are still prisoners, and they are well treated by the Germans. They get parcels from home and it is not fair that they should be fed from England and Ireland by these parcels.

"From time to time we were taken one by one before the Irish Brigade authorities, asked if we knew why we were brought there, and what we thought about joining. It was no good, however, and when they found this out the good treatment we were given previously at Lemberg was stopped. After that we were again treated like dogs. I myself, although minus my left hand was brought before the Irish Brigade authorities, and this led me to believe it was a show of men from Irish regiments they wanted to boast about for than anything else.

"When you see postcards from fellows who are prisoners in

Germany who say they are well treated pay no heed to that. They must say that to get their postcards through at all. If they write the truth the postcards are censored and never sent, and the fellow who does that rarely escapes punishment. To give you an example: I remember once before permission was given to prisoners to write asking for bread or other eatables, I wrote home, If you don't send me on a 'Bolands' (meaning bread, of course) you can send on a habit. I was brought up for that, and they tore up the postcard before me. They said they were not fools, and knew what I was writing about. It was not to occur again or I would be punished. Later an order came out allowing us to write for bread or any other eatables, but we had always to say we were well treated by the Germans. Of course, the fellows said so in order to get food. There has been no doubt for a long time that food is short in Germany.

"Amongst the Naas men in Lemburg with me were Privates J. Doran, Corban's Lane; Joe Hickey, Back Lane; P. McCann, the Harbour, and Walsh, who was born and reared in Naas, but prior to the war was living in Limerick. I was the only Dublin Fusilier who was sent home from Lemburg Camp. All these Naas men mentioned were unwounded except Hickey. All prisoners who are capable of work must do it. An order was read obliging all prisoners of war to work. If they refused they were compelled at the point of the bayonet. Most of the men have been engaged at farm work from time to time.

"Our officers were not with us. They were all taken to Berlin. There were, however, five Russian officers who were given ten days to consider whether they would take down their 'Zeppelins' as we called their rank badges. I don't know what the idea was except it was to degrade the officers, but to a man they refused to remove their badges. I saw one of the officers afterwards being taken to a bunk, where they took off his uniform to wear.

"They gave us no particular prisoners' uniform beyond striping our clothes with red paint and giving us a little round cap with a big red cross painted across the front of it. Last winter I was going almost without boots, shivering and half clad like all the others until we began to get clothes, etc., from home. Every German I met seemed down on England. They said all the others were beaten except England, and that should would soon be. From the tales told by them and by a paper called the *Continental Times*, published in Berlin and printed in English, we imagined on returning to find very little of London left. They had tales of German victories everywhere; of British trenches captured without the loss of a German soldier; of the way Zeppelins were blowing London to bits, and other nonsense of that sort. We paid very little attention to the German victories, as reported in the paper.

"We nearly always knew when a visit might be expected from the American Ambassador. Everything was changed while he was about. Even large hose pipes were laid around to show that they were prepared to cope with an outbreak of fire in the camp. But, once the Ambassador had gone, these were all taken away and things generally became as bad as before. The first time the American Ambassador came he gave each man a cigar and some cigarettes, which were a welcome treat. Prior to that we got nothing to smoke, and for three months you should see the fellows who had pipes to smoke taking the bark off trees and using dried tea or coffee leaves for smoking. This was the condition we were in until parcels began to arrive from England. Frequently things were missing from the parcels. A fellow one day got a big box. On opening it he found it contained nothing but the paper in which some things had evidently been packed.

"The grub given us by the Germans was:-
Breakfast   Black coffee and black bread.
Dinner   Horse beans, with perhaps, a bit of margarine dropped to grease them, and a herring and black bread for supper.

Guests of the Kaiser

"I remember last Christmas Day (1914) my fare was:- Breakfast: Black coffee and no bread; dinner, chopped cabbage and the water it was boiled in, and grease to thicken it; supper, a cup of black coffee, a bit of sausage and black bread. It didn't make one feel much like Xmas!

"A fortnight before I left Lemburg I got word that I was amongst the prisoners to be sent home. I was forbidden to take any documents or papers of any sort with me, and I was told if I attempted to do so I would be sent back. I had a copy of the little book distributed by Sir Roger Casement, but was not allowed to bring it. I left Lemburg with two Canadians and an Irish Fusilier on the 4th December. We were taken to Holland and handed over to the Holland Red Cross, who escorted us to England, where we were handed over to our own people. There was a great cheer when the boat taking us back home came into harbour. We were taken to Milbanke Military Hospital, and from that I was sent to a convalescent home near Hyde Park. There I was treated splendidly, and finally got away on Christmas Eve to come home.

"Some of the people here, I believe, praise the Germans and say they are good fellows and would give Ireland her liberty. I've had a taste of their liberty, and want no more of it. It's a pity those who believe the Germans to be such good fellows don't get an opportunity of testing how good they can be to a wounded prisoner of war. It would give them some idea of the sort of liberty the Germans give. They are not civilised at all! They are savages. If they were civilised they would not treat us as they did. All may be fair in war, but war on crippled soldiers in the treatment they gave us is typical, as far as I could see, of German Kultur. (culture).”

Another returned prisoner was Pte. Brennan, Irish Guards, from Sallins and housed at Lemburg. There were 600 prisoners in the Lemburg camp and sixty-two died between December 1914 and

Guests of the Kaiser

October 1915 from hardship and poor diet. Pte. John Nelligan, from Co. Kildare, serving with the Chesire Regiment, died while a POW. There was only one pump in the camp for drinking and washing purposes. The food, as described by Pte. Higgins and other returned prisoners, was poor and insufficient. It was only with the arrival of food parcels in January and February of 1915 that prevented more deaths. Conditions at the other POW camps were no better. Committees were organised in Kildare to send parcels and letters to the prisoners in Germany and they were very successful in helping the prisoners and keeping up morale. Medicine was rare and morphia treatment - consisting of morphine drops - was the norm for every ailment. One returned prisoner, Pte. T. Donohoe, Naas, serving with the Dublins and captured at Mons and held at Senlager, claimed the German medical orderly was not too particular about the dosage and that some men never woke up after their treatment.

Lieutenant R.S.T. Moore, from Killashee, Naas, was repatriated from Switzerland in September 1917. He was the only son of Colonel St. Leger Moore, C.B. Lieut. Moore went to France with the original BEF and following the battle of Mons was reported killed in action. For some time the family mourned his loss until it was confirmed, by a fellow officer, that he was a POW. Lieut. Moore was severely wounded and after some time in hospital was transferred, under the care of the Swiss Red Cross Association, to Switzerland, where he resided for two years until his repatriation.

When news of the first soldiers captured reached Kildare a local committee, the County Kildare Prisoners Committee, was formed with Colonel Briggs, Commanding the Royal Dublin Fusiliers Depot at Naas, as Chairman. There were about 500 RDF prisoners, 360 of them at Lemburg. The Co. Kildare Committee sent out fortnight parcels of food to all the RDF prisoners at over 20 different camps. The parcels were sent from Berne, Switzerland and comprised of a parcel of bread, and also of tobacco, cigarettes, etc. Local dances and func-

Guests of the Kaiser

tions were held to raise money to fund the parcels. The committee was voluntary and without any expense, except the necessary printing, advertising and postage etc.

Food parcels were a great bonus to the POWs as otherwise they had to exist on a diet similar to that of the German population. The most nutritious of food went to the men at the front and those employed in the war effort, while the rest went to the ordinary population and prisoners. The POWs were also able to draw money through clearing banks in Holland. However, the Germans only allowed a rate of 20 marks to the pound, when the going rate was over four times that. With money prisoners could buy such luxuries as wine, cigars, wood and coke for their stoves, and sometimes beetroot or rhubarb.

Camp life was boring for the prisoners and there was nothing to do except roam the compound listlessly. Many enlisted men were forced to work on farms or in mines on poor rations. Escape was hazardous and while many attempted it, few were successful. Most POWs were, if not happy to be prisoners, at least content to be out of harms way. While the conditions of camp life were bad, the front line conditions were considerably worse, with the added danger of being killed or badly wounded.

When the Armistice was signed on November 11 1918 the POWs waited anxiously for their release. They were at first handed over to the Red Cross and then to the RAMC for health assessment. Most of them made their way back home at the beginning of 1919.

Pte. John Doran, 2nd Royal Dublin Fusiliers, and a POW since the retreat from Mons, received this letter from the King, on his release.

"The Queen joins me in welcoming you on your release from the *miseries & hardships, which you have endured with so much patience and courage.*

"During these many months of trial, the early rescue of our gallant officers & men from the cruelties of their captivity has been uppermost in our thoughts.

"We are thankful that this longed for day has arrived, & that back in the old country you will be able once more to enjoy the happiness of a home & to see good days among those who anxiously look for your return.

George RI."

Pte. John Doran did live a full life after the Great War returning to see his son Johnny, known as 'Mons', and born while the great battle was raging and he was fighting for his life. Less than twenty years later, both his sons had joined the British Army, just in time for another World War. Pte. John Doran died in 1961 at the age of 75.

CHAPTER 7

The War at Sea

Until the creation of the German Imperial Navy, after the turn of the century, Great Britain had been the unchallenged ruler of the seas. If there was one single reason for Britain's decision to enter an alliance with France against Germany, it lay in this threat to her naval supremacy. At the outbreak of war, while the Germans had a formidable navy, Britain had managed to keep ahead. Both powers had colonial fleets deployed around the world and it was here, far away from Europe, that the first rounds of the war at sea began as German ships attacked British commercial shipping. Seafaring men from landlocked County Kildare were not uncommon, the most famous being Admiral John de Robeck. Another seafarer was Captain Nagle, a native of Celbridge. Captain Nagle was in command of the *Niceto* when it was sunk by the German cruiser *Karlsruhe* on October 6 1914. The *Niceto* was little more than a week out of Buenos Aires when she was captured by the *Karlsruhe*.

"About three in the afternoon," Captain Nagle said, "we saw a passenger steamer steering about east south east. We asked her by wire-

The War at Sea

less what her name was and she replied that it was the *Principi de Udine* and that she was bound for Santos. That, of course, was entirely wrong, as we could see, for she was not steering right for that direction. This vessel must have communicated our whereabouts to the *Karlsruhe*, for half an hour later the cruiser came into sight on the horizon. She bore down on us and signalled to us to stop our engines, meantime hoisting the German flag. Then she fired a gun that brought us to. A boarding party of about a dozen men under charge of two officers put off from the *Karlsruhe* and came aboard our vessel. The first thing the officer in charge said to me was tell your men to pack up and be ready to leave inside half an hour. For a considerable time thereafter I was engaged with this Chief Officer, who asked me a great variety of questions as to the nature of our cargo, our destination, and so on. It seems he was not altogether satisfied with the report I gave concerning our cargo, for he told me that I should have to go before the Commander of the *Karlsruhe*.

"Accordingly, shortly after half-past five, I was taken off to the *Karlsruhe*, where I had an interview with Commander Kohler, a fine tall and very gentlemanly officer. My statement appeared to give satisfaction to him and I was allowed to leave. By the time I had been rowed back to my ship I found my crew were being taken on to the *Crefield*. I was not allowed to go on board my own vessel again but joined the *Crefield* like the others. It was now seven o'clock and quiet dark. The work of sinking the *Niceto* was done immediately. Three charges of dynamite were exploded in different parts of the ship, and by two o'clock in the morning she had disappeared.

"We remained on board the *Crefield* until October 22, when we were put ashore at Teneriffe. On the *Crefield* we found the crews of several other vessels which had been similarly dealt with before our turn came, and we saw still others raided and sunk in the same way later on. On board the *Crefeld* we were treated very well. The Naval

The War at Sea

officers who had to deal with us were thorough gentlemen, and their crew acted like gentlemen too. Indeed it was the servant of one of the officers who boarded my ship who packed up my clothes for me. I had time to save only a few bits of things and I owe even that to the courtesy of a German bluejacket."

Captain Nagle added that in a conversation he had with one of the *Karlsruhe's* officers he learnt that they cheerfully accepted as a foregone conclusion that the cruiser would be overtaken in due course and sunk.

"He acknowledged that if the *Karlsruhe* were tackled by any of the British cruisers in pursuit their only policy would be to make a bolt for it. They would not attempt to engage with a British cruiser for the *Karlsruhe* is so lightly armed compared with our cruisers that they know she would stand little or no chance."

Joseph Freeman of Hodgestown, Kilcock, was a stoker on board HMS *Powestott*, one of the British battleships engaged in the battle near Heligoland. This was the first naval encounter of the war as Royal Navy ships ambushed a German convoy, on August 28, during which a destroyer and three cruisers were sunk by superior British forces.

In February 1915 Germany declared the waters around the British Isles a war zone and warned that neutral ships which strayed outside a 'safe passage' north of the Shetland Islands would be liable to attack. It was in accordance with this declaration that the passenger liner *Lusitania* was torpedoed and sunk on May 8 1915 off the southern coast of Ireland. The attack outraged the American public since 128 of the 1,200 passengers drowned were US citizens. The Germans claimed the *Lusitania* was transporting munitions, a claim which has never been proven. The Americans and British denied the charge. As a result of the outrage, Germany abandoned the policy in August and

The War at Sea

returned to the practice of sinking ships only after the crews and passengers had been given the chance to escape. This policy, of course, did not apply to naval vessels.

Among the survivors of the *Lusitania* disaster was a young man named Thomas McCormack, a native of Robertstown. Thomas McCormack was returning to Ireland after spending two years in America. He had no thoughts of danger and was unaware of any threat on the part of the Germans to sink the ship. The first he heard of submarines was on the Wednesday preceding the disaster, when he saw the ships' life boats hung over the sides. He inquired of a sailor the reason for this and was told it was done so as to be prepared for attacks coming near England, and also that there was no cause for alarm as it was done on all trips then.

On May 8, the eventful day, Thomas McCormack said they sighted land about 11 a.m., and they were beginning to consider themselves safe. He was walking on the main deck about 2 o'clock when he heard two bangs. They were not very much, he added, and he did not know what was wrong until he noticed the ship keeling over to starboard and saw a bit of panic with people tumbling over one another running for life belts. He also went to procure his life belt, but as he was travelling third class, his berth was situated three flights of stairs below, and before he descended more than half way he found himself knee deep in water. He returned to the deck to find the ship was almost on her side, with the bow dipped low and the stern high in the air. The boats were being lowered and large numbers of people were standing around. No life belt was available, so he decided to jump. Jumping from the side on which the deck was nearest the water, he said, meant certain death, because it was becoming a howling mass of people clinging to one another in groups and as he had no life belt he was afraid a drowning person might catch on to him and "if you have no life belt it is all up." He scrambled up towards the stern, the

The War at Sea

deck being now almost perpendicular with the stern towering upwards of 40 feet in the air. He stripped himself of his coat, vest and boots and made that fateful jump. On rising to the surface he started swimming away from the ship, and got to a safe distance before the *Lusitania* disappeared. Then came the explosion, which threw water and wreckage high in the air.

Thomas McCormack kept afloat for about an hour and a quarter until he found a life belt and donning it he survived the ordeal until he was rescued about 6 p.m. by a trawler. On reaching the deck he fell, having temporarily lost the power of his legs. The trawler, he said picked up a large number of people wearing life belts, but many of them died before reaching Queenstown. While in the water McCormack also saw many dead bodies of children floating about. He had learned to swim as a child in the canal and spent most of his time in the water in the summer months. He was later employed as a boatman and it was no doubt these experiences that had saved his life while many more perished. Ironically, he also said that on the trip from America he saw people throwing wreaths and flowers into the sea, and on asking the reason was told that they were passing over the *Titanic*. The *Lusitania* attack coming only three years after the sensation of the *Titanic* sinking seemed like a deliberate re-enactment of a natural disaster.

Kildare's most famous seafarer was Admiral Sir John Michael de Robeck, brother to the Baron de Robeck, Gowran Grange, Naas. During the Gallipoli campaign he replaced the local Admiral of the Fleet who collapsed with a nervous breakdown when floating mines had led to the loss of four vessels. Initially the Gallipoli campaign was supposed to be a naval operation involving the bombing of Constantinople by Allied ships. On his appointment Admiral de Robeck advised Sir Ian Hamilton, Commander in Chief of the Allied forces, that he would require the aid of land troops if the campaign

The War at Sea

was to be successful. Acting Vice-Admiral de Robeck was mentioned for distinguished services in connection with the Gallipoli campaign.

Soon after dawn on the morning of March 18 Vice-Admiral Sir John de Robeck gave orders for the Fleet to clear for action in an attempt to force the passage of the Dardanelles by naval power alone - a feat accomplished a century before by Admiral Duckworth in the *Royal George*. But by 5 p.m. three battleships, *Bouvet, Irresistible* and *Ocean*, were out of action and the naval attack was called off. The Fleet withdrew to the island of Lemnos until the Turkish mines were dealt with. If the Allied Fleet had succeeded in forcing the straits the Gallipoli campaign would have never taken place and the war might have ended sooner.

Lieutenant Walter Borrowes, Barrettstown, was killed in action on board a submarine in 1915. The twenty-three year old son of Sir Erasmus Borrowes, Bart., of Barrettstown Castle was buried at sea. Commander Hubert Henry de Burgh, RN, eldest son of Colonel de Burgh, Oldtown, Naas was awarded the DSO for rescuing seven Germans under heavy fire. The official record of his conduct was as follows;

"For his services in command of a destroyer in the action with enemy destroyers off the Belgian coast on June 5 1917 when one of the enemy's destroyers *S20* was sunk. Commander de Burgh succeeded in saving seven men of *S20's* crew while under heavy fire from the shore batteries and with three German seaplanes hovering overhead."

An unnamed Naas cadet on his way to training college at Madras, India, was a passenger on *City of Birmingham* when it was torpedoed by a German submarine. He sent his parents the following letter, dated December 2 1916.

The War at Sea

"We were sitting in the music room, which is forward, having a lecture on Hindustani when suddenly there was an explosion which made the boat quiver from stern to bow. It was a most sickening thud. We stood up, Mr. Trail said 'Steady, steady,' and the chaps after the first rush (about 5 seconds) trooped out as steadily as veterans. I was about the last out.

"The torpedo had hit us astern, so she did not develop any decided list to one side or the other, but gradually settled down in the stern. (The author of the letter took several photographs of the sinking ship from his lifeboat.) The boat sank in 40 minutes. It was a grand, but awful sight, to see the bows in a perpendicular position, take a terrific plunge and disappear. We saw the steam rushing out as the boilers burst. All this time we could see the periscope of the submarine nutting round at a terrific pace. As soon as the boat had sunk she made off."

The passengers from *City of Birmingham* were picked up by a French ship and put off at Alexandria, Egypt. German submarines continued to be a major scourge until the entry of America into the war in 1917. With a vast army to transport across the Atlantic the Americans threw their navy wholeheartedly into the war against the U-Boats. Merchant ships were convoyed through dangerous waters and new depth charge bombs began to take toll on the U-Boats. The successes of the German submarines began to wane and the blockade of the North Sea ports had a telling effect on the population.

CHAPTER 8

Attack
– The March Offensive

As the war dragged into 1918 the morale of the British troops had reached an all time low. They no longer expected anything more from the war than pure survival. All eyes were on the arrival of the fresh American Army ('Yanks and tanks') to change the fortunes of the war. The Germans also knew that the coming of the Americans would decide the outcome of the conflict and had devised their own plans to end the war in one bold stroke. On March 21 they struck. The place selected was on the Somme, in a sector the British had recently taken over from the French, where the line was consequently in a poor state of repair and, most important, where a wedge could be driven through the Anglo-French front. Once through, the Germans were to turn northward and 'roll' up the British line, while a subsequent attack in the north at Hazebrouck would split the British front in two. General Erich Ludendorff and the German High Command believed this double stroke would be sufficient to end the war, if not victoriously then on terms acceptable to Germany.

The losses of 1917 and the continued lack of replacements from

Attack! The March Offensive

Ireland meant that the 16th and 36th Divisions had to be reorganised - the BEF had also found it necessary to reorganise. The 36th had suffered so badly that replacements to it were drawn from all spectrums of Ireland's religious and political spheres and it lost its distinctive 'Ulsterness.' The 16th fared no better. Like the 36th some of its battalions were disbanded, and the men posted to their regular battalions. The British front had not been so undermanned since Ypres in 1915. Twelve British divisions were facing 42 German divisions. The Germans were extremely confident after knocking Russia out of the war. (Russia had signed a truce with Germany in December 1917.) The German troops were told this was to be the decisive battle of the war and if they performed well the war would soon be over.

The German Army employed new tactics in the offensive. The German bombardment was to last only four hours and to 'neutralise' rather than kill the defenders. The first hours of a bombardment were deemed the worst, when the noise and concussion robbed men of their senses. Specially picked squads of stormtroopers would attack as the bombardment lifted and pass through the weak points in the enemy defences and keep going into the rear areas and spread confusion and terror. Behind the stormtroopers would come columns of infantry specially trained to move and fight in small groups exploiting the gains of the *Sturmtruppen*. Overhead, ground-attack squadrons would patrol, bombing and machine gunning surviving enemy points of resistance. (Twenty-one years later an Austrian veteran of the war, Adolf Hitler, would open the Second World War employing these same tactics.)

At 0440 hours on March 21 when mist lay thickly all over the valley and plain of the Somme over 10,000 guns and heavy mortars opened a tremendous bombardment on the British front. A deadly mixture of chlorine, mustard and tear gas swamped the lines first, followed by high explosive shells on every British position for a depth of

Attack! The March Offensive

15,000 yards, while mortar fire flattened the forward defensive wire. It was the most devastating and effective bombardment of the war: all communications were cut; movement on the front was severely disrupted as the shelling hit all rear and forward areas; and prolonged wearing of gas respirators on men - and horses - caused disorientation and confusion. The fog blanketed the German movement. Many British positions were annihilated by artillery fire before a single German appeared. After over four hours of shelling the German assault divisions moved forward. By the evening the situation was drastic; the British Fifth Army Forward Zone and a great part of the Battle Zone had been over-run. In two days fighting, despite heavy losses, the Germans had captured the whole of the British defended zone on either side of the Somme and were poised to push out into the country. By March 24 they had broken through and had advanced 14 miles in four days, the greatest gain of territory since 1914. Before them the British Fifth Army was in full retreat, while the Third Army in the north would soon follow.

On that first day of the 'Kaiser's Battle' , over a distance of approximately two miles, 1062 men of the 1st and 2nd Dublin Fusiliers were gassed, blown to bits, missing or taken prisoner by the Germans. Lance-Corporal John O'Brien, New Row, Naas serving with B Company 8th/9th RDF was killed in action on the first day of the March offensive. He was 48 years old and a married man. Sergeant Clarke Hewitt, Naas, also serving with the Dublins, was captured. He was reported 'missing' for weeks until news arrived in May that he was a prisoner of the Germans.

A survivor of the March offensive Pte. Michael Dennison, Eadestown, serving with the 10th RDF, received the parchment certificate of the Irish Brigade for gallantry and devotion to duty during 1917. The certificate which was signed by Major-General W. B. Hickie stated "Your name and deeds have been ordered to be entered in the

Attack! The March Offensive

record of the Irish Division. " Pte. Dennison, who enlisted in 1915, was a veteran of many engagements and was wounded previously in France.

Britain looked towards Ireland for men to replace those lost in the March offensive. Conscription had been introduced in Britain in 1916 and John Redmond had insisted that only an Irish parliament could make such a serious decision for Ireland. Now, Britain proposed to introduce compulsory military service in Ireland for all males between the ages of 18 and 51. Overnight the entire atmosphere in Ireland towards Britain changed, more so than the events of Easter 1916 could ever hope to produce. Nationalists in Ireland united against conscription and Home Rulers and Sinn Feiners formed a committee to resist its implementation. Despite John Dillon's objections, the conscription bill was passed by the House of Commons. In protest John Dillion led the Home Rule Party out of the House of Commons and home to Ireland. The Catholic bishops, meeting in Maynooth, issued a strong condemnation of forced conscription. The Irish trade unions organised a one-day general strike in protest. Recruits flocked in their thousand to the Irish Volunteers pledging to fight all attempts by Britain to introduce conscription. By the autumn of 1918 the Volunteers had 100,000 members. Eventually the British authorities were dissuaded from introducing conscription simply because they realised that it would require more troops to police conscription than its enforcement would produce.

On the morning of April 9 a bombardment which rivalled in intensity that of March 21 erupted on the British front from Lens to Armentiéres. Again aided by mist and fog, forty-two German divisions assaulted and broke the British line from Wytschaete to Givenchy. Parts of the British Second and First Armies were overwhelmed and once again the BEF was in retreat. The German attacks continued until April 30 but failed to break the stubborn resistance of the BEF,

Attack! The March Offensive

who for forty days had withstood, practically alone, for French help was minimal, everything Ludendorff could throw at them. The crisis passed and the German offensive began to run out of steam. Ludendorff switched his attack to the French front on May 27 and by June 3 was at Château-Thierry, only 56 miles from Paris. Here the Germans ran out of time, for among the hastily-assembled reserves into which they eventually ran were the American 3rd Infantry Division and 2nd Marine Regiment. On June 6 the Marines counterattacked at Bellau Wood after the immortal cry "Retreat! Hell! We only got here."

Photo: J. MARSH

James Marsh, Sallins (right) and friend.

far from the short grass

Attack! The March Offensive

The German offensive slowed down as the Allied line held fast. The German effort had failed to achieve its objective and with the arrival of the American divisions the Allies at last had adequate reserves. The Germans had exhausted their reserves and the offensive had destroyed the ability of the German army to prolong the war. The front stabilised and the Allies prepared for a counter offensive.

The losses in the Irish divisions during the March and April offensives were very high - 6,435 killed, wounded and missing in the 16th and 6,109 in the 36th. The divisions were taken out of the line to be refitted and reorganised. The 10th Division's battalions - there were only three Irish battalions left in the division after its 'Indianisation' - arrived in France in May after service in Palestine and to the shock of all, both the battalions of the 10th and 16th were distributed to other divisions on the Western front. By 1918 the Irish had few friends in Whitehall and the disbanding of the 'Irish' divisions was seen as an act of policy by the War Office. Chief of the Imperial General Staff was Sir Henry Wilson, an implacable foe of Irish Catholic Nationalism and no friend of anything 'Irish'. Since the Easter Rebellion the British authorities had been systemically reducing the 'Irishness' of the Irish units. Irish drafts were sent to non-Irish units while English drafts were sent to Irish battalions. Wih the mass opposition of Ireland to conscription and the rise of Sinn Fein the War Office was again questioning the validity of having distinct 'Irish' divisions in the army. The mistrust of Irish regiments had no foundation. They stuck to their task in many cases to the bitter end and despite these obstacles the Irish regiments soldiered on. They continued the fight through the hard battles of the Hindenburg Line, Second Cambrai and the recapture of Mons.

Private Patrick 'Paddy' Murray, Naas, joined the 1st Dublin Fusiliers early in the war. Though badly wounded he returned to the front and died of gas wounds on May 13. Private James Marsh, from

Attack! The March Offensive

Sherlockstown, Sallins, serving with the RAMC, died on July 16 in Durban, South Africa, of dysentery, while en route to India or German East Africa. It is possible he had been gassed on the Western Front and was being transferred to a warmer climate. His younger brother, John, also served in the RAMC. He survived the war and returned home to Sallins. (Their cousin, Rifleman Michael Murphy, 12th Royal Irish Rifles, died of wounds on February 7 1918. His regiment was with the reorganised 36th Division in the lines at St. Quentin at the time.)

On August 8 the Allies launched an offensive that began to force the Germans back over the ground they had recently won. Ludendorff

Photo: M. CULLEN.

Maurice Cullen
Athy,
Killed in Action
1918.

Attack! The March Offensive

called August 8 the 'black day of the German army.' The British used the same tactics the Germans had used in the March offensive, exploiting their breakthroughs with a force of 554 tanks, some of them new 'Whippets,' fast light tanks. The bulk of the infantry were Australian and Canadian. These tough 'Colonials' had not suffered as much trauma as the rest of the British infantry in the March and April battles. By the evening of the first day the British had advanced seven miles, taken 15,000 prisoners and destroyed six out of the ten German divisions in the line. The next day the French advance began. By the middle of August, Ludendorff knew the Germans would not achieve a victory and would have to negotiate. After much political wrangling the German High Command began talks with a neutral power to arrange negotiations. But events were moving much faster. The Americans launched their offensive on September 12 and follow-up attacks by the Allies breached the Hindenburg Line, Germany's last defensive position.

The Irish Guards were positioned at Ayette, as the Germans pulled back. Here they lay out in the sun and rested and prepared to attack across the Canal du Nord. Pte. Maurice Cullen, Foxhill, Athy, was serving with the 1st Irish Guards as the last Allied offensives began. His brother, George, was serving with 2nd Irish Guards. The Germans were in a wood facing them. On September 9 Maurice Cullen was shot dead by a German sniper, concealed in a tree. The sniper had already shot several other victims before hitting Pte. Cullen, but his location was spotted and he was shot dead by Maurice's comrades.

In September the British and French armies on the Salonika front combined with the Serbs and forced Bulgaria to surrender, laying open the way to the Danube and a back door into Austria. On the Italian front the Allies shattered the Austrian army at Vittorio Veneto and on November 3, Austria, now frantic, signed an armistice. Turkey signed a local armistice with the British in the Middle East on October

Attack! The March Offensive

30 allowing the Royal Navy to steam up the Dardanelles and occupy Constantinople. Hungary signed a separate truce on November 7. Ludendorff and Hindenburg, seeing Germany's position was hopeless, sought an armistice on fair terms. The Allies insisted on unconditional surrender and the Kaiser's abdication. The German navy mutinied at Kiel and with food in short supply disturbances spread. With Germany hovering on the brink of civil war and the loyalty of the army in question, the Kaiser abdicated on November 9 and fled to neutral Holland. A Republic was proclaimed in Germany and negotiations to end the war began.

At 11 o'clock on the morning of November 11 1918 the guns on the Western front fell silent. An Armistice had been signed six hours earlier in a railway carriage parked in a siding in a forest in Compiègne between the Allies and representatives of the new German socialist republic. The War to end all Wars was over.

CHAPTER 9

All Quiet on the Western Front

When the guns fell silent on the eleventh hour on the eleventh day of the eleventh month in that last year of the war there was little celebrating in Ireland. The wind of change had come and with it a new chapter in Irish history. The men of 1916 were the heroes now and those who had donned khaki were quickly forgotten as the country mobilised behind Sinn Fein. Armistice Day was a day of celebration throughout the Empire, but in County Kildare the altered political climate caused the occasion to be muted. In Naas the Union Jack was hoisted over the Court House and the *Kildare Observer* reported that 'there was a general feeling of relief, if there was little outward manifestation of jubilation. Towards evening there was some flag waving by the military, who later indulged in pranks and demonstrations to show their joy at the termination of the war.' Some of the shops and houses in the town and its vicinity also displayed the British flag.

In Newbridge and the Curragh the *Kildare Observer* also reported that the military had celebrated 'with flag waving, cheering and other

All Quiet on the Western Front

Photo: P. GOREY.

Sgt. Major Joseph Bermingham, Kilina (2nd from right), served with an artillery regiment 1914-1918.

demonstrations of joy.' The town of Celbridge was brilliantly illuminated for the victory celebrations and celebrating went on in the streets until the small hours of the morning. The Newbridge Town Commission passed a resolution of congratulations to the Allies on their victory.

The Great War claimed the lives of 49,400 Irishmen, while many thousands more were wounded or maimed. On demobilisation, 248,000 men returned to Ireland alone, and based on the number of Irishmen serving in the Allied armies of America, Australia, Britain, Canada, New Zealand and South Africa, historians estimate that almost 500,000 Irishmen served during the First World War. Around

All Quiet on the Western Front

23,000 men from Kildare served in those ranks. In the years following the war the memory of their great sacrifice and their countless deeds of valour and heroism became lost in the rise in national sentiment and the emergence of the Irish State which had created a new set of heroes. The men who had fought for 'the freedom of small nations' were looked on as having served the wrong cause. There was no 'land fit for heroes' waiting for them.

Those who had survived the nightmare of the Great War bore strong witness to the cruelty of modern war: missing limbs, blinded, gassed, shell-shocked or forever haunted by the deeds they had witnessed, or committed. They lived out the rest of their lives on their modest war pensions, pushed into the background by the new war raging in Ireland and the struggle for independence. The families of the dead were left to pick up the shattered pieces of their lives and some would never recover. Whole generations had been wiped out. Some families had lost a father and son, others had lost all the surviving males in the household. The Halligan family of Dublin Road, Naas lost three brothers, Matt, Michael and Mark while the Curtis family of Kilcrow also lost three sons, Patrick, John and Laurence. There was hardly a house in the back streets of Athy, Naas or Newbridge which wasn't affected by the war.

Many veterans appeared untouched by the years of savagery and conflict. They just pushed it to the back of their minds, never spoke about it, and got on with the rest of their lives. Tom Bergin, from Rowan Terrace, Newbridge, survived the Great War intact, and died in 1996, aged 97. So too, did Paddy O' Brien, Limerick Bridge, Jigginstown. Though wounded in the leg, he returned home and died in the early 1980s aged 84. Others choose to stay in the British armed forces rather than return to Ireland, where poverty and political turmoil awaited them. Denis Lawless, Naas, enlisted in the RDF in 1916, when

All Quiet on the Western Front

he was only seventeen. He served in Salonika and France, where he was wounded in the neck. When the Dubs were disbanded, in 1922, he re-enlisted in the Dorsetshire Regt., serving in Egypt, Malta and India. He retired a Sergeant in 1937, after 21 years service.

Five-hundred and sixty-seven Kildaremen lost their lives in the Great War: 193 died serving with the Royal Dublin Fusiliers; 51 with the Irish Guards; 41 with the Leinster Regiment and the rest were distributed over the other services. The family of Private Andrew Delaney, gassed in Flanders, were left with a death grant of £7 and a shiny medal accompanied by a letter saying that it would have been presented to her husband had he been still alive. All families of the dead were given a large memorial medal in honour of their sacrifice. It was 4-4½" wide approximately, and when felt, is as cold as a tombstone - "cold comfort for a families' loss."

Lance-Corporal J. "Bossy" Doran, one of several Dorans from Naas to serve with the RDF, came home from the war with a severe leg wound. He was looked after by his mother at Fair Green, Naas, but died of his wound on August 24 1919. He was 45 and is interred in St. Corban's cemetery, Naas. He was one of many who lingered after the war carrying the scars and wounds which would ultimately cut short their lives. Many veterans suffered from gas wounds and were tormented all their lives by the pain and misery that most cruel of weapons caused.

Peter Buckley, from Celbridge, died on April 6 1918 before the Armistice was signed. He had been severely wounded on February 12 1916 while serving with the 4th RDF. Pte. Buckley was wounded in the back by a shell in the Dardanelles fighting. He was invalided home and developed consumption from the hardships he endured. He ended up in Peamount Sanatorium and then Celbridge Workhouse Hospital

All Quiet on the Western Front

where he died. His brother, Hugh, died of wounds on November 3 1914, while serving with the 2nd Connaught Rangers in France.

The 'War to end all Wars' had been the most devastating conflict ever. Ten million soldiers had died; another twenty-two million were wounded or maimed; ten million civilians had died and another ten million people died from a war-spawned plague of Spanish influenza. The veterans swore 'Never again'. So, too, did the politicians gathered in Versailles to sign the peace. But the Germans signed only under duress. The Treaty was forced upon them without discussion and they were forced to pay war reparations by the victors. They did not forget and soon a leader arrived to remind them of their humiliation. Twenty years later he sparked off a firestorm that overshadowed the War to end War.

PART II

"On the far off shores there is an abiding memorial that no pen or chisel has traced."

Pericles

CHAPTER 10

The Phoney War

On September 1 1939 Germany invaded Poland. Britain and France, tied to Poland by treaty declared war on Germany and so began the Second World War, the most devastating conflict in history. The new Free State of Ireland, or Eire, remained neutral throughout the war, though the government offered as much valuable assistance to Britain and her allies as was possible for a neutral country. While there was no shortage of volunteers from Southern Ireland recruiting was not what it was during the First World War. It was only less than twenty years since the rampages of the Black and Tans and the 'Troubles' were still fresh in the memories of the Irish people. Despite this 80,000 Southern Irishmen fought with the British forces during WWII, 10,000 of them been killed in action. (38,000 Northern Irishmen fought during WWII with 4,500 of them *hors de combat*.) The reasons so many joined up in the Second World War were as diverse as those in the Great War. A chance for adventure or an escape from poverty were the main reasons - Independence had made no difference to the poor of Ireland. Like the Great War everyone thought it would be over by Christmas.

The Phoney War

Britain began mobilising for war at once. Kildareman Major Charles Clements, was in England when war once again came to Europe. Born in 1904 in Killadoon, Celbridge, Charles Clements had joined the 4th Queens Own Hussars in India in 1924. A keen huntsman his team had won the Muttra Cup in 1928. On September 2 he was driving to Portsmouth. "I passed two loads of children from London and Southampton," he wrote "each labelled with the name of their school taking their cargo of evacuees to the little Hampshire villages. At every small railway station, transport and guides were waiting to take off those arriving by train. There was an even bigger traffic block than usual in Winchester and I could not help feeling what chaos one well directed bomb could cause.

"In the country few people except the evacuees were carrying respirators, but as I approached Portsmouth they became far more common. The pavements of Portsmouth were swarming with people. Naval and military reservists were reporting at the many barracks in the town. Others, partly equipped, were being marched about from place to place, and high overhead swung seven barrage balloons. A very inadequate protection, I thought, to this highly vulnerable target."

With the independence of twenty-six counties of Ireland from Britain after the Anglo-Irish Treaty of 1921 the bulk of the Irish line regiments of the British Army were disbanded. The Royal Dublin Fusiliers, Connaught Rangers, Leinster Regiment, Royal Irish Regiment, South Irish Horse and the Royal Munster Fusiliers were disbanded in a sad and moving ceremony in July 1922. Surviving regiments were the Irish Guards, Royal Inniskilling Fusiliers, Royal Irish Hussars, Royal Irish Fusiliers and the Royal Irish Rifles who became the Royal Ulster Rifles.

Although there had been three full Irish infantry divisions in the First World War the largest unit of Irishmen to serve together as infantry in the Second World War was the 38th (Irish) Brigade, consisting of the

The Phoney War

Photo: S. MAHON.

Michael "Mickser" Mahon and Jackie Sheridan pictured in 1939 soon after enlistment.

1st Royal Irish Fusiliers, 6th Royal Inniskilling Fusiliers and the 2nd London Irish Rifles. During the Second World War it was not too easy to get into an Irish regiment and many Irishmen fought individually in different British regiments. Naas men Jackie Sheridan and Michael Mahon travelled to Belfast to enlist. Both had only turned eighteen. Michael Mahon, or Mickser, was born in New Row in 1921 and had just left his job in Odlums mills. Jackie was employed with Peter Lawlor and had a row over overtime and asked Mickser to join the British army. (Jackie's uncle, Paddy Sheridan, was killed in action in France, while serving with the 8th Royal Dublin Fusiliers, on February 16 1917.) Neither of them had said anything to their parents about enlisting. Mickser had tried to join the Royal Navy but he was too young. He went to a Warrant Officer in Rathmore and a warrant was sent out for him to go to Belfast. His father went mad when Mickser

The Phoney War

told him. Mrs. Sheridan did not know anything until the morning Jackie left when she saw Mickser waiting outside their house, 4 Caragh Road. "I'll never forget Jackie with his little suitcase under his arm," Mickser said "as he headed off that morning at 6 o'clock, whistling. We caught the train to Belfast. They were not worried about our age. We were examined by nine doctors to make sure we were fit and well. From Belfast we went to Scotland and then to our first camp in Reading. We knew our close order drill in a week and the British were going to send us home, because they thought we were deserters from the Free State army."

While training together the two boyhood friends incurred the wrath of an English Lieutenant. One morning while on parade the English officer approached Jackie Sheridan and noticing his dark stubble barked, "Did you shave this morning, Private Sheridan?"

"Yes, sir," Jackie answered.

"Well, shave again, Private Sheridan," the Lieutenant said. "You are not in the dirty Irish Army now."

With that Mickser went for the Lieutenant and was promptly marched off to the glasshouse. (The Lieutenant was later killed at El Alamein.)

The two friends enlisted in the 1st Battalion, Royal Sussex Regiment, which had been formed in Belfast in 1701. They were sent to France in 1940 but had to withdraw over the Channel as the Germans swept through the Low Countries. Mickser was home in Naas on fourteen days leave when the Germans attacked and had to rush back to his unit. They were not the only Naas men facing the German onslaught. Brothers Johnny and Billy Doran from Fairgreen, Naas were also in the ranks at the outbreak of war. Johnny, known as

The Phoney War

'Mons' since birth - he was born while his father, also Johnny, was fighting at Mons in 1914 - (see page 98). The two brothers joined the Royal Artillery at York Barracks, Bristol, in 1935. (Ireland was not declared a Republic until 1949 and until then all citizens of Ireland had, under the terms of the Anglo-Irish Treaty, dual membership and could hold an Irish and a British passport.) Pte. Johnny Doran went to France with the BEF in late 1939. His brother, Billy, was stationed in Bristol in an anti-aircraft unit. He remained there for the duration of the war.

It was not long before the reality of war was brought home to Kildare. Third Officer Patrick Donnelly-Swift was on board the SS *Yorkshire,* out of Liverpool, when it hit a German mine on October 17 1939. Twenty-seven year old Patrick, was from Kildare town and was soon to have being promoted to Captain. He was also soon to wed. His mother heard the news on the radio, and without hearing the name of the ship, knew it was her son's which had been sunk.

From the end of the war with Poland in September 1939, there were no further German military operations until April 9 1940 when the Nazis attacked both Denmark and Norway. The new tactics of modern war were known as 'Blitzkrieg'- Lightning War. Parachute and glider troops would seize important objectives such as river crossings from an unexpected direction, while Stuka dive-bombers relentlessly pounded enemy defences and airfields in pre-emptive strikes. Then the Panzers (tanks) would exploit the confusion and uncertainty, using their speed and momentum to carry the war where it was lest expected. It was not a new concept, for cavalry had been used in this way for hundreds of years. But the concept of Blitzkrieg had been evolved by progressive German Generals such as Heinz Guderian and Erich von Manstein and worked to deadly effect in the early days of 1940.

On April 8-9 German troops landed at Tromsö and occupied

The Phoney War

Photo: K. DONNELLY-SWIFT.

3rd Officer Patrick Donnely-Swift, (right) Kildare, on board the SS Yorkshire.

Narvik, Bergen and Oslo. Denmark was occupied with little resistance on April 9 while the Allies declared their intention of defending Norway. 2nd Lieutenant Darby Michael Kennedy, Bishopscourt, Kill, serving with the 1st Irish Guards, was over the moon when he heard this. He told his batman to, "Pack my Colt and Mauser, and the Remington with the telescopic sights, and put the small pistol and the knuckle-duster somewhere handy." D.M. Kennedy, or John, as he preferred to be called, was born at Bishopscourt in 1919. At the beginning of 1939 John Kennedy made his way to England to join the British Army. At that time it was not too easy to secure a commission or join a regiment of your choice. With the assistance and help of an

far from the short grass

The Phoney War

old family friend and neighbour, General Fanshawe, John applied for, and was accepted by the Irish Guards.

On the morning of April 15 the British 24th Guards Brigade, including the 1st Battn., Irish Guards, was landed at Harstad on the island of Hinnöy - some 60 miles from Narvik, separated from the port by a sea channel and snow-covered mountains.

John Kennedy wrote, "This place must be heavenly during the summer and all the mountains are snow covered and the hillsides purple with shrubs. Even now it has its 'looks' as one might say, because it is all snow and when the sun catches some of the peaks it reflects their shadow into the water. Still, I would sooner be at home today and see the unforgettable gorse at Punchestown."

More British troops arrived, but unlike the Germans, the British troops were not equipped for mountain fighting. The landing of more British, French and Polish troops could not redress the situation and it was decided to abandon central Norway and concentrate all available forces against Narvik. On April 12 eighty-three British aircraft - Blenheims and Wellingtons - attacked targets off Norway at Stavanger. George Fawcett, 23, from Straffan, was serving with 50 Squadron, RAF, and was based at Waddington. Twelve aircraft were shot down, among them George Fawcett's. His body was never found.

On April 24 the 1st Irish Guards became the first Irish infantry unit to clash with the German Army in World War Two. Dennis McLoughlin, from Millicent, Sallins, was serving with the Irish Guards in Norway. He had joined the Irish Guards the previous year and was accompanied by his father, Pat, to England on that occasion, as he had only turned nineteen. (One had to be eighteen to join the British Army, and usually needed references of good character, while you had to be nineteen

The Phoney War

to serve overseas.) It was a great honour to join the Irish Guards, or 'The Micks', as they were affectionately known. Dennis McLoughlin was a very tall and imposing youth and his family were proud he had joined this prestigious Irish regiment.

With the south of Norway now free of Allied troops, the Germans were free to use all available troops to push for the relief of Narvik. The Allied Command decided to stall the Germans at Mö, the narrowest part of Norway. The 1st Scots Guards were sent there and on May 13 the Irish Guards were put on the *Chobry* en route for Mö to help the Scots Guards hold. Two days later, the *Chobry* was bombed by three Heinkels. Fifty tons of ammunition were in the hold and the whole midship of the *Chobry* became a raging furnace. The bombs all landed near the senior officers cabins and the battalion commander, Colonel Faulkner, and several senior officers were killed. The German bombers circled overhead as the battalion was ordered up on deck. It was too cold to jump overboard and the Guards waited patiently until the escorting destroyers pulled alongside to evacuate them. As the fires raged ammunition and green and red flares exploded forcing isolated men overboard. 694 men were evacuated in 16 minutes, but there were many casualties and all the battalion's equipment was lost. Guardsman Dennis McLoughlin was one of the fatalities. The survivors of the battalion were picked up by various ships and brought to Harstad to refit. 2nd Lieut. John Kennedy was one of three officers mentioned in the official report: "These officers displayed great calmness and courage and did valuable work in rescuing and caring for the wounded; they were amongst the last to leave the ship. Many lives were saved by this display of coolness and their ability to organise the men."

French and Norwegian troops captured Narvik on May 28, but it was decided to abandon Norway altogether. Narvik's port installations were demolished and the 25,000 men of the Franco-Polish-British

The Phoney War

Expeditionary Force were evacuated to Scotland on June 7.

The British Expeditionary Force arrived in France in October 1939, a full month after Britain's declaration of war. From then until the German invasion of the Low Countries the Allies idly faced the massed forces of the Third Reich - a period known as the 'Phoney War.' Expecting a replay of the Schlieffen Plan Britain and France had to wait for Germany to violate the neutrality of Belgium, Holland and Luxembourg, as the impregnable Maginot Line protected France's border with Germany and the only route into France was through the Low Countries.

Major Charles Clements, from Killadoon, Celbridge, arrived in France, with elements of the 3rd Division, in October 1939. "We travelled in considerable comfort." he wrote. "I had a cabin *de luxe* all to myself for the first time in my life, and nearly every sergeant had at least a berth and no one was really uncomfortable. We sailed after dark and when I got up in the morning after a very good night's rest we were off the French coast at a point which we were presently able to identify as the entrance to the harbour of Brest. We had not been in convoy, but had had an escort of one or two destroyers most of the way."

The 3rd Division, moved to Evron, near Lille, to take over a section of the line from the French on the Belgian border. "Time rolled on uneventfully up to Christmas." Maj. Clements wrote. "Christmas Day was the first holiday that many of the men had had since the war started and even then they could not all have it. It was certainly my first half holiday (not that I was overworked, life was not nearly such a strain as it had been in the summer) still the fact remains that I had not had a minimum of a full morning and at least two hours work sometime after lunch.

The Phoney War

"It was frightfully cold after Christmas. My men, who were constantly in the open on point duty etc., stuck it magnificently." Major Clements returned to his regiment, 4th Queens Own Hussars, Royal Armoured Corps, in England on January 22 1940 after four months of the 'Phoney War' in France.

When the Nazi war machine rolled into Belgium and Holland on May 10 the BEF and the French 1st Army moved north in response. While Bock's Army Group B kept the British and French pinned down in Belgium, Rundstedt's Army Group A reached the Meuse River by attacking through the supposedly impregnable Ardennes. The Panzers broke through the French line at Sedan and the path into northern France lay open.

By May 20 the German Panzers had reached Noyelles in France, splitting the Allied forces in half. On May 21 the British attacked at Arras and while the attack was at first successful it was soon driven back by the Germans. The following day the Panzers began moving north toward the French ports of Calais and Boulogne. By May 23 the Germans had cut off the BEF, the Belgian and French 1st Armies in northern France. Two days later the Panzers stopped for repairs and Lord Gort, the British commander, decided to withdraw the BEF from Belgium and move it to Dunkirk to save as much of his force as possible. Gort reasoned it was better to save the BEF to fight another day. The surrender of the Belgian Army on May 28 sealed the fate of the French 1st Army around Lille. The BEF had already began its retirement to the port of Dunkirk and ultimately its evacuation from France.

All the regular Irish regiments in Europe were in action during the German invasions and the retreat to Dunkirk. The 2nd Irish Guards were sent to Holland after Germany invaded the Low Countries and after assisting in the safe extrication of the Dutch Royal Family, moved to France. They were evacuated from Boulogne after sustaining over

The Phoney War

200 casualties. The Inniskillings suffered heavy casualties with only 215 officers and men escaping from France. Both the Ulster Rifles and the Irish Fusiliers managed to evacuate around 600 troops. The Royal Irish Fusiliers, or 'Faughs' (Gaelic battle cry of 'Faugh A Ballagh' - 'Clear the Way') had held up the 7th Panzer Division, commanded by no less than Major General Erwin Rommel, for several days on the Béthune-La Bassée Canal.

Photo: F. McCORMACK.

Jack McCormack, Newbridge (right), with two of his brothers, Terry (centre) and Jimmy.

The Phoney War

Guardsman John McCormack, Newbridge, was serving with the 2nd Irish Guards. John, or Jack, was from Dawson Street in Newbridge. His father, Patrick, moved to Newbridge from Fermanagh in 1902 and married local woman Bridget Flood. Their first child, Jimmy, was born in Newbridge. Four more, Frank, Jack, Terry and Crissie were born in India. Patrick McCormack ended up a Sergeant-Major farrier, and returned to Newbridge after 12 years service in India. Three sons, Jack, Frank and Jimmy joined the British Army while two, Terry and Ernie, joined the Irish Army. Jack McCormack joined the Irish Guards in 1933 when he was twenty-four and a married man.

On May 13 the 2nd Irish Guards landed at the Hook, in Holland, and took up defensive positions to hold the village and keep the road and port open. About midday, Queen Wilhelmina of the Netherlands, and her entourage, arrived and were taken on board the HMS *Malcolm* bound for England. Later that afternoon the Dutch Government and the Diplomatic Corps were also evacuated. That night and the next morning German air raids killed eleven Guardsmen. Following the raids the Irish Guards were evacuated back to England. There was very little rest for Jack McCormack and the rest of the Irish Guards. On May 22 they arrived at Boulogne, as part of 20th Guards Brigade, to guard the Channel ports.

It was raining heavily as the Guardsmen lined the decks wearing their long oil-skin gas-capes. Hordes of panic-stricken refugees waited on the dock ready to rush the ships. Guardsmen with fixed bayonets had to clear a path through the mob so that the battalion could disembark. They took up positions around the town to await the Germans. Around three o'clock the Germans attacked with tanks, infantry and aeroplanes. Dawn brought German reinforcements and heavier attacks and No. 1 and No. 4 Companies both suffered heavy losses - 60 and 88 men respectively. The Guards were ordered to

The Phoney War

evacuate and withdrew to the harbour and barricaded the streets around it. The Germans were closing in as the destroyer HMS *Whitshed* came alongside the quay. With the Irish Guards and a Royal Navy landing party giving covering fire, many soldiers and wounded were evacuated onto the boats in the harbour. An eyewitness recalled: "as the German infantry now passed ahead of their tanks and infiltrated closer and closer to the quays, the fine discipline of the Guards earned the awed open-mouthed respect of all. Watching them in perfect order, moving exactly together, engaging target after target as though on parade ground drill, it was difficult to realise that this was the grim reality of battle. They were truly magnificent, and no sailor who saw them could ever forget the feeling of pride he experienced."

The Irish Guards were last to re-embark. At half-past nine, with the Germans continually firing, the last Bren Gun section ran for the boats as tanks rumbled up to the quayside to duel with the guns of the destroyers pulling away. The Irish Guards reached Dover at midnight and entrained reaching Tweseldown Camp. When they returned to England Jack McCormack recalled the authorities wanted to make them pay for the equipment they left behind!

The evacuation of the BEF from France began on May 26. Adolf Hitler had foolishly ordered the Panzers to halt their advance giving the British vital time to start the evacuation. From Britain a motley fleet of coastal ferries, coasters, barges and lighters sailed with the Royal Navy to re-embark the BEF. After news of Operation Dynamo broke many boat owners from England simply set sail to Dunkirk to assist in the evacuation. The BEF in disarray poured on to the beaches through the burning rubble of Dunkirk. They were exhausted from days of frantic fighting. Supplies and rations were running out and no one knew how close the German panzers were. All thought was of escape. The troops were demoralised and hungry and had to wait under a hail of shells and bombs from the dive-bombing Stukas wailing overhead.

far from the short grass

The Phoney War

Dunkirk town and harbour were a shambles so troops had to be re-embarked from the beach and the East and West Moles. The East Mole was a precarious jetty extending nearly a mile out to sea while the West Mole was dangerously close to oil storage tanks on the docks. Improvised jetties were made by driving trucks into the sea. On May 27 Hitler resumed the Panzer attack. However, most of the British divisions and all but V Corps of the French 1st Army had got inside

Photo: R. WILSON.

Johnny Doran, (left) Naas, and comrade.

The Phoney War

the Dunkirk perimeter. As the evacuations went on the British and French continued to pull back.

On the beaches and the jetties orderly lines of men waited patiently for their turn to be re-embarked. Sometimes men cracked under the strain and orderly lines would again have to be formed at gunpoint. Some men appeared singly, or in groups. Other units arrived in good order and in good spirits. On the open beaches the troops had no shelter from the bombs of the Luftwaffe, but surprisingly low casualties were suffered as much of the explosion of German bombs was muffled by the sand. Above them the RAF fought unseen dogfights with the Luftwaffe greatly helping their stricken comrades below.

Over the next few days the Royal Navy, assisted by the civilian flotilla, evacuated 338,226 men from the beaches of Dunkirk turning a bitter defeat into a victory of sorts. Pte. Johnny Doran, Royal Horse Artillery, was evacuated early in that crucial week. He could not swim and along with other non-swimmers he was tied to a fellow soldier who could and 'towed' out to an awaiting boat. He later recalled that everything looked white from the dust of exploding German bombs; houses, fields, even themselves. At one stage on the retreat through the Dunkirk perimeter Pte. Doran helped to bury some dead soldiers at the side of a road. They were no sooner buried when they were unearthed again by bombs from German Stukas.

All evacuees from Dunkirk were returned to ports on the South-east coast. They were tired, dirty and hungry. Some had not slept or eaten in days. Many arrived in their stocking feet. Others were in their shirt sleeves or in torn uniforms. All of them were glad to have survived their ordeal. As they arrived they were met by local people who brought them blankets, sheets, cups of tea, sandwiches and cigarettes. When their stocks ran out they sent schoolboys with barrows

The Phoney War

around appealing for help. The barrows came back piled with food and hundreds of cigarettes.

When the last of the BEF had been evacuated from Dunkirk there were still 140,000 British soldiers left in France, among them the 51st Highland and an understrength 1st Armoured Division. Captain Jenico Gormanstown, 16th Viscount, of Naas, was serving with the 2nd/4th Battn., King's Own Yorkshire Light Infantry and was fighting with the British and French forces around Rouen. He was the son of the 15th Viscount Gormanstown and of Eileen Viscountess Gormanstown (nee Butler) and husband of the Viscountess Gormanstown (nee Hanley) of Naas. Twenty-five year old Capt. Gormanstown was killed in action on June 9, as the British prepared for another evacuation from La Havre. His body was never found. On June 12 the entire 51st Division was defeated and taken captive at St. Valery. The 'grand excursion to France' was over.

CHAPTER 11

Balkans Interlude

On October 28, 1940 Italy invaded Greece, expecting to overrun the country within weeks. The Greek Army, though heavily outnumbered, put up a spirited resistance, even chasing the Italians back into Albania. Winston Churchill offered troops and aid and in March 1941 British, Australian and New Zealand troops landed at Piraieus and Vulvos. In April Germany arrived to Italy's aid, swept through Yugoslavia in 12 days, and invaded Greece on two fronts - through Bulgaria and Yugoslavia.

"We were sent to Greece to fight the Italians," Major Charles Clements, 4th Hussars, wrote. "When we landed Greece and Germany were not at war and the German Military attaché watched us disembark. He could not have been very impressed by our 'Tanks' which were only tanks in name. In fact the Mark VI B Tank was in reality a lightly armoured machine gun carrier on tracks. Used in this capacity it would have been efficient, but, unfortunately as it was

Balkans Interlude

called a 'Tank' the Higher Command used it as such, in which capacity it was useless having neither a gun that could hurt an enemy tank nor the armour to keep out their fire."

Major Clements had been stationed in England during the invasion of France and after Dunkirk the 4th Hussars were one of the only fully

Photo: MRS. C. CLEMENTS.

Charles Clements, Celbridge, 4th Hussars.

Balkans Interlude

intact units awaiting the German invasion. In October 1940 he had returned on leave to Killadoon, Celbridge, aware that he was going overseas and would probably not return for a long time. (Overseas leave was not granted until September 1944.) Shortly after the 4th Hussars sailed to the Middle East. The 4th Hussars were a proud regiment, whose cavalry record went back to the Charge of the Light Brigade during the Crimea War, and before that to Wellington's campaign in the Peninsula. Now they were part of a hastily gathered British Expeditionary Force sent to curb Italian expansion in the Balkans.

"We were part of the armoured division, really a 'Brigade Group' consisting of ourselves, the '3rd Royal Tank Regiment' - medium tanks with a two-pounder gun, heavy but not quite equal to most of the German 'Panzers' which we met. The 'Northumberland Hussars' a territorial artillery regiment, and an extremely good one, also with two-pounder guns, carried on trucks, but supposed to be dismounted for action and the 'Rangers' a very bad London territorial regiment. Only the 3rd Tank Regiment had seen previous action in the war.

"We were later joined by Australian and New Zealand Divisions. Personally I had to fudge a Medical Board to get to the War at all; as my knee kept giving out and when it did I could scarcely walk for the next 48 hours. When I had gone with the 3rd Division to France in 1939 I had to be carried onto the boat. I was in command of B Squadron, which consisted of a HQ of four tanks and five troops of three tanks each."

The 4th Hussars spent over a month at Ynitsa, near Salonika, and when the Germans invaded on April 6 they were withdrawn from the Salonika front towards Monastir. The German panzers reached Salonika on April 9 and the 4th Hussars were ordered to hold Ptolemais to allow the remnants of the Greek 7th Army to escape into

Balkans Interlude

the comparative safety of the mountains. Major Clements wrote: "Struggling across the valley in a never ending line, worn and depressed, walked the remnants of the 7th Greek Army. They do not march, they have no formation and apparently no officers, they just shuffle along, mostly carrying some sort of weapon and each man carrying a pathetic bundle of belongings. Occasionally a cart or wagon drawn by emaciated ponies has a place in the queue and now and then a troop of Cavalry complete with officers clatters by. It is a rabble but it is not yet a rout. They have been told where to go and they are going there by path and track avoiding the roads. As I find out later their artillery are on the roads.

"The problem was what to do now. I thought that my duty and therefore my object was to get what remained of the regiment out of Greece. If we could hold up the German advance it would increase our chances. We could not block the road as any block could be easily by-passed and also I did not know if any other of our troops were retiring upon Kalamata."

On April 22 the Greek Army capitulated in Salonika and the BEF began to withdraw south for evacuation. Maj. Clements was in the retreat towards the port of Kalamata where the British, Australians and New Zealanders were attempting to re-embark. "We drive on through the night," he wrote. "It is obvious by now that the Campaign is a failure. I am too sleepy to take much interest. There are Greeks all over the road, walking and riding. They are soldiers. There are never any refugees. As dawn breaks we reach Larisa and join the main axis of retreat. Somebody else is doing rear-guard so we pull up for a rest, clear of the town."

While resting the squadron was attacked by German bombers. "We watch with some interest the reactions of the troops on the road. On sight of an aeroplane most people leave their trucks and bolt for

Balkans Interlude

cover. The Germans bomb the verges and machine gun the road. They don't want to spoil the surface for their own transport. I try potting aeroplanes from my tank but it is a profitless occupation with the sights provided."

The squadron proceeded on to Athens and then Corinth where they located the rest of the regiment. "Our task is to prevent the Germans getting into the Peloponnese from which our troops are being evacuated. I chase on after my Squadron. When I catch up I find they are in trouble. They are burying 8 men killed by a bomb dropped from 10,000 feet. I feel they ought to be getting on but don't say so. They are obviously shaken by our first deaths when it almost looked as if we should get away with it. The wounded are sent to hospital at Corinth. Several 4 Hussars have been killed but none in B Squadron up to now. Somebody produces a prayer book and I read the burial service."

B and C Squadron engaged the advancing Germans near Kalamata but after a short battle the panzers broke through. "I, with the remains of B and C Squadrons, took to the hills. We kept together for about three weeks, encouraged by constant rumours of ships coming to take us off. At the end of this time I got passage in a small Greek boat making for Crete, to try to make personal contact but we were picked up by the Germans on the island of Anti Kithyra."

For this action Major Clements was awarded the Military Cross. His citation reads as follows: "Throughout the operation in Greece in April 1941 Major Clements commanded his squadron with marked skill and gallantry. On 26 April 1941 when his regimental headquarters were overrun by parachutists, he took command of the three scattered isolated squadrons in the North-west corner of the Peloponnese. He handled them most effectively after putting up an excellent resistance, finally extricating them most skilfully and with-

Balkans Interlude

drew them to the Kalamata area, where they were most unfortunately cut off."

German paratroops had landed on the south bank of the Corinth Canal on April 25 and an armoured division simultaneously began crossing the Gulf of Patros in makeshift craft. The Germans poured out on to the roads of the Peloponnese while the Royal Navy hurriedly evacuated as many troops as possible. The Navy miraculously managed to re-embark 50,732 British, Australian and New Zealand troops, while over 12,000 were killed, wounded and missing, including 9,000 prisoners, two-thirds of whom were captured at Kalamata.

Three weeks after the last Allied evacuations Major Clements secured a place in a small motor boat in which several Greeks were attempting to reach Crete. His intention was to arrange with the Royal Navy to pick up his men, left behind in Greece, at a pre-arranged rendezvous. The motor on the boat broke down, but they were able to continue their journey by sail.

"Early on the second morning the sky was filled with German aeroplanes towing gliders." Maj. Clements wrote. "They were flying just above sea-level. The invasion of Crete had begun. The Greeks and I were unable to communicate owing to language difficulties and they panicked, but it was obvious to me that the Germans were too busily engaged to take any notice of a small boat and as we approached land I was able to watch Stukas diving on some object just out of sight on the other side of a cape. Anti-aircraft fire was clearly visible but alas to no effect. What I was seeing was the sinking of the cruiser *Gloucester,* the ship which had taken us to Greece."

On May 20 German paratroops landed on Crete in the first stage of the German invasion. The next day an air and seaborne invasion of the island began. The Royal Navy attacked the seaborne forces but

Balkans Interlude

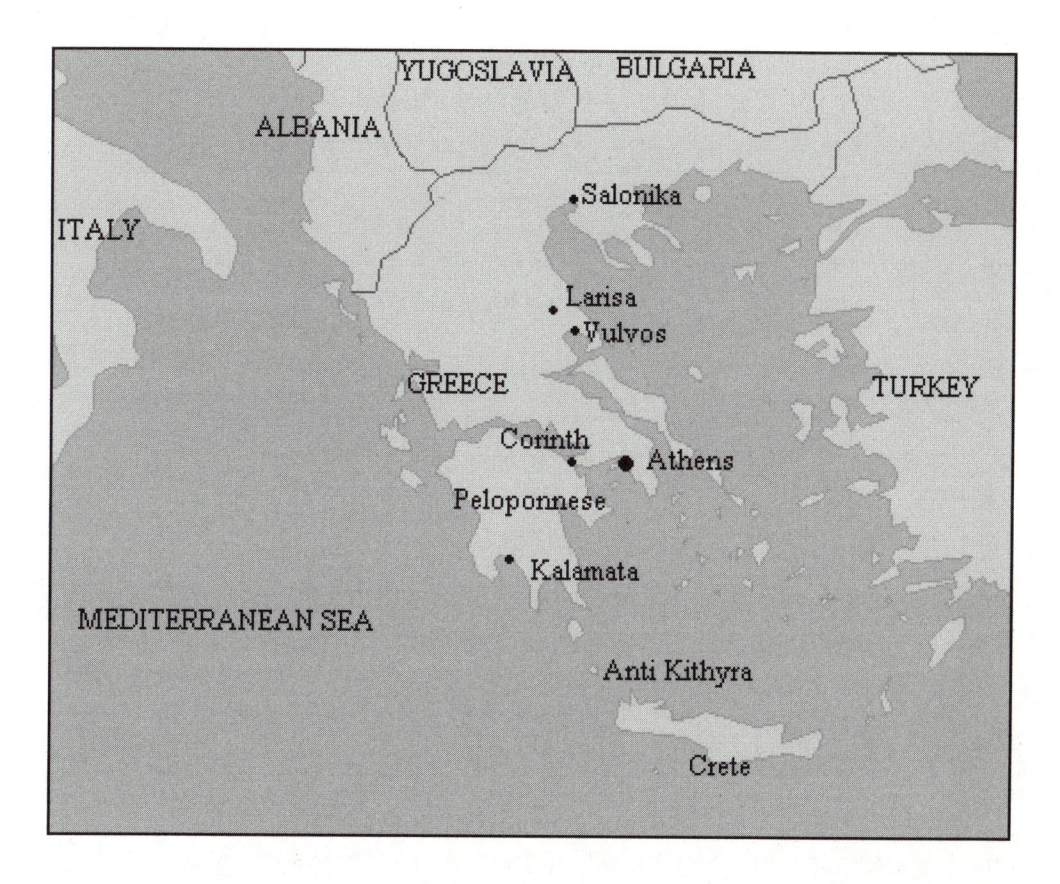

[Map of Greece and surrounding region showing Yugoslavia, Bulgaria, Albania, Italy, Greece, Turkey, with cities Salonika, Larisa, Vulvos, Corinth, Athens, Kalamata, and islands Anti Kithyra and Crete in the Mediterranean Sea]

the Luftwaffe sank the cruisers *Gloucester* and *Fiji* and damaged two battleships. The defenders of Crete were expecting the invasion and when the German paratroops landed they endured heavy losses. In spite of this the Germans soon overran the island. The Royal Navy managed to evacuate over 16,000 troops but left behind, in killed, wounded and captured, over 14,000.(Total British and Empire prisoners were 11,835.)

When Maj. Clements and his small party sailed into the bay - of what he later learned was Anti Kithyra - they were spotted by German soldiers and the Major was taken prisoner. He was approached by the Governor of the island, who asked him his name, rank and regiment.

Balkans Interlude

Maj. Clements gave him his name and rank and the German Governor again asked the name of his regiment. "I am not allowed to tell you," Maj. Clements said. "but you can look at my cap badge if you like."

The Governor looked at Maj. Clements cap badge and said, "You are a cavalry officer I see. I told you I was Governor of the island but I am really a cavalry officer too. Come and have a drink."

They had lunch and afterwards Maj. Clements was treated with the utmost courtesy and respect. One morning the Governor said to Maj. Clements. "I have bad news for you. Your battleship *Hood* has been sunk." The next morning he said, "There is good news for you, but bad for me. Our battleship *Bismarck* has been sunk."

Maj. Clements replied, "That makes us all square."

"No it does not," the Governor said. "You have other battleships, *Bismarck* was our only one."

A week later Maj. Clements was taken by supply ship to the mainland. He was again treated very well by the men on board, some of whom were wounded paratroopers. He was wined and dined - on captured British foodstuffs - and the paras told him to fill his pockets with cigarettes and chocolates, as there would be no luxuries where he was going. Maj. Clements was taken from Greece to Bibarach, in Germany, where he was held for a few weeks until he was transferred to Warburg. He remained a POW for the duration of the war.

CHAPTER 12

The Desert War

The Desert War began in September 1940 when Italy invaded neutral Egypt from Libya which was then part of the Italian Empire. Italy had declared war on Britain and France in June of that year and saw the Allies weakness as a chance to capture all of North-east Africa, including the gleaming prize of the Suez Canal. Under the Anglo-Egyptian Agreement of 1937 Britain was pledged to defend the Canal Zone - something she would have done anyway. The Italian invasion was both ill-conceived and mismanaged. The Italians were not even properly equipped. Their weapons were obsolete and they were short of mechanical transport. Nevertheless, the sheer size of the invasion force was such that the handful of British troops in the Middle East at the time had no hope of stopping the Italian onslaught and they fell back without giving battle. The Italian 10th Army only advanced fifty miles into Egyptian territory before digging in at Sidi Barrani to await supplies. The British had hurriedly assembled a mechanised army in Egypt and went on the offensive on December 9, catching the Italians completely by surprise.

The Desert War

Photo: SHERIDAN FAMILY.

Summer 1941. Mickser Mahon and Jackie Sheridan, Naas, pictured on their last leave home together. It was alas, their last picture together.

Sidi Barrani was captured on December 11, Bardia on the Egyptian border on January 5, Tobruk on the 23rd. The Western Desert Force, commanded by Irishman Lieutenant General Richard O'Connor, pursued the Italians right across the Cyrenaican bulge and only stopped at El Agheila when the tiny army was stripped of men and material for the ill-fated expeditionary force to Greece. The British operations in North Africa had proved to be a remarkable feat. In six weeks the WDF had fought its way across 200 miles of barren waste and destroyed a largely superior force, capturing 113,000 prisoners, 700 guns and a vast amount of much needed supplies. In February 1941 the German Africa Korps, under the command of General Erwin Rommel, arrived in Libya to save the Italians from imminent defeat. The Desert War had entered a new phase.

Naas men Mickser Mahon and Jackie Sheridan arrived in the Western Desert in August 1941 to become part of the newly formed

far from the short grass

The Desert War

8th Army. They were just in time for Operation Crusader, the follow up British offensive to the failed Operation Battleaxe, which was designed to push back the advances of the German-Italian forces. Mickser and Jackie had been given two weeks leave prior to shipping out for the Middle East. They had returned to Naas where Jackie had announced he was not going back. He wanted to stay home and marry his sweetheart, Dinie Kavanagh, who lived nearby and was also serving in the British ATS (Auxuliary Territorial Service). He said he had a premonition of his death, but his family and friends persuaded him to return to England. It was the last time the two friends returned together to Ireland.

The trip to the Middle East was long and dangerous. German U-boats were constantly on the prowl. The troop transports went half-way out into the Atlantic and around Africa, pulling in at Freetown, Sierra Leone, up through the Red Sea and into Egypt. There was a great fear of U-boats and the men were constantly on watch for the dangerous 'Wolf Packs'. On board the troopships conditions were rough. The men had to be constantly 'entertained' for the whole trip would take six weeks. Beer was available, though strictly rationed.

When they arrived in Egypt everyone got 'Jippy-tummy.' The heat and flies were difficult to get used to. One veteran recalled how they were first billeted near an Egyptian peanut farm. "Our camp was behind an Egyptian peanut tree farm. Each morning the Arab men came out and done their 'jobs' on a patch. The next day they all moved on to another patch. The women had their own area secluded from the men. The smell around our camp was terrific and the flies were everywhere."

The trip to Egypt took about six weeks and when the transports docked in Suez there was a great feeling of relief. Egypt was technically an independent kingdom prepared to grant Britain military and naval base facilities by treaty. Although the occupation was over, Egypt was still under effective British military control. The Egyptians were not too friendly to the British and until the tide turned against the Axis in 1942 the prospect of a pro-Axis rising was always present. It did not take long to realise how hated the British were in this part of the world. The Egyptians were waiting for complete independence, which they thought would appear when the Germans arrived. In the meantime they contented themselves with superior smiles and smug remarks and the knowledge that the British honeymoon was nearly over.

When the Allied troops arrived in the Middle East the historic sights were, of course, foremost on their minds. For young Catholics from Kildare, and Ireland, Jerusalem was first on the agenda. They journeyed over miles of desolate stony hills and entered the town via the modern sector. This was of no great interest and they proceeded to the wilderness of narrow passages and streets of the old town. Here they saw the Via Dolorossa along which Christ bore His cross and the Holy Sepulchre, containing the tomb of Christ. Bethlehem and Gethsemane were next. In Bethlehem they visited the Church of the Nativity, descending a steep stair into a small cave-like room, where the Manger was built into the rock wall. Bethlehem had more the feeling of the real Holy Land than Jerusalem. At Gethsemane they visited the modern and impressive Church of All Nations. The Garden of Gethsemane was in good preservation and with its ancient olive trees was very peaceful and serene.

Cairo was another place of great interest, though some of the men had only one tourist stop on their list - the Berkah - Cairo's infamous brothel area. The Pyramids and the Sphinx were the most appealing. In the blazing sun they climbed the exteriors and the interior of the great Pyramid. They endured an exhaustive climb through the narrow tunnels to the King's and Queen's chambers. The climb was done by

The Desert War

Photo: SHERIDAN FAMILY.

Jackie Sheridan and Dina Kavanagh's sweetheart photograph.

the light of a flickering candle held by a native guide. It was all typical tourist fare, with the natives trying to sell anything from 'pieces' of the pyramids to young children for prostitution. A tour of the native markets, or souks, was inevitable and after awhile it all became tiresome. The natives never let up and when you knew they did not like you it was hard to be nice. They were under the illusion that the coming of the Germans and Italians would solve all their woes.

The British had a precarious hold on Egypt and Palestine and, despite the resentment of the native populations, used these countries as their Middle East strongpoints. Alexandria was the main British base. As in the Great War women played a major role in the British army, undertaking many duties which would normally be done by men. Some women served in the Auxiliary Territorial Service (ATS). Sisters Eileen and Georgina Baldrie, from Naas, served in the Middle East with the ATS. Many women served as nurses or otherwise

The Desert War

helped in hospitals or elsewhere in the medical services. Blood transfusion and plasma units were available close to the front, and with them came surgical teams and nursing sisters. Lieutenant-General Bernard Montgomery cancelled the order that forbade nurses working in the forward areas when he came to North Africa in 1942 saying their presence comforted and calmed the nerves of many seriously wounded men, who knew they would be properly nursed.

Further afield conditions in the Western Desert were harsh. Living off the countryside was impossible. There was nothing but a interminable belt of flat and stony desert, broken only by occasional low ridges or watercourses (wadis), the latter dry throughout the year except when converted to torrents by highly infrequent cloudbursts. Water, the most vital commodity in the desert, was always scarce. The local water wells varied widely in taste and mineral content, often verging on the undrinkable - some guaranteed instant diarrhoea. There was either too much salt or too little in the water. Too much salt made it impossible to brew drinkable tea, or coffee, and the intense temperature drop during the night made hot drinks essential in the desert. The normal water ration was a half gallon per man per day, and he had to wash, shave, keep his clothes clean and brew tea with this sparse amount. (Food was basically tinned bully beef and biscuits).

Water was not the only problem in the desert. There were other enemies apart from the Germans and Italians - the broiling sun, flies, fleas, scorpions, dysentery, jaundice, sand fly fever and other ailments and pests. Living in hot and unpleasant conditions, with temperatures reaching 50 degrees took its toll on men. Jackie Sheridan was down for several days with sand fly fever, missing out on his battalion's first encounter with the enemy. He had been guarding tanks for five days and nights. Jackie had a heavy growth of beard and got sick when he shaved. He was sent to hospital in Cairo.

The Desert War

Photo: M. BYRNE.

Eileen Bladrie (extreme left) and friends, from the ATS, at the Great Pyramid, Egypt.

Mickser Mahon was not so lucky. He had tried to join the newly formed Paratroops, but three-quarters of the applicants were rejected. The Paras got 2s extra a day duty money. The 1st Royal East Kent Regiment, known as 'The Buffs', were short and requested forty volunteers. Mickser was sent there instead. The Buffs were a sister regiment of the Royal Sussex and along with the Sussex formed part of the 4th Indian Division. The Division was involved in the drive to relieve Tobruk, where the garrison was holding out since April. Operation Crusader began on November 18 coinciding with a breakout by the Tobruk garrison. Tobruk was relieved on December 8 and Rommel's forces began a general retreat. As the Axis forces continued to retreat to the inland extremity of the Gazala position the weather deteriorated into violent storms and torrential rain. On December 13 the 1st Buffs captured Point 204 on the Alam Hamza Ridge, but the Italian *'Trieste'* Division successfully defended Point 208 from the attack of

The Desert War

the 4th Rajputana Rifles. This left the Buffs precariously lodged on Point 204, within striking range both of the Italian 'Ariete' Division and the German 8th Panzer Regiment. On December 14 another British attack failed to carry Point 208, while the Buffs beat off a succession of probing attacks. The British decided the only way to get the advance moving again was an all out attack by the XIII Corps on the Alam Hamza position.

On December 15 the attack was launched and by mid-afternoon the British had been fought to a halt all along the line from the coast to Alam Hamza ridge, with the 'Ariete' still holding Point 208. It was at this point that the 8th Panzer Regiment was unleashed in a devastating counter-attack against the Buffs on Point 204. The German attack proceeded on classical lines with Panzers and Panzergrenadiers supporting each other. The Buffs were surrounded and then crushed in converging attacks from 1400 to 1530. It was a hard fought battle in which the Buffs fought to the last round, inflicting heavy casualties on the German attackers, but nothing could stop the relentless advance of the panzers across the British position.

The Buffs Commanding Officer remained at his wireless transmitter until the very last moment, passing back information as to the progress of the battle and directing his own troops. Finally most of the Buffs and 31st Field Regiment were overrun. The Commanding Officer had three Matilda tanks around him in a phalanx and they were firing everything they had. As the panzers got closer the C.O. put a bullet through the transmitter so that it would not fall into enemy hands. About 1,000 men surrendered, sending shock waves through XIII Corps. One of those captured was Pte. Michael Mahon.

"I fought in the best army in the world." Mickser Mahon said. "The 8th Army. It was my first time in action and I was disappointed to be captured. The Germans treated us well, but they handed us over to

The Desert War

the Italians. They were no good. They treated us badly, beating up some of our lads. I had no intentions of staying with them and when the first opportunity came I escaped. I had no time for the Italian soldiers. They didn't want to fight."

There was a great feeling of pride among the 'Desert Rats' of the 8th Army and that same feeling ran through Rommel's Afrika Korps. Between the two foes there was a mutual feeling of respect and honour. The Desert Rats even adopted the Afrika Korps marching song, *Lilli Marlene,* as their own.

'Underneath the lantern by the barrack gate,
Darling, I remember
the way you used to wait;
'Twas there that you whispered tenderly
That you loved me
You'd always be
My Lilli of the lamplight.
My own Lilli Marlene.'

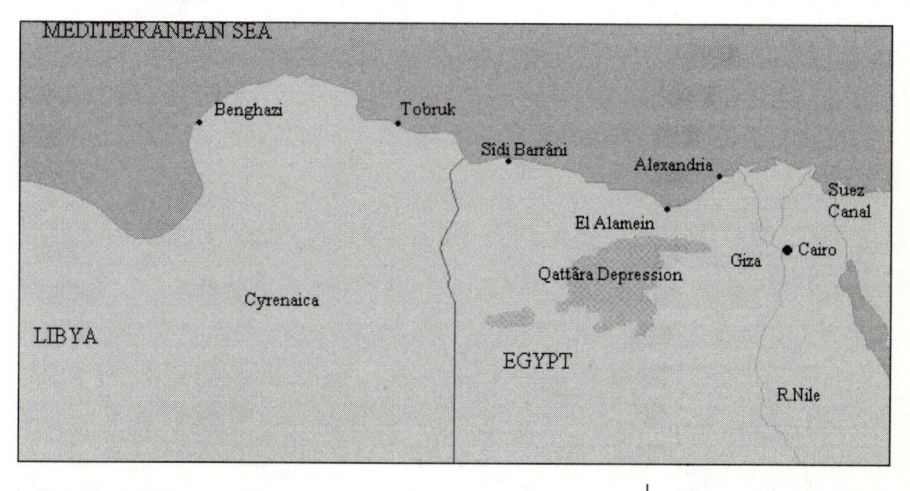

The Desert War

The weather in the desert deteriorated and rain fell unceasingly on the battlefront for weeks as both sides huddled in their greatcoats wondering how conditions in the desert could be so bad. Christmas passed quietly and the men were glad of the respite. Morale was kept up by playing football and listening to BBC news broadcasts and hearing the stirring chimes of Big Ben. But on January 21 Rommel took the Allies by surprise and recaptured El Agheila. On the evening of the 29th Rommel appeared unexpectedly outside Benghazi, where for logistical reasons the 4th Indian Division had got no further forward. The Desert Fox almost took the 4th Indian Division with him, but it managed to break free at the cost of over 4,000 killed, wounded and missing. The battered division was sent to Cyprus to refit and reorganise and did not return to join the rest of 8th Army until July 1942 at El Alamein. Pte. Johnny Doran, Naas, was serving with the Royal Artillery as the desert war see-sawed back and forth across the Cyrenaican bulge. Pte. Doran was a veteran of Dunkirk, from where he had been safely evacuated. He always said, "No matter where I went, Jerry kicked my arse."

At El Alamein the 8th Army prepared to fight the decisive battle of the Desert War. Tobruk had fallen and Rommel had chased the 8th Army to Mersa Matruh, inflicting heavy casualties on the Allies. The 8th Army was in a sorry state when they retreated to the Alamein position. Here the British worked frantically to prepare defensive positions. The El Alamein 'Line' was the last possible defensive position west of the Suez Canal. Alexandria was 34 miles away, less than a day's march if the German armour broke through. El Alamein took its name from a small railway station a mile or so from the coast, which carried the coastal road and the railway connecting Alexandria with Mersa Matruh. Here the desert narrows down to a 40 mile (64 km) bottleneck - bounded on the north by the Mediterranean and on the south by the inaccessible wastes of the Qattara Depression. Across this bottleneck the 8th Army had dug a line of trenches, with strongpoints and defen-

The Desert War

Photo: M. BYRNE.

Jackie Sheridan, Naas, sent this photo to his aunt 4/4/42, possibly from Cyprus.

sive 'boxes', covered by minefields and by artillery fire. Dominating the area was the bare stony Ruweisat Ridge - a narrow hill about eleven miles long and half-a-mile deep on either side.

Being the tail end of summer climatic conditions were oppressive. The air was heavy and there was little natural shade and no water. The men lived in holes in the ground praying for the implacable sun to go down. The detritus of battle was everywhere and the smell of human waste mixed with the heavy sweetish carrion smell of the dead. Flies were a constant source of irritation. Water was too scarce for washing and the men were filthy and unshaven. On August 5 1942 Prime Minister Winston Churchill visited El Alamein and two days later Lieutenant-General Bernard Law Montgomery was appointed commander of 8th Army. The Desert Rats had a new and determined

The Desert War

leader and now for the first time unlimited supplies, effective 6-pounder anti-tank guns and 250 American M4 Sherman tanks, a worthy rival to the German Panzers. The stage was set for the most decisive of British battles.

Ptes. Jackie Sheridan and Mickser Mahon were at Alamein with the 4th Indian Division. The offensive commenced at 9.40 pm on the moonlit night of October 23. A thunderous 882-gun bombardment opened along a six mile front in the northern sector near the Mediterranean. As the barrage rolled forward thousands of men from four divisions - 9th Australian, 2nd New Zealander, 1st South African and 51st Highland - began to advance. Soon the infantry were engaged in hand to hand fighting with the Germans. Allied casualties were heavy, about 6,000 men and 300 tanks and 4th Indian Division, in reserve, replaced the New Zealanders. By now Rommel had returned (he had been in Germany on sick leave) but it was too late to save the day. Low on petrol and ammunition by November 3 Rommel had no option but to retreat. The Allies broke through his lines in several places that night and the Axis began an orderly retreat the next day.

Mickser Mahon met up with Jackie Sheridan in the confusion of battle and they "fought side by side in the advance on the German front." Their division had replaced the New Zealanders and on D+1, October 24-25, the Buffs had advanced one mile taking hundreds of prisoners. Later on the Buffs were unlucky in capturing another, more important, prisoner. Mickser delighted in recalling how he and his squad over-ran Rommel's tent. "We missed him by minutes." Mickser joked. "His bed was still warm!"

Rommel tried to halt the British advance at Fuka on November 5 but he was pushed back again. On November 8 British and American troops landed in Morocco and Algeria signalling the beginning of the

The Desert War

end. Not even the skill of the Desert Fox could prevent the inevitable collapse of an understrength Afrika Korps fighting on two fronts. The Axis forces were simply not strong enough to stand up to the 8th Army and withdrew eastwards as the Anglo-American force landed behind them.

Captain John de Burgh, Oldtown, Naas, landed in Algiers in command of a troop of the 16th/5th Lancers. The 5th had once been the Royal Irish Lancers, but amalgamated with the 16th Lancers after the Irish Cavalry regiments were reorganised in 1922. The amalgamated regiment still carried some Irish distinctions, notably an Irish harp on its NCOs' chevrons. The regiment had been in India when war broke out but returned to Britain to train for Operation Torch. Commander of the 16th/5th Lancers was Colonel E. A. Fanshawe, from Rathmore, Naas. Also in the Lancers was Major Robert Gill, from Yomanstown, Naas. John de Burgh was eighteen when war was declared, but he had already made up his mind to join the British Army. "I knew a war was coming. After the First War the peacemakers were a disaster. The terms of the Versailles Treaty left the way open for another war. I had made my mind up before the war started and was commissioned into the army. After three months training I was commissioned a 2nd Lieutenant. 6th Armoured Division was formed six months before landing in Africa. We finished our training in Scotland."

The 16th/5th Lancers trained in Ayrshire along with other units of the 6th Armoured Division, including the 38th (Irish) Brigade, for the Anglo-American invasion of French North Africa, code-named Operation Torch. The Americans wanted to invade France, but the more realistic British preferred to finish off the war in North Africa first and then invade Europe through the 'soft underbelly' of Sicily and Italy. In the end, though not without misgivings, the Americans went along with the British plan.

The Desert War

However, it was not going to be easy. Morocco and Algeria were under French control and Vichy France, under Marshall Philippe Petain, was pro-German. There were 100,000 French and native troops in North Africa and it was unknown whether they would oppose the Allied landings. Anti-British feelings were strong due to the bombardment of the French fleet at Mers-el-Kebir by the Royal Navy in July 1940, when over a thousand French sailors were killed. Because of this it was decided that the bulk of the troops involved in Torch should be American and that the overall commander would also be an American, Lieutenant-General Dwight D. Eisenhower. The Americans would land at Casablanca and Oran, while a British/American force would land at Algiers.

"Our group formed up in the Clyde," Captain de Burgh said. "It was a magnificent sight to see. Battleships, flat-tops and transports. We went around Northern Ireland and passed Gibraltar at night. We landed at night, unopposed. There was a heavy aerial bombardment and torrential rain. We didn't know what side the French were on and we did not get a great reception. The French were not too pleased to see us. The Americans were very gung-ho, but they were badly led. They could not accept casualties. They were very inadequately trained. But they very quickly learned the job. You had to. You had to be good to survive. I was fortunate to be with a first class regiment and a first class division."

The French resistance was confused and scattered and depended on the locale but most opposition was encountered from shore batteries and naval units. The French commander in chief, Admiral Jean François Darlan, was willing to cooperate with the Allies and issued a cease-fire order to come into effect on November 10. The cease-fire was the end of Vichy France. A furious Hitler ordered German forces to march into unoccupied France. German reinforcements were rushed to Tunisia and by the end of the month there were 24,000 Axis

The Desert War

troops around Tunis. The Germans prepared for battle on two fronts. The Allied troops - now renamed 1st Army - began the long haul towards Tunis. By November 20 the Allies were in contact with Axis units and a series of short sharp battles took place as the 1st Army tried to force their way through to the Tunisian capital.

"Tunisia was a fast moving war. The Irish Guards were with us and so were the Irish Brigade." John de Burgh said. "The Germans fought clean and we fought clean. At a very early age you learned the value of trust and friendship. Your men had to have faith in you." Captain de Burgh was only twenty-one and won the Military Cross in one of his first encounters with the Germans in Tunisia. "Just being there at the right time," was his explanation. "Nobody went out to be a hero. You did not let friends down. That's all. I was mentioned in dispatches. It was one of the first MC's in the regiment and the first major encounter with crack German troops. The 6th Armoured was the elite of the 1st Army. Very highly trained."

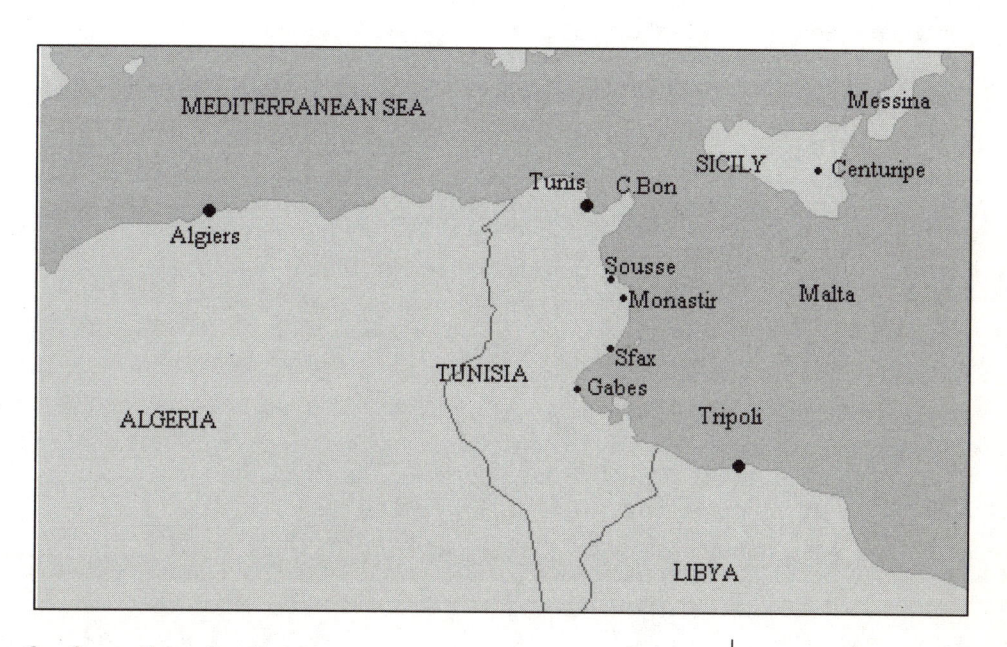

The Desert War

Fusilier Dennis Carroll, from Pound Lane, Maynooth, (His father, also named Dennis, served in WWI with the Dublin Fusiliers.) landed in Algiers on November 22 with the 6th Royal Inniskilling Fusiliers. The 'Skins'- the nickname is said to have originated in 1805 when a bathing party was caught unawares by the French and went into battle naked - along with the 1st Royal Irish Fusiliers and the 2nd London Irish Rifles formed the 38th (Irish) Brigade. The Irish Brigade was formed the previous January - amidst vigorous opposition by the government of Northern Ireland - to attract the maximum number of recruits throughout Ireland. It was the brainchild of Winston Churchill, who also wanted to form an Irish Wing or Squadron of the RAF to make the Irish contribution to the war effort more visible. Churchill was aware of the high number of Irishmen in all three services and he knew that most of them came from what was a neutral country.

"I joined the British army in the latter half of 1940 in Belfast," Dennis Carroll said. "with a fellow named Shanahan from Kildare town. I was sent to the 6th Inniskillings. You were rarely sent where you wanted to go. You were usually sent where needed. I later heard the other chap was killed. We landed in Algiers and went west to meet the 8th Army, who were coming from Libya. We were with the 1st Army, which was made up of British and Americans. We were on the go all the time. The Americans were very green at first. They had the best of weapons, artillery and tanks. Even their infantry weapons were better. But they didn't adapt as quickly as we did, though they did eventually. There was less discipline in the American army. Discipline kept you in line and had a certain influence on you.

"It was bitterly cold in the desert at night. You would be lying out all night. We had shorts for during the day and long trousers for at night. If you left your canteen out at night, it would be like taking it out of a fridge. A few minutes later, after the sun came up, the water would

The Desert War

Photo: R. JOCELYN.

Major John Kennedy M.C., Bishopscourt, taken from a group photograph of Irish Guards Officers.

be boiling. That was Tunisia." The Inniskillings were in action around Goubellat and a series of hills around the Bou Arada plain against crack German paratroops, who they would meet again in Italy.

The rest of the year ended in a stalemate as the weather deteriorated and German reinforcements poured in. On February 14 the Germans attacked and the inexperienced American troops were thrown back in disorder. The German attack was halted by the 6th Armoured Division and the regrouped Americans, who endured heavy casualties in their first encounter with the Afrika Korps. Rommel called off the Kasserine attack on February 22 and returned his attention to the 8th Army. The 1st Army pressed on and the casualties mounted. Captain John de Burgh was wounded twice, "though not too badly. I was sent back to hospital in Algiers and the second time found it full of Irish Guards. I was one of many lucky to survive. Others were not so fortunate. If you did not shoot first the other bugger did. Our objective was to capture Tunis and cut off the German supplies. We expected to do it in two months, but it took us six months."

One of the wounded Irish Guards was Captain John Kennedy, from Bishopscourt, Kill, a friend of Capt. de Burgh. Capt. Kennedy arrived in Algiers on March 9, with the 1st Battn., Irish Guards. It was two-and-a-half years since they last saw action. Now the Guards were part of the 1st Division and they went into the line on March 19 after a memorable Saint Patrick's Day celebration of wine and song. In the next two months the Micks suffered heavy casualties. Facing the Guards in the drive to Tunis was a long, steep razor-backed hill called Recce Ridge. At 1 a.m. on March 30 103 Guardsmen, of No.2 Company, embarked on a raid on German positions on Recce Ridge. Capt. Kennedy and Major Gordon-Watson moved up to a barn to get a closer view of the battle. In the short sharp fight on Recce Ridge 19 Guardsmen were killed and over forty wounded, including Capt. Kennedy, who was slightly wounded in the leg. He spent a time in hospital in Algiers, but quickly got fed up and discharged himself. He hitched a ride back to his battalion, just in time for the last push to Tunis.

On January 23 the 8th Army entered Tripoli and by the beginning of February most of the Axis were behind the Mareth Line - an improvised Maginot line built by the French to keep the Italians out of French North Africa. The Mareth Line stretched from the sea to the Matmata Hills. It consisted of strongpoints and blockhouse. 4th Indian attacked through the Matmata Hills in an outflanking move over very difficult terrain. On March 26 the Allies broke through the Tebaga Gap leaving the Axis with no alternative but to abandon the Mareth Line and beat a hasty retreat to the Wadi Akarit line, pursued by 4th Indian, which had simultaneously, if with difficulty pushed through the mountains towards Matmata itself. The Axis fled north through the Gabes

The Desert War

coastal gap to form a new defensive front between the sea and an area of marshes and water at Wadi Akarit. It was a very defensible position where the Axis could block the sole and narrow passage between the sea and the vast trackless marsh called the Chott-el-Fedjadj. Not even the arrival of some new tanks, the mighty 'Tiger' and the formidable 'Panther', could stem the tide of Allied victory. The Tiger weighed in at 50 tons and was armed with an 8.8cm gun, which proved so deadly to the Allies in the earlier stages of the Desert War. Pte. Jackie Sheridan, 1st Royal Sussex, got his picture taken at Wadi Akarit and sent it home with a letter to Naas. It was the last picture taken of Jackie. A year later his premonition would come through.

On April 6 and 7 a strong frontal attack breached the Wadi Akarit position and the 8th Army broke through into the Tunisian plain beyond. From then on the Axis were in full retreat, except here and there where some natural feature afforded them an opportunity of delaying the Allies for a few hours. The final all-out drive on Tunis occurred on May 6 and the city was entered the following day. "We were thrusting from the east while the 8th Army was coming from Libya." Fus. Dennis Carroll said. "The two Allied armies met in Tunis. We packed up at a place called Sousse and Monastir. There was nothing there except camels and ponies." (Today Sousse and Monastir are popular tourist destinations, especially among Irish holidaymakers.) The surviving Axis forces tried to retreat into the Cape Bon peninsula, pursued by 6th Armoured and 4th Indian Divisions. On May 13 the Axis forces finally capitulated. The Desert War was over. "We had great respect for the Germans," Capt. John de Burgh, 6th Armoured, said. "At the end of the North African War, when the 90th Light surrendered, the Jocks were shaking hands with the Germans and giving them cigarettes. It was like the end of a football match."

CHAPTER 13

The Long Haul
– Sicily and Italy

Sicily was the next Allied target after North Africa had been secured. Defeat in Africa had marked the end of Italy's Empire and induced a great war weariness among the Italian people, who had never wholeheartedly wanted war in the first place. Morale in the armed forces, never great, was at rock bottom. The Allies hoped that Italy's sudden collapse would put greater strain on Germany, already reeling from the defeat in Stalingrad and the loss of North Africa. An invasion of Sicily and then an assault on mainland Italy might be the final nail in the Italian coffin.

The invasion of Sicily was the first amphibious assault on a defended beach since Gallipoli in 1915 and the Allied planners were mindful of what a disaster that had proved to be. The chosen landing beaches on the south-eastern end of the island were divided into three sectors - British, American and Canadian. The British 8th Army were given the primary role while the Americans were required to protect Montgomery's flank and rear. The British 5 Infantry and 51st Highland Divisions and the 231st Independent Brigade with Commandos land-

The Long Haul - Sicily and Italy

ed astride the Pachino peninsula. Despite some minor shelling, the troops quickly moved inland and by evening secured all their objectives.

The topography on the island of Sicily favoured the defenders, who were the 8th Army's old foes from North Africa - the *Fallschirmjäger* - and other crack German troops from the *Herman Göring* and the 15th Panzer Grenadier Divisions. The worth of the Italian troops on the island was dubious and the Germans had a contingency plan in case they collapsed and the Wehrmacht were forced to assume their responsibilities. The terrain was harsher than Tunisia and to add to the hardship it was the middle of summer. The slightest exertion caused sweating and it was very dusty and there seemed to be no escape from the Sicilian dust. Thankfully the veterans of the 8th Army were used to the heat and dust, but it was murder on new replacements.

"We landed in Sicily from Bizerta," said Fusilier Dennis Carroll, 6th Inniskillings."We came ashore at Syracuse and Augusta and moved up. This was after the main landings." The Irish Brigade were visited on June 30 by General Montgomery who informed them that they were being shifted to the 8th Army. They landed without incident on July 25 and travelled around 90 miles to a concentration area near Syracuse. Their objective was Centuripe, a heavily defended town on the way to Messina. Centuripe was defended by men of the *Herman Göring* Division and 3rd *Fallschirmjäger* Regiment. It was an ideal defensive position with the town sitting on a hill. Terracing six feet high - for cultivation - had been cut into the hill. Steep slopes had to be negotiated to approach Centuripe. The Inniskillings and Faughs (Irish Fusiliers) met determined German resistance and after heavy fighting gained a foothold in the town. The Germans retreated across the Salso and Simeto rivers putting up stubborn resistance. On August 5 the Irish Brigade was pulled back for a rest. "At Centuripe the Irish Brigade done a great job. Even Churchill congratulated us. It was a

The Long Haul - Sicily and Italy

tough battle. It was all over by the middle of August. The Germans pulled back and crossed the straits of Messina to Italy. We had a rest period then until the invasion of Italy in September."

Frederick Kelly, Newbridge, fought with the Irish Fusiliers on Sicily. Fred Kelly left 475 Ballymany Cottage, Newbridge, at the age of seventeen to join the British Army. His father, James "Stim" Kelly, was a WWI veteran. He had served with the Dublin Fusiliers and had been wounded in action, though not seriously. Fred's mother died when the children were all young and James Kelly found it hard to rear seven children on his own. Reluctantly, but out of necessity, Fred left home for Armagh to join the Royal Irish Fusiliers. He served with the Faughs in Egypt, Iraq and Jordan before the Irish Fusiliers joined the 8th Army for the Sicilian campaign.

With the fall of Sicily the next objective was the Italian mainland. On September 3 the 8th Army attacked across the narrow strait of Messina, separating Sicily and mainland Italy. The Allies needed a major port quickly and Salerno was chosen for another attack on September 9, with General Mark Clark expecting to take Naples five days after the Salerno landings. While the invasion fleet was heading towards Salerno, ships' radios carried the news that Italy had surrendered. All seemed to be going well for the Allies, but Hitler was not going to give up Italy without a fight. The American 5th Army - actually there were more British troops than American in the newly formed unit - hit the beaches on September 9 and ran smack into the 16th Panzer Division, which was completing its take-over of the Italian positions. The Allied 8th Army was still 200 miles (320 km) away to the south and the Germans were able to reinforce the beachhead with ease. It was touch and go for a few days as the Germans counterattacked and tried to drive the Allies into the sea but the guns of the Allied fleet gave them the upper hand and the Germans began an orderly retreat northwards. Southern Italy was of no tactical use to the

The Long Haul - Sicily and Italy

Germans and they skilfully delayed the Allied advance while work went ahead on the Gustav Line which, anchored on the town of Cassino, Field Marshall Albert Kesselring, German C-in-C Mediterranean, intended to hold until the spring of 1944.

While preparing for the invasion of Italy Pte. Jackie Sheidan had a chance encounter with fellow Naas man Michael 'Barreller' Byrne in North Africa. Michael, known as 'Barreller' was from Rathasker Road, Naas. (His father, Michael, and also known as 'Barreller', was a veteran of the Great War.) Barreller had joined the British army in 1939, shortly after the outbreak of war and had fought all through the desert campaign with the Royal Field Artillery. It was a million to one chance that two men from the same town serving in different regiments would meet and both tried to make the most of it. Jackie drew his beer ration. (Troops were not paid in the desert, as there was nothing to spend it on. All men were entitled to two bottles of beer and some cigarettes when the supplies arrived. Beer was usually a Canadian, Australian or New Zealand brew and came in litre bottles. It was, one veteran recalled, "dangerous stuff.") He planned to meet Barreller later that day for a drink, but Barreller's unit shipped out first and the two friends never met again.

On September 18 an 8th Army advance party coming from the south reached the Salerno beachhead. Naples was not taken until October 1. Once liberated, Naples was soon in service as a major supply port. "We landed peacefully at Naples," Captain John de Burgh said. "and moved up to Cassino. Italy was not tank country. There were too many mountains. We had Shermans and Churchill tanks. The Shermans had 75mm guns and were a match for the German Mk IV. The 1st Guards Brigade were with us and were our infantry."

Italy was not ideal tank country, but both sides employed armour at every opportunity. The most feared tank was still the Tiger, which

The Long Haul - Sicily and Italy

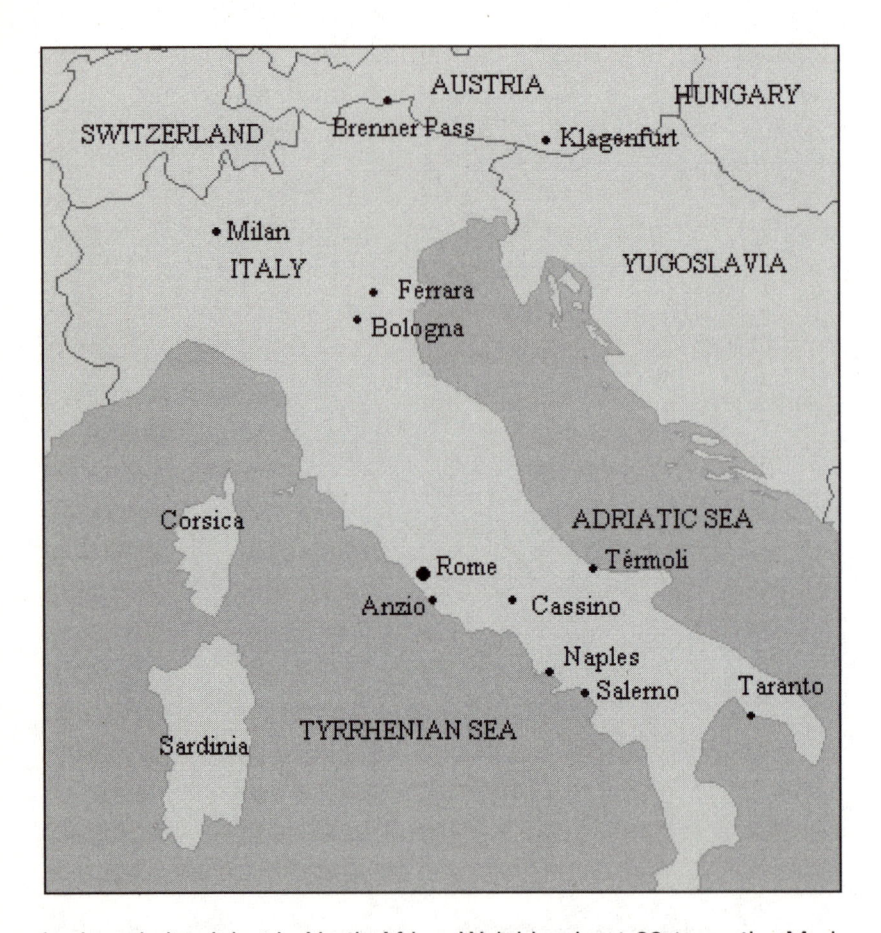

had made its debut in North Africa. Weighing in at 60-tons, the Mark VI was clumsy and slow, but its armament - the feared 88mm gun and two 7.62mm machine guns - and its armour - 5.9 inches in front and 7.3 at the turret - more than made up for its shortcomings. The American Sherman and the British Churchill were no match for the Tiger, though they could easily take on the German Mark IV. The Sherman was fast and reliable, and was armed with a 75mm gun and two .30 calibre machine guns. Its armour - 75mm max. and 15mm min.- and its tendency to 'brew up' so quickly, gave it the nickname 'Ronson' by the Americans (because it lit first time) and 'Tommy cooker' by the Germans. The Churchill, armed with a 1.6-pounder gun, had

The Long Haul - Sicily and Italy

good armour and excellant cross-country ability, especially in mountainous terrain. Its main drawback was inferior fire-power compared with contemporary German tanks.

The Irish Brigade landed at Termoli on the night of October 4. As soon as they arrived they went into the front line as the Allies were expecting a German counterattack at any time. "We landed in the south," Fusilier Dennis Carroll said, "and made slow progress all the way up through Italy. The Germans had fortified positions and concrete pillboxes built into the mountains, along with the natural defences of hills and rivers. We used to say, 'One more mountain to climb. One more river to cross.' But, every time you went up a mountain there was a river at the bottom. We made slow progress through Italy, but gradually pushed the Germans back to the Gustav Line."

"We landed at Taranto," Corporal Mickser Mahon, 5th Buffs, said "and moved up through Italy. I was in Cassino for three months. It was rough. Like the First World War. Trenches and that. We lived in the trenches for weeks. The Yanks had taken heavy casualties (the American 36th Division were first to attack Cassino). They didn't seem to mind the losses. The Americans suffered an awful lot in Italy. They wasted a terrible amount of lives and materials."

Cpl. Mickser Mahon was in the line on Christmas Eve night 1943. The front was quiet in the run up to Christmas and it was hoped all the men would get their Christmas dinner out of the trenches. Despite the hardship the men were in good humour. Many of them were replacements for those lost in the long haul through North Africa and had yet to see action. The troops had got their extra Christmas ration; 200 Capstan cigarettes and a belt of rum. Then they were given a small bottle of beer. Anyone who did not drink - and there was a few - gave their beer to the ones who did.

Later in the evening the Germans, who were only a few hundred

The Long Haul - Sicily and Italy

yards away, called over to them *"Froeliche Weihnachten"* (Merry Christmas). Then the strains of *'Silent Night'* reached them, sung in German, which makes this most beautiful of hymns sound even lovelier. "The Germans called to us singing *'Silent Night',*" Mickser Mahon said. "We did nothing for an hour. The men wanted to go out to meet the Germans, just like in the First War. But, I didn't trust them and told the men to stay where they were. They kept calling us, 'Merry Christmas, Tommy. Peace on earth.' The Germans pretended to be drunk, staggering around with bottles in their hands. So about ten o'clock the lads went out to join them. They were waiting for us and opened up on us with everything they had. They were crafty bastards, the Germans. You could never trust them."

When the British went out into no-man's land a flare shot into the sky as heavy machine guns opened up. Machine-pistols rattled and grenades exploded, followed by artillery and mortar fire. The British ran back to their own lines, screaming and cursing. Some fell and lay still. Others were wounded and crawled towards their own lines and safety. "They threw everything at us for over an hour, until near midnight." Mickser said. "I was glad I didn't go out." When it was all over a cold calculating voice called over, "Merry Christmas, Tommy." The Buffs had been initiated into the Italian campaign. It was a foretaste of the horrors to come.

The war in Italy was an expensive campaign for the Allies. The Italian terrain favoured the defenders. River valleys run across the peninsula and each provided a line of defence. Ridges and mountains gave the Germans the advantage of height with good observation and excellent fields of fire. The few roads were open to attack and off the road tanks and vehicles were useless. It is footslogging country and the greatest burden fell on the 'Poor Bloody Infantry.' The weather was also an inconveniance and an appalling hardship for troops in the field. Sleet, snow, rain and gales made life almost unbearable and

The Long Haul - Sicily and Italy

conditions were unremittingly grim. Troops in the line lived in holes in the ground, usually cold and wet. Pte. Johnny Doran, RHA, recalled sleeping out in the Italian Winter. He slept fully clothed with his blanket pulled over his head. When he awoke the next morning he said he would not know which way to turn to get out, as the snow could be a foot or more on top of him.

The German Winter Line, or the Gustav Line as it had been named, stretched from Gaeta on the west coast through Cassino and along the Rapido valley into the Maiella mountains and along the Sangro valley to the east coast. The little town of Cassino lies on the river Rapido astride Highway 6 and is dominated by the historic Benedictine monastery atop the 1,693-foot (516m) massif of Monte Cassino itself. Known as Monastery Hill to the Allies, this was the main obstacle. On January 20 1944 the US II Corps began the attack on Cassino and two days later the Allied VI Corps landed at Anzio in a vain attempt to cut Kesselring's line of communication between Rome and Cassino and break the stalemate on the Gustav Line. German reinforcements poured into Cassino, including the veteran 1st Parachute Division. The exhausted Allies began receiving reinforcements too. Three fresh divisions - 2nd New Zealand, 4th Indian and 78th British - arrived under the command of Lieutenant-General Bernard Freyburg, who insisted that the prying eyes of the monastery should be closed.

Freyburg believed the Germans were using the monastery as an observation post, which was untrue. He was not alone. Many of the troops on the ground also believed it. On February 15 the monastery was destroyed by a powerful Allied airstrike. The soldiers in the front line cheered as the bombers pounded the Abbey and the peak, delighted that the prying eyes of the monastery were closed. The Germans now moved into the ruins of the monastery, turning the rub-

The Long Haul - Sicily and Italy

ble, huge craters and deep indestructible cellars into a veritable fortress.

The 1st Royal Sussex were astride Snakeshead Ridge, seventy yards from the Germans and 1,000 yards from the monastery. Their objective was Point 593 or Monte Calvario. On February 16 Pte. Jackie Sheridan went into action with the 1st Royal Sussex in their bid to capture the shell-torn peak of Monte Calvario, ominously dubbed Hangman's Hill. Cassino could not be taken as long as Hangman's Hill remained in German hands. As they prepared to attack British shells burst among the leading companies and Battalion Headquarters, inflicting several casualties. After two nights of bitter fighting the Sussex failed to capture the hill. They lost 12 officers and 162 men. In two days a fine battalion that had fought since the earliest days of the war was shattered. Pte. Jackie Sheridan was wounded on February 20 and had to endure the painful journey down the treacherous slopes to a field hospital. His friend, Englishman Norman Taylor, watched as Jackie was taken away, glad that his pal was out of harm's way. A month later, on March 20, Jackie Sheridan was killed by 'friendly fire' while recovering from his wounds in a field hospital. Nine men were killed by the British shelling. Jackie Sheridan received a shrapnel wound to the chest. With his belongings sent home to his family was his paybook, which he kept in his breastpocket. The paybook was torn where the shrapnel had struck. Mrs. Sheridan wrote to the mother of Norman Taylor, Jackie's friend, informing her of Jackie' death. A month later Mrs. Taylor returned a letter to Mrs. Sheridan informing her of Norman's death in action.

Sheets of rain began to fall on the battlefield as Mickser Mahon prepared for the third big push, unaware his best friend and neighbour, Jackie Sheridan, was badly wounded. The slightest movement of Allied troops attracted sniper and shellfire from the Germans, who seemed to be everywhere in and around Cassino town. On March 15

The Long Haul - Sicily and Italy

J. Sheridan, Naas, killed by friendly fire at Monte Cassino.

a huge bombardment destroyed the town. The rain continued incessantly as the Buffs moved in to relieve the New Zealanders in the railway station, often having to bridge flooded craters. The fighting was ferocious. The bombardment hindered rather than helped the Allies. After fierce hand-to-hand combat they succeeded in capturing some neighbouring peaks, such as Castle Hill and Hangman's Hill. But still the Allies got no nearer to Monte Cassino itself. On March 23 the attack was called off.

The Long Haul - Sicily and Italy

Bren carrier of the 6th Inniskillings passing through London Irish Rifles positions, Cassino.

The 6th Inniskillings, along with the rest of the Irish Brigade, relieved French troops north of the monastery on the slopes of Mount Cairo on March 28. The Skins were the closest to the monastery, with one position actually looking down on the battered ruins. German artillery fire was so accurate movement by daylight was impossible. A call of nature was unadvised too, as German snipers had everywhere monitored. Food, ammunition, mail and everything else came up at night. The smell around Cassino from unburied corpses was tremendous. Rats as big as cats, infested the area. The ground was rocky and prevented troops from digging in. "All you could do was build a little sangar of rocks around yourself for protection." Fusilier Dennis Carroll said. "We were to the right of Cassino. I met a nineteen year old, whose hair had turned pure white from the constant bombing and shelling at Cassino. There was no cover. The rocky terrain made the shelling worse, as not only was there shrapnel from the shells, but little sharp pieces of rock added to the chances of injury.

"We picked up an Italian interpreter. He had ginger hair, which was

page number 176 | far from the short grass

The Long Haul - Sicily and Italy

unusual for Italians. He was brilliant. He organised billets for us and so on. He was at staff meetings and was very helpful. One night we were to attack across the Garigliano river. We had to get into canvas boats and pull ourselves across by rope. As we lined up to get into the boats the Germans bombed us. Their fire was very accurate and we lost thirty blokes that night. It turned out our ginger-haired Italian was a spy for the Germans. He disappeared that night, but was later seen in Rome and picked up. He was shot for spying.

"Later that night I walked into a tripwire. There was a mine attached to the wire and it blew the pack off my back. I got shrapnel wounds all along my right leg, calf and knee. I was out for a couple of weeks and then I was sent to Anzio. This was after the initial landings. The British and Americans landed at Anzio and could have went on to Rome, which was undefended. Yet, they dug in and waited. By then it was too late. The Germans rushed up reinforcements and the chance of taking Rome was lost.

Johnny Doran, Naas, sent this photo home to his sister from Italy.

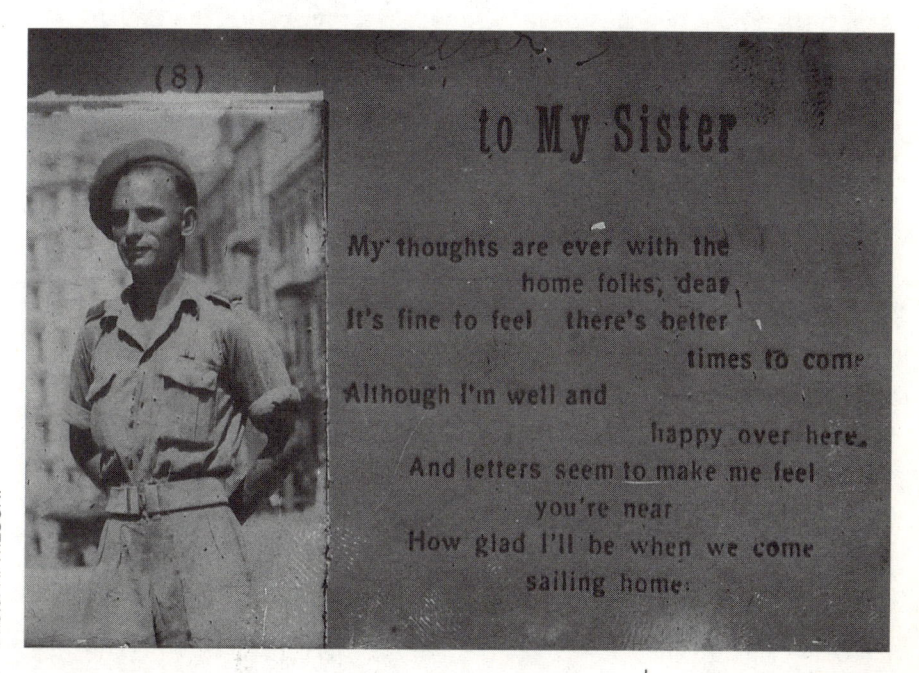

Photo: R. WILSON.

(8) to My Sister

My thoughts are ever with the
    home folks, dear,
It's fine to feel there's better
        times to come
Although I'm well and
        happy over here,
And letters seem to make me feel
    you're near
How glad I'll be when we come
    sailing home.

The Long Haul - Sicily and Italy

"I remember one incident when, after an attack our lads left a Bren gun hanging on the barbed wire. A Northern Irish chap named McMullan went out and took it off. Everyone stopped firing, probably in amazement. It was just a Bren gun. Nobody was going to get in trouble for leaving it behind. Not long after I was building a sangar with sods. We were digging on reclaimed marshes and everytime you dug up a sod, water filled up the hole. The sangar was oval shaped. I wasn't long building it when a six barrelled mortar - 'moaning minnies' we called them - landed. I was hit a fair whack in the back from shrapnel. I was sent to a hospital ship off the beachhead. Loads of ships were sunk, including the steam packet, the *Leinster*. I got on a ship to Naples. From there I went to Pompeii, where I lay on a stretcher outside a building, which was requisitioned as a hospital. It was packed with wounded. An ambulance took me to a hospital in Manfredona, a little fishing village, where I had an operation to get the shrapnel out. I was in the hospital for a month and then I was sent to a transit camp to be relocated to my unit. As soon as you were patched up you were sent back. The Americans gave out medals for anything. The British were not as generous. A few MMs and an odd MC. A DCM was as a rare as Red Indians in Manhattan."

Twenty-two year old Murtagh Doyle, from the Curragh, was also at Anzio, serving with the 2nd Battn., Sherwood Foresters. Two divisions, one British and one American, had landed at Anzio on January 22 in a bid to break the deadlock at Cassino. A co-ordinated attack on both fronts was designed to force the Germans to withdraw from their defensive positions. The VI Corps commander waited too long to build up his forces giving the Germans time to rush up reinforcements to an otherwise undefended route to Rome. When the Allies attacked on January 29 they were met by stiff German resistance.

The 24th Guards Brigade, which included the 1st Irish Guards, along with the 3rd Infantry Brigade led the British attack. The

The Long Haul - Sicily and Italy

Sherwood Foresters came under heavy German fire in their bid to take Campoleone. In the fierce fighting the Foresters were all but destroyed. Because there was practically no rear area on Anzio the depleted Foresters were once again in action when the Germans counter-attacked on February 3/4 and again from February 7 to 10. The Foresters fought bravely in the cold and pouring rain suffering more casualties. As the month wore on and the Allied attacks petered out the front settled down to a form of static trench warfare characteristic of the Great War. The winter conditions inflicted undue hardship and a great war weariness settled upon the Allied troops as they dug themselves in deeper into the mud. Nowhere was safe on the beachhead. Some sick and wounded men would not even report back to the field hospitals, as their proximity to the Allied supplies made the hospitals targets for Geman fire. Pte. Murtagh Doyle, after surviving the Allied attacks and German counterattacks of February, was killed in action on March 1.

The 1st Irish Guards had landed at Anzio on January 22 after the beachhead had been secured. On January 26 the Germans launched a spirited attack, involving nine tanks and three companies of infantry, on the Irish positions. Captain D. M. Kennedy, No. 3 Company Commander, watched the Germans advancing through his field glasses and called down a mortar barrage on the exposed troops. Within moments the German attack was broken by the deadly barrage. Capt. Kennedy then proceeded to direct artillery fire on the German tanks, driving them off, too. The *Times* of London later had this to say: "During a subsequent advance German troops who had penetrated within 100 yards of a company headquarters were all killed, captured, or chased away by a counter-attack. That fight was scarcely over when it was reported that another German company was approaching. Most of them were caught in the fire of Bren guns; the remainder fled to cover, where they were caught by artillery fire laid on by Major D. M. Kennedy."

The Long Haul - Sicily and Italy

Three days later the Irish Guards were on the offensive in the attack on Campoleone. It was a bloody day and casualties were heavy. The Guards had the assistance of American M10 tank-destroyers. Capt. Kennedy left this account of some of the fighting: "As we hit the side road we were well spread out, our guns facing east and west alternately down the column. Behind us came the carriers looking very small in comparison to the M10's. The sun was now up, shining like a big red ball of fire, bringing to us a new day and new spirits. I signalled to the Guardsmen on the tanks to man the .55 Browning machine guns, and to open fire when they saw us do so from the leading tank. They had not long to wait, for the first target was the house where we had lost Lieutenant Musgrave the night before. We all opened fire on it like a line of old men-of-war engaging the enemy at sea. No fire was returned, but all of a sudden some men ran out waving a Red Cross flag. Some Guardsmen ran over to them to discover what was up and he M10's pulled into some dead ground. Almost immediately the Germans started to shell us in earnest. The Company dismounted and took cover. I gave them an impromptu lecture on 'Infantry Tank Tactics,' and we prepared to clean up every single house in the district. This task turned out to be easier than we expected, because one sniper in a house only a hundred yards away gave himself up, as he could not bear the suspense of having tanks so close to him. He was a Frenchman and gladly gave us the location of every German position he knew. No. 13 Platoon, under Sergeant Dunne and two tanks, advanced to attack the first house covered by fire from the other two tanks. The attack went very smoothly and far faster than we expected, as Sergeant Dunne went through the house like a dose of salts, driving 'Krauts' out in all directions. The two covering tanks then moved up to the next farm-house where more Germans surrendered, again from all directions. From this farm-house No. 15 platoon, under Sergeant McKeown, and a section of No. 13, under Corporal Kane, launched a successful attack on a strong German force entrenched in an embankment. They returned plus pris-

The Long Haul - Sicily and Italy

oners and spoil, and the whole Company and the tanks concentrated round the farm-house." Kennedy and his men bagged fifty-five prisoners in all and managed to fight to a point just short of the Campoleone railway line. After this action John Kennedy was promoted to Major and awarded the MC for his part in stopping the German advance.

On February 4 the Irish Guards were withdrawn to some caves to recuperate. Another story surfaced to add to the Kennedy legend. The Italians living in their separate cave had, so far, taken no part in the war, but one of them, called Vittorio, was the owner of a farm-house known as "Ration Farm," and he was depressed by this turn of events. He came forward with the story that it was all due to some Fascist

Irish Guards, Anzio area.

spies, and that he could show the Irish Guards where these spies were and so contribute to the Allied victory. He was put in charge of Guardsmen Montogomery and Adamson, two of the most forbidding-looking and resourceful men in the battalion. They returned after about an hour with a small Italian Army captain, a smaller and even more terrified civilian, and a huge Alsatian dog. From the conversation which followed the Italians got the impression - which was entirely possible - that they were going to be shot out of hand. The two fell on their knees weeping bitterly. Vittorio, the informer, repeated many tmes that, since the dog was an Alsatian, it must have been supplied by the Germans for the special purpose of carrying messages. The Italian captain swore that it had been his since it was a puppy, so the Sergeant-Major suggested a simple test. The dog was led away round a corner, and the Italian captain was told to call it. The Italian began confidently, but when no dog appeared, his voice rose in tones of shrill despair, particularly when he noticed Guardsmen Montgomery and Adamson shifting their Tommy guns from hand to hand. The Adjutant decided to look at the dog before doing anything hasty. He went round the corner and found the Alsatian struggling desperately and half-strangled by a rope tied to its collar. Holding on to the rope was Major Kennedy. "A grand little dog," he said. "It took to me at once." The Italians were reprieved and sent to Brigade H.Q. , who sent them to a holding 'cage'.

The Irish Guards went back into the line on February 17 and stayed there until the 25th. Here men like Major Kennedy and Guardsmen Montgomery and Adamson ruthlessly hunted down Germans turning the gullies of Anzio into a murderous maze. The actions of Major Kennedy and these fierce Guardsmen no doubt saved countless lives on the Anzio beach-head. John Kennedy was not only admired by his own troops. The Americans were also full of praise for him and called him the "Mad Irishman", devoting a full column on his exploits in their paper, 'Stars and Stripes.' Towards the

The Long Haul - Sicily and Italy

end of the fighting in the Wadi's Maj. Kennedy was wounded in the chest and evacuated to Naples.

On March 7 the 1st Irish Guards sailed away from Anzio to Naples with 20 officers and 247 other ranks. Originally, 794 men had went to Anzio along with 286 replacements. Over 800 men had become casualties in two short months, a casualty rate of 94 per cent. The Guards remained in Italy for another month then sailed back to England to prepare for the invasion of France. The 1st Battalion was so devastated it never fought as a unit again in the war.

On March 2 Company Sergeant-Major Fred Kelly, Newbridge, was with D Company, Royal Irish Fusiliers, who were ordered to clear the enemy from a wadi on Anzio. The Germans held the higher ground here overlooking the Allied lines, where the men had to crawl about in the holes and gullies keeping out of sight. The Faughs attacked the German wadi and partially cleared the enemy but owing to darkness, the thickness of the scrub and casualties from shell fire, it was not possible to finish the job that night.

The next day the remnants of the company went forward to complete the job. The company commander was hit and CSM Kelly received a bullet wound to the chest. Although there were only 15 men left in the company CSM Kelly carried on and saw the task completed and remained there to see that the position was held until it was possible to get reinforcements under cover of darkness. For this action Fred Kelly was awarded the DCM. His dispatch read: "CSM Kelly's example of courage and his determination to see the task completed, under the most trying conditions, were beyond praise."

The Allied line at Anzio remained virtually the same as it had been at the end of the great German counterattack on February 20. There were some alterations in the next few months but they were minor

The Long Haul - Sicily and Italy

Photo: IMPERIAL WAR MUSEUM.

Camouflaged Sherman of the 16th/5th Lancers, with supporting infantry, near Cassino.

ones. Some parts of the front were more active and dangerous than others. Week in and week out the weary troops defended the line, as the Allied build-up continued. On May 11 the last great offensive on the Cassino front began. In a brilliant attack the French Expeditionary Corps pressed up the Ausente Valley reaching San Giorgio. On May 17 Kesselring gave orders for the evacuation of the whole Cassino front, since the successes of the French and the Americans in the south had rendered it untenable. On May 23 the Allies began the breakout from the Anzio beachhead linking up with the advancing US II Corps two days later.

"The bombing of Cassino was a tactical failure, but regrettably good for morale." Captain John de Burgh, attached to 16th/5th Lancers, said. "We could not get through with our tanks. There was a lot of house-to-house fighting and the German paratroopers were

far from the short grass

The Long Haul - Sicily and Italy

excellent fighters. We had the French with us and I met some very fine French officers. They had Moroccan troops with them, who were great fighters. The French got around the mountains, leaving the Germans little choice but to retreat." French General Alphonse Juin was the Allies most ablest commander in Italy. The French Expeditionary Force had Moroccan and Algerian troops, native mountain people, led by superbly trained French staff officers. They were equipped with modern American equipment and were formidable opponents.

The honour of taking the heights of Monte Cassino was given to the Polish Brigade, who also had suffered terribly in the battle. But the bulk of the Germans had left quietly during the night and the Poles found only the wounded and dead remained. As the Gustav Line collapsed the Irish Brigade, with the 16th/5th Lancers in support, were given the objectives of cutting off Highway 6 - the escape route of the Germans from Cassino. German resistance was strong and had been stiffened by a number of paras withdrawn from Cassino. The Allied infantry and tanks, fighting through cornfields and terraced olive groves, came under a deadly storm of mortars, artillery and machine-gun fire. Major Robert Gill, from Yomanstown, Naas, leading a support squadron of 16th/5th Lancers, was killed when his tank was hit, in the early stages of an attack launched on May 17. The bulk of the Germans escaped, fighting another spectacular rearguard action.

The battle for Cassino was a tough battle fought over the most rugged terrain and for the most part in miserable weather. It was fought in conditions reminiscent of the First World War. After five months of fighting over 200,000 soldiers had been killed or wounded. On June 4 1944 the Allies entered Rome. The capture of the Italian capital was soon overshadowed by other events - the invasion of France - and the Italian campaign became a mere side-show as all reinforcements and attention were switched to France.

The weary 8th Army bivouacked on the banks of the Tiber down-

The Long Haul - Sicily and Italy

stream from Rome and then began the advance northwards. The Allies had invaded France on June 6 and Lady Astor, speaking in the House of Commons, had said the men in Italy were 'dodging D-Day.' It was a grievous slur on the brave men who had fought and died on the road to Rome. Unable to hit back publicly, they wrote new words to *Lilli Marlene,* the marching song they had learned from the Afrika Corps in North Africa:

'We are the D-Day Dodgers,
Out in Italy,
Always on the vino,
Always on the spree.
Looking round the mountains in the mud and rain,
There are lots of little crosses, some which bear no name.
Blood, tears, sweat and toil are gone.
The boys beneath them slumber on.
These are your D-Day dodgers who'll stay in Italy.'

As the Allied Generals pranced and posed in Rome the battle for Northern Italy went on. Pte. James McGowan, Suncroft, was serving with the 6th Battn., Black Watch, a Scottish regiment. He had survived the fierce fighting around the Cassino front but was killed in action, on June 11, north of Rome. Captain Ian Blacker, Castlemartin, Kilcullen, serving with the 10th Battn., The Rifle Brigade, was also killed in action in the push after Rome, on June 22, near Rivotorto.

The Irish Brigade was withdrawn from the line in July and sent to Egypt "for what they called refitting." Fus. Dennis Carroll said. "We arrived in Alexandria and everybody had a good time there, for awhile. Then we were sent back to Italy. The 6th Inniskillings was amalgamated with the 2nd. There was not enough men to keep all the battalions going. Casualties had been very high. We moved back to Italy. It was all foot slogging. The further north we went, the bigger the hills

The Long Haul - Sicily and Italy

got. We were in the hills overlooking Bologna that winter, lying in the snow. We could see Bologna in the distance. We patrolled at night and lay in the snow from 4.30 in the evening to daybreak the following morning. No smoking or nothing and no one ever got hypothermia. The snow was four foot high at times. I was a corporal at the time. The Germans were a hundred yards away. We could hear them and I'm sure they could hear us, too. But, there was an unspoken agreement not to fire on one another.

"Once up in the mountains I spotted a German gun hidden in a mountaintop cave. It came out and fired one round, to get our range. I spotted the muzzle flash and with my binoculars found the location of the gun. With that they fired another round. Paddy McCarthy and an English sergeant were standing together. The shell landed between them. Paddy McCarthy was unhurt, just blown off his feet. The English sergeant was killed outright, though there was not a mark on him. The shock had killed him and even though there was only a few feet between him and McCarthy, Paddy was unhurt. It was strange. The gun disappeared after that... The Germans were very cocky. The 1st Paras were the toughest. I remember the body of a German lay beside a road for days. It was booby-trapped. Eventually it went black from the cold.

"We came across an empty house near Bologna. It had a huge wine vat with a wooden spigot and we all sat around drinking wine. Eventually some of the lads got curious and got on top of the vats to see how much was left. They looked in and found the naked body of a woman. She had been raped and murdered by the Germans and her body dumped in the wine vat. Her body was pickled. Another time we found a motorbike built into the wall, hidden from the Germans."

CSM Fred Kelly was with the Irish Fusiliers at the Gothic Line and years later wrote how he lost one of his best friends in unusual cir-

The Long Haul - Sicily and Italy

cumstances. "It was September, 1944, during the heavy tank and infantry battles in the Gothic Line near the village of Croce and Coriano where the incident took place. My company had taken a ridge near Croce with casualties, and Paddy's company was moved behind us as reserve to help to hold the position.

"The enemy were quick to retaliate and we were shelled for about ten minutes. We did not have any casualties so I decided to go back to the reserve company to see how they fared, and to arrange about our move forward as we expected. On arrival at Paddy's area I was greeted by him and 'Anything to drink, Tim?' were his first words (I was "Tim" to Paddy, although Fred to my family).

"I must explain that, as Paddy knew, I usually kept a concoction in my spare water-bottle (I carried two), and so, after a swig, and a chat about liaison, etc. I decided to return to my area, but before leaving I said, 'Get that ruddy almond tree cut down, Pat' (It grew beside his Company HQ slit-trench). He made a witty retort that it could keep the sun off, as he'd had enough sun in India in pre-war days.

"I had no sooner returned to my own area than the shelling was resumed. It was really heavy this time. Then, during the lull, we checked our casualties, which were light, but my CO said, 'I think they have copped it in the Reserve Company.' I said I would go back again, and I took two men to assist if possible.

"On arrival at Paddy's area, the OC was totally shaken. He said, 'Paddy's gone,' and indeed, they were just removing his body, and that of his company runner. An enemy mortar bomb had struck the almond tree which deflected the bomb below to the slit trench, killing both men instantly. There was nothing I could do except to return and report, and feel pretty rotten. I had lost a true friend through that almond tree, a friend whom I shall never forget."

The Long Haul - Sicily and Italy

The Gothic Line was breached in September as the Allies continued the long haul up the boot of Italy. Hope of reaching the Po valley soared, but then faded with the coming of the autumn rain. Torrential rain turned streams into raging torrents that surged over the plain and became more of an obstacle than the mountains. As the weather deteriorated the troops in Italy settled down for another cruel winter. Heavy snow followed by freezing cold rain made conditions unbearable and sapped the strength and morale of the men. That winter in the mountains was particularly grim and very unpleasant. Morale was dangerously low because of exhaustion after the previous hard fighting and the widespread feeling that Italy was merely an unimportant side-show of the war. Some of the best units of the Allied army in Italy were withdrawn for the fighting in Northern Europe and the 5th and 8th Armies were all understrength. Desertion rose alarmingly but was dealt with sensitively. With the severe weather conditions it soon becme clear that no further offensive could be launched until the spring. The battle for northern Italy settled into a stalemate in conditions which were commonly associated with the Western Front of the Great War.

On April 9 1945 the 5th and 8th Armies began their final offensive. The Germans performed with great valour but little hope and were quickly forced back, caught between the pincers of the two Allied armies. Fighting was still severe and Sergeant John Mulpeter, Rathangan, serving with the 7th London Rifle Brigade, was killed in action on April 22. Thirty-two year old Sgt. Mulpeter was a veteran, having joined the army in the early days of the war.

"When spring came we attacked and the Germans fell back. This was 1945." Corporal Dennis Carroll, 2nd/6th Inniskillings, said. "After Bologna we were out on flat land and we pushed on to the Senio river. There were high dikes on each side of the river and the land was lower. The Germans were on one side and we were on the other. You

The Long Haul - Sicily and Italy

couldn't dig in, because a few hundred yards up the Germans were on the same side. You couldn't look over the floodbanks or you'd get a bullet in the head. I saw one officer stick his head up and Bang! He got a bullet through the head. We had periscopes, but every time they went up they got a hole through them. We ran out of periscopes and started using bean and sardine tins. We put them on our bayonets and stuck them up. You were guaranteed to get a hole through them.

"The Germans had a wooden bridge sunk under the water. They were very ingenious. We were all night chucking grenades at them. Our platoon easily threw a hundred grenades. Just as a deterrent to keep them from coming over. In the daytime we done nothing, just lay there. The grenades kept coming up. There were no shortages of them." The Irish Brigade spent over two weeks on the Senio floodbanks. The fighting was reminiscent of First World War trench fighting and casualties were very high.

The main Allied offensives began in April. After nearly two weeks heavy fighting the Germans were in full retreat and their situation, even to their commanders, was obviously hopeless. "The Germans were pulling back. They had no fuel for their tanks and were short of men. On one occasion we captured a father and son. The lad was only sixteen. They gave themselves up and were glad to be out of it. POWs were well treated. They were given cigarettes and tea. It was a clean war. They were rationed just like us and got cigarettes every day. This was more or less coming into the last push. I remember going into this house. Inside was a table with a Luger sitting on it. A Luger pistol was a prize trophy, but it was too obvious. I had a look at it. There was a wire coming out the barrel. Once you moved the Luger something would happen, so I left it there. I don't know what happened to it.

"On that same occasion a regiment of tanks from the Queen's Bays were told there was an 88-mm gun up the road. They refused to

The Long Haul - Sicily and Italy

go up. They were ordered to, but they refused. The following day or two we pushed on to Ferrari. We had air support. American Mitchell's softened up the German guns. We hadn't much problems. We stopped overnight and started with a creeping barrage the next morning. Our shells would land 100 yards in front of us and then lift as we moved forward. Later, Colonel Clarke said to me we were very lucky as the guns were firing short. It happened a lot. It was probably only one gun. The barrels wore out and you would have to check the range of every one of them to see which one was firing short."

Despite their imminent defeat the morale of the German troops remained high. While the troops were tired from five years of fighting they could not envisage a German defeat. They fought on in the hope that something would turn up - secret weapons that would turn the tide of war or a falling out between the Allies.

"The Germans were packing it in now. We captured about twenty of them. They came out with their hands up. When we captured them

Photo: R. WILSON.

Johnny Doran and Austrian family he befriended.

far from the short grass | *page number 191*

The Long Haul - Sicily and Italy

we usually took their watches. It was the same if they captured us. I approached one fellow and took his watch, pen and pencil. He asked me not to take them as they were a present from his mother. I was too soft and gave them back. I'm sure someone else down the line took them anyway. The Germans started mortaring. I took a watch from another German and had no luck for it, as I was hit by shrapnel in both hips. I picked up the transmitter as the signaller was lying down and he was decapitated. We shoved the German prisoners under a bridge. I was able to walk back to the dressing station, but the wounds put me out of the picture. I was sent to a camp outside Naples. The battalion went on to Austria, but my war was over. I was sent back to England."

The war in Italy was practically over. The German commanders approached the Allies to surrender. On April 29 surrender terms were agreed; the cease-fire coming into effect on May 2. The long haul through Italy was over.

Sergeant Mickser Mahon was no longer with the infantry. He had volunteered for a military police detachment. "I was fed up getting shot at," he said. "All my friends were gone, either killed or wounded. It seemed to be only a matter of time before I was next, so I got out of the infantry. I had been fighting since 1941 and everyone who had started out with me was gone. Jackie was dead, and all the rest." While British casualties were only a third of what they were in the Great War it is rarely realised that the front-line troops suffered just as heavily in the Second World War. "I seen Mussolini hanging by the feet in Milan. I was with the MP's then and the war was just over. We drove into the square and he was hanging up like a pig."

The Italian Dictator, Benito Mussolini, was captured with his mistress, Clara Petacci, and some Fascist followers. They were shot by partisans without ceremony on April 28 in the small town of Dongo,

The Long Haul - Sicily and Italy

near Como. Their bodies were taken to Milan and dumped in front of a garage in the Piazzale Lortetto, where partisans had been shot in reprisals by Fascists a year before. They were strung up by their ankles and people hurled waste and filth and spat at the already disfigured corpses. One woman fired five bullets into Mussolini 'to avenge her five dead sons.' It was a fitting death for one who had led his country to ruin and destroyed millions of lives to create his 'New Roman Empire.'

Sergt. Mahon was heading for Austria when news came through of the surrender of the German Armed Forces and with it the end of the war in Europe. "We were crossing the Brenner Pass into Austria when word came through of the German surrender," he said. "We were given a half-pint of beer as a celebration." The end of the war came as a bit of a shock to the troops. It was difficult to absorb the news immediately. So many had died and the survivors felt that sad twinge of guilt that they were still alive. There were so many memories of comrades and so many feelings of loss that it was difficult to comprehend. Many men had been fighting for years. Some had left school and went straight into the army.

"I was a solid three years fighting." Major John de Burgh, serving with the 6th Armoured Division, said. "That is a long time. I was fortunate though, to belong to a good regiment. We looked after everybody, our wounded and so on. It had always been important to keep up morale. If some chap's wife had run off or someone's house had been bombed, it was important to know. That last winter in Italy was very unpleasant. The only way we could be supplied was by mule. Everything came up by mule, and it was very, very cold. We finished up in Austria and north-east Italy, trying to contain Tito's partisans and the Russians. We were given an amiable welcome by the people there."

The Long Haul - Sicily and Italy

The 6th Armoured Division had moved into Klagenfurt, capital of the Austrian province of Carinthia. The area was teeming with many nationalities; Germans trying to surrender to the British before the Russians arrived; Yugoslav partisans trying to take over Carinthia province; Bulgarian troops, now on the side of the Allies, looting and murdering and a Cossack Corps, fighting on the Axis side, who were prepared to fight rather than return to Russia. The Russians were only too glad to see the British and were keen to see everything was done properly. SS troops of the 16th *Reichsführer* SS Panzergrenadier Division and the Cossack Corps were anxious to surrender to the British.

"We started racing and show-jumping as soon as the war ended." Major de Burgh said. "We had a lot of good racing going. Anything but soldiering. We got a lot of our best horses from the Cossacks, who had about 30,000 horses. We were involved in the surrender of the Cossacks, but fortunately we were not involved in sending the Cossacks back." About 7,000 Cossacks, their families and thousands of horses, mules and other animals had surrendered to the British. But under the terms of the Yalta agreement all POWs and captured nationals were to be returned to their native country. The Cossacks claimed they would be slaughtered and amidst protests they were forcibly herded onto trains and repatriated to Russia. Most of them were brutally killed by the Russians and their commander hanged in Red Square as a war criminal. "I said 'We cannot send Boris and Vichy (two Cossacks he had befriended) back.' I told them 'to bugger off' and then come back. I took several Cossacks to Germany with me in charge of our racehorses. When we returned to the UK, I arranged for them to go to Canada. Years later I met Vichy in New Jersey while visiting the American equestrian team and he told me they were all quite happy in a little Russian community in Canada.

"I spent two years in Austria after the war and learned to ski, raced and had a top class show jumper. At the same time the aftermath of the war was appalling. I was in Hamburg and the destruction was unbelievable, and everywhere there was that awful sweet smell of death. The Marshall Plan was brilliant. Our soldiers grumbled about why we were sending all this 'money to the Krauts,' but because we did all the old enmities were very quickly forgotten. The First War politicians had handled the peace very badly. We did not make the same mistake. Winning the peace is often harder than winning the war, and we won both."

CHAPTER 14

Bomber Command

In the dark days of 1940, following the surrender of France, Britain stood alone in her fight against Nazi Germany. While Britain took a bated breath the Wehrmacht was assembling a huge invasion force in Boulogne and other Channel ports for 'Operation Sealion'- the invasion of Britain. But before any invasion could be launched Germany had to have air supremacy. In preparation for the invasion the German airforce, the Luftwaffe, began an offensive against British ports, shipping, radar stations and airfields. The Battle of Britain began in earnest on August 13 when 1,485 Luftwaffe planes took to the skies. Luftwaffe commander, Reichsmarschall Herman Göring, assured Hitler of a swift, glorious victory. But it was not to be. While the Royal Air Force sustained heavy losses they inflicted greater damage on the Luftwaffe. The invasion of Britain, set for September 15, was postponed to September 21. The most crucial battle for control of the skies occurred on September 15 when 250 Hurricanes and Spitfires took on 1,090 German bombers and fighters. The RAF chased the Germans from the sky, shooting down 60 aircraft. This massive defeat forced Hitler to postpone the invasion of Britain indefinitely. British Prime Minister Winston Churchill paid tribute to the triumphant fighter pilots in one of his many stirring speeches: "Never in the field of human conflict was so much owed by so many to so few." Out of the

Bomber Command

total of 3,080 pilots who fought during the Battle of Britain, 10 of them were from Ireland.

At the beginning of September, after an accidental bombing of south-east London and RAF reprisals against Berlin, Adolf Hitler ordered the Luftwaffe to begin a reprisal campaign against British cities. The examples of Warsaw and Rotterdam, which had produced sudden collapses in Polish and Dutch resistance, were a clear inspiration in this new policy. The difference was that the British population soon proved to be made of sterner stuff than Hitler and his generals believed. The London Blitz began on September 7 and soon spread to other major cities, including Belfast and Derry. The bombing campaign, designed to break the spirit of the British public, continued until May 1941 and resulted in over 30,000 deaths. (Five civilians with Kildare connections were killed in air raids - Thomas Behan, a WWI veteran and winner of a MM and *Croix de Gurre*, son of Patrick and Mary Behan, Derrymullen, Robertstown, was killed on November 2 1940 in a raid on Coventry; Kathleen Whelan, 22, daughter of Murtha and Margaret Whelan, Curragh Camp, was killed in an air raid on August 30 1940 at her home in Liverpool; Patrick Barnwell, 29, son of Patrick and Julia Barnwell of Lough Brown, Newbridge, died of injuries received on May 4 1942 in an air raid on Ryde; Josephine O' Connor, 34, whose parents were from Rathangan, died in a raid on Wansworth on February 19 1944, while Bridget Nevin, 73, daughter of James Nevin of Sallins, was killed in a V1 rocket attack on August 2 1944.) Thousands of children were evacuated from the cities and sent to live in the countryside, while many more were shipped to Canada and the United States or to relatives in Ireland. My mother's cousin, ten year old Eddie Cannon, came to stay in Naas, after Liverpool was severely bombed. It was said that unblacked-out Southern Ireland helped the German navigators to find Liverpool, just across the Irish Sea.

Bomber Command

"I would have dearly loved to have dropped a bomb on lit-up Dublin," said one Irishman serving in the RAF. "It was a dead give-away for the Jerries."

Ireland in 1940 and 1941 was in fear of both a German and British invasion. It was only when the Americans arrived in Northern Ireland in January 1942 that this fear subsided. Unhappy that Ireland would not come in on the Allied side or give Britain access to Southern Irish ports Winston Churchill sparked off a major political crisis on May 19 1941 by suggesting the possibility of introducing conscription in Northern Ireland. Amid major protests in Nationalist areas of the North and hostility from the South and the de Valera government and reservations from President Roosevelt and the Canadian and Australian premiers, Churchill was overruled on the issue by his cabinet.

While the Blitz continued the RAF sporadically attacked targets in Germany, but it was not until 1942 that any serious bombing began on the part of the RAF with a 1,000 plane raid on Cologne. By then the entry of Russia and America into the war in 1941 had changed the whole course of the conflict. On June 22 1941 Germany turned her attention away from Britain and invaded Russia. It was one of her first two great blunders. On December 7 the United States entered the war when Japan bombed her Pacific fleet in Pearl Harbour. Two days later Germany and Italy foolishly declared war on the United States. From then on the outcome of the Second World War was never seriously in doubt.

The first units of the US 8th Air Force arrived in Britain in July 1942 to take part in the night bombing raids of RAF Bomber Command, or so the British believed. The Americans disagreed with the British tactics and opted for daytime bombing raids or what they called 'precision bombing.' Their objectives were well-defined targets like factories, construction-yards and assembly-shops which to a degree were,

Bomber Command

though this was unknown to the Allies at the time, fairly successful. As it operated by night, the RAF could not expect results like these, and so performed area bombing. In addition to H.E. bombs, they used a great variety of incendiary devices, some packed with jellied products of horrifying efficiency. Air Chief-Marshall Arthur "Bomber" Harris, A.O.C. Bomber Command, did not limit his task to the simple destruction of the Third Reich's war potential, but aimed also at destroying the morale of the German people.

The RAF's night offensive was based on three types of four-engined plane: the Avro Lancaster; the Handley-Page Halifax and the Short Stirling. Their armament of eight, nine and eight .303-inch machine guns, respectively, were insufficient to allow them to carry out daylight raids. A blind-bombing device guided the bombers and gave them their position at all times and enabled them to locate their targets with considerable accuracy. The objective was also indicated by pathfinders using coloured flares.

For obvious reasons the Americans rarely sent in more than 200 planes while at night the RAF were able to send in three and sometimes five times as many. RAF raids lasted as long as possible with thousands of tons of bombs being dropped. Casualties amongst civilians were heavy - 38,142 died in six attacks on Hamburg alone. Allied aircrew suffered terribly, too. The bombers were up against fighters and batteries of anti-aircraft guns and 55,000 British airmen never returned home.

To keep the air offensive going, huge back-up and supply crews were needed. Maintenance requirements for Bomber Command were as much as those for an army in the field. Thousands of Irishmen - and indeed dozens of Kildare men - joined the RAF, most of them attracted by the colourful reputation of the air arm.

Bomber Command

Photo: M. COADY

Michael Coady, Naas, (centre) and friends.

    The Battle of Britain had made the RAF, and in particular, the fighter pilot the most glamourous of the war. Everyone wanted to be a pilot, but pilots, navigators and bomb aimers tended to be drawn from the University and Grammer School element of aircrew intakes. Many recruits would never become pilots – "only gentlemen could fly" – and ended up as ground crew or air gunners – the latter one being the most dangerous of jobs.

    Michael Coady, Rathasker Road, Naas, joined the RAF in June 1942 at the age of seventeen - even though the legal age was eighteen. Both his father and grandfather served in the Royal Dublin

Bomber Command

Fusiliers and his uncle, Mikey, died from gas wounds. "Four of us from Naas joined up together." Michael Coady said. "Myself, Sean (Jack) White, Paddy Goulding and Jim Grehan, brother of Jack Grehan. We were all split up. (Paddy Goulding was from 15 Caragh Road; Jack White was from 12 Caragh Road, while the Grehan brothers lived over the family shop at Main Street, Naas. Jack White was posted to India, where he served until the end of the war.) After training I went to a transport command on a Canadian heavy bomber base in Yorkshire. They were mostly French-Canadians and half the time we didn't know what they were talking about. There was a lot of Irish in the Canadian airforce, too. We were loading them with bombs and handling metal strips, (designed to obstruct radar) which at the time we didn't know what they were used for.

"From there I went to a base in Grantham, near Spalding in Lincolnshire, then to Gunnery Training in No.1 Gunnery School, in Port Talbot, Wales. Everyone wanted to be a tail gunner. Sometimes you were told they had enough planes and no gunners. Other times they had enough gunners and no planes. We were not allowed to wear our uniforms when we were returning to Ireland on leave. We returned in civvies, where I met German prisoners, in uniform, on leave in Naas." German airforce personal who landed in Ireland were interned by the Irish government, as indeed were Allied airmen, at the Curragh camp. Interned officers were allowed out on parole, as long as they gave an undertaking to return, and usually headed to Naas and Newbridge for a night out, where Luftwaffe pilots, in their dashing uniforms, proved reasonably popular.

Brendan Conlan joined the RAF in the middle of 1942 in Belfast. He had already served one and a half years as an apprentice fitter in the Board of Works. His older brother had died the previous year, while serving with the Irish army when a mine he was helping to lay exploded, killing him and five of his comrades. His father, Frank, as a railway

Bomber Command

employee, was an intelligence operative for Michael Collins. He also played senior football for Kildare, playing against Kerry in 1905 and Galway in 1919. The Conlans lived over their shop on Edward Street, Newbridge and Brendan's enlistment in the RAF was met by disagreement in the household, but Brendan insisted "It was nothing to do with politics. There was nothing in Newbridge at the time. It was a chance for adventure."

Brendan recalls six other Newbridge men joining the RAF. The recruiting officer asked him if he wanted a week to make up his mind. "I told him if he wanted me to wait for a week I wouldn't be back." He spent two weeks in Newtownards and then was posted to Ardbroath on the east coast of Scotland. After completing his training, and finishing his apprenticeship, Brendan Conlan was posted to Waterbeach, Cambridge, to 514 Bomber Command. Here he worked on 514s bombers "first Stirlings and then Lancasters. We signed for everything we worked on and I probably went up three times a week to check for malfunctions. Everything was rechecked by engineers and if there was any faults you would be reprimanded.

"There were dozens of Irishmen in the RAF and many of them never came back. A friend of mine, he was a Corkman, and who was in the same billet as me, never came back from a bombing mission. The tail-gunners had an awful job, cramped in that little position. I seen some of them come back splattered. One time a bomber exploded on take-off. The whole crew went up in a fireball. It was not thought too much of, as aircrew were lost every day."

1943 was the bloodiest year of the air war when 2,314 RAF planes were lost and German night-fighter defences were at the summit of their wartime effectiveness and strength.

"While stationed in Blackpool the man in charge of us was a fellow

Bomber Command

Photo: B. CONLAN.

Brendan Conlan (left) with a DC9 at Lydda Air Force base.

named Stanley Matthews. Bob Monkhouse was also serving in the same unit." In 1944 514 Bomber Command was transferred to the Middle East to become 514 Transport Command, ferrying troops to the Far East. The Desert War was over so it was safe to travel through the Mediterranean, rather than round the Cape Horn, as Middle East and Far East bound convoys had to do prior to the Allied victory in North Africa. Over 1,000 men were on board the troop transport. Aircraftman Conlan recalled his greatest fear was of German submarines. "In the Bay of Biscay the waves were 30ft high. We were five days at sea and we first docked at Algiers, then went on to Port Said. We travelled by train - which had no windows - to Shaloufa on the

Bomber Command

Suez Canal and then to Cairo. I found the pyramids fascinating and marvelled at how man could create such fine work. While in a tented transit camp we slept eight to a tent. The nights were very cold and we dug ourselves a shallow grave to sleep in. When we woke up sand was everywhere and in everything."

AC Conlan was sent to the permanent base at Lydda, 18 miles outside Tel Aviv, in what was then Palestine. "Tel Aviv is a beautiful city," he said "and I was enthralled with the magnificent buildings and avenues, though we were not allowed in the old city at night. The Palestine police were mostly British and they had a cushy time, were well paid and with their own houses and private swimming pool. We got paid once a fortnight and had plenty of time off. The army called

Photo: B. CONLAN.

Brendan Conlan, Newbridge, (at back), pictured at the Sea of Galilee.

Bomber Command

us the 'brylcream boys.' There was an American base camp nearby and we got all our films from them." Movies were shown at outdoor cinemas and were usually subtitled in four different languages.

"We worked from early morning till twelve noon and were busy all day. We worked in shorts as the weather was very warm. The only consolation was we had an outdoor swimming pool. Sometimes we went swimming in the Sea of Galilee. Our work was very tedious, but interesting. There were over 200 billets in our camp. The huts were wooden on concrete bases with galvanised roofs. We were baked inside them and needed mosquito nets at night. It was a great experience and I had no regrets. I loved the Holy Land and met many Irish priests and even served mass in the Garden of Gethsemne."

Jim Cullen, from Kilcullen Road, Naas, joined the RAF in late 1943 at the age of seventeen. He travelled to Belfast with two other Naas men, Tommy O'Shea and Paddy Gogarty. A well-known local woman helped forge birth certificates for lads who were still under age. "We did not want to be turned down again." Jim said. "The first time we went to Belfast to join up we were turned away and we had to walk home. It took us nearly a week. You only had the train fare for one way. This time they took us in and we sold our suits of clothes to keep us going until we got paid. There was terrible poverty in Naas at the time. You had to go out to the bog for work and you spent all day footing turf for a half crown, or five shillings, if the man was generous. Half of Naas went to England for work and one time I was amazed to see so many Naas men working on an RAF base." (There were so many Kildare people in England that Capt. John Kennedy wrote home in 1942: "Naas will soon be getting jealous of London W.1. becoming 'Kildare's other capital'.")

Jim Cullen travelled from Belfast to Padgate, in Lancashire, and

Bomber Command

Photo: P. GOREY.

Norman Robinson, 3rd from left, with his crew in training uniform.

after passing out was promoted to Flight Sergeant. He met his future wife, Mary, who was training as a nurse in London, while V-1 rockets were falling on the city. "It turned out to be a good time to go as the heavy bombing was over and casualties were not so bad. So many men were lost over Cologne and Hamburg. They would send even four or five planes to Cologne. So many Irish lads lost their lives in incidental missions. I thought it was a terrible waste of life."

Pilot Officer Norman Robinson, Carbury, was shot down over Germany in November 1943. He was piloting a Lancaster III and had flown a total of 26 flying operations. Aircrew were usually stood down from flying after 30 missions. Norman Robinson's squadron, based in Lincolnshire, had a gruelling six hour, and more, flight to their targets in Berlin, Dusseldorf, Dresden and Peenemünde. Norman's family

far from the short grass

Bomber Command

noticed the strain on him when he returned home to Carbury on his last leave in the summer of 1943. He was very tired and had lost a lot of weight. From November 18 1943 to March 30 1944 the RAF mounted 9,111 sorties aginst Berlin in 16 major attacks, in what became known as the Battle of Berlin, and 11,113 sorties against other cities for a loss of 1,047 aircraft. With these devastating results both the Stirling and Halifax bomber were withdrawn from all operations against Germany.

Berlin, Dusseldorf, Dresden and Peenemünde were protected by a formidable force of night-fighters and anti-aircraft defences and struck terror into the hearts of Allied airmen. The Germans were perfecting new retaliatory weapons (V1 and V2 rockets) at the Peenemünde testing station on the shores of the Baltic. Hitler boasted that London would be levelled by the end of 1943 and Britain forced to capitulate. On the night of August 16-17 597 four-engined bombers of Bomber Command raided Peenemünde. On take-off the pilots were warned that in case of failure they would begin again without regard to the losses sustained. The raid was a magnificent success. Damage to German installations was heavy, for a loss of 40 British bombers and 32 damaged. After this, production was shifted to a number of underground factories and the first V1's did not hit London until mid June 1944.

The system established in 1943 continued into 1944 as Air Chief-Marshall Harris stuck obstinately to his theory that Germany could be forced into defeat merely by the effects of strategic bombing. Sergeant Michael Breen, Decoy Farm, Naas, serving with the RAF Volunteer Reserve, was shot down over Germany on February 11 1944. From January 1 1944 the Allied airforces had increased their target load, even raiding Vienna and the East Prussian city of Marienburg. In the month of February they were still fighting the Battle of Berlin and were concentrating on the German aircraft industry. Sgt.

Bomber Command

Breen was only eighteen and had only recently finished his training when his plane was lost. The first five operations were the most crucial for the new crews with odds of 10 to 1 against surviving. Having survived 15 ops., the odds became even. 35% of crews survived a tour of duty – 30 operations.

As the year dragged on Allied planes reached further and further into the heart of Germany nearly destroying the Third Reich's capability of manufacturing synthetic fuel - a vital component in the war effort - and petrol and diesel fuel production. As the Allies advanced in Italy newer bases for bombers cropped up making it easier to bomb the southern extremities of the Third Reich. From bases in North Africa the RAF, and USAAF, flew support missions for the Mediterranean theatre of operations. The Mediterranean Allied Air Force incorporated Mediterranean, Strategic, Tactical and Coastal Air Force. Nineteen year old Sergeant James Holland, from South Main Street, Naas, was serving with 114 Squadron RAF Volunteer Reserve - known as the Hong Kong Squadron. He was the son of Major J. A. Holland, formerly RAMC, of Naas, and a nephew of WWI Victoria Cross winner John V. Holland. On March 5 1945 his plane was lost over the Mediterranean. His body was never found.

In the last year of the war the vast bombing effort found the best target: the German transport system, and the industrial centres producing artificial rubber and petroleum products. The elimination of these produced almost immediate results - German troops could not be moved adequately and their transport and tanks were constantly short of fuel. Moreover, the Luftwaffe was practically grounded for lack of fuel. On the ground the Allied armies pushed through occupied Europe and into the heart of the Third Reich. Air Gunner James Burns, Curragh, was serving with 78 Squadron, RAF. His squadron was part of 4 Group Bomber Command and were based in Southern England. They flew Halifaxes and Lancasters. On April 4/5 4 Group

Bomber Command

A photo captioned "13 Pals" sent home to Ireland and signed by the men with Kildare connections, among them Jack White and Jimmy Sheridan, Naas (front row second left) and Daniel Sheehan, Newbridge.

attacked targets in Hamburg. Three aircraft were lost and James Burns was among the fatalities.

The final RAF operation in Europe was three weeks later with a double attack on the night of April 24/25 against Hitlers' redoubt at Baerchtesgaden and Naval installations at Sylt, on the Dutch/German coast. By the end of the war Bomber Command had flown 372,650 sorties and dropped 1 million tons of bombs for a loss of 8,617 aircraft and 47,268 aircrew – the highest pro rate loss of any Allied military unit.

CHAPTER 15

Fortress Europe

Plans for the invasion of France had been in the pipeline once the United States entered the war in 1941. In January 1942 the first American troops arrived in Northern Ireland and Southern Ireland breathed a sigh of relief, aware that the chances of a German, or even a British invasion, had diminished greatly. As the might of the American industry shifted into top-gear the build-up for the invasion of 'Fortress Europe' began. Troops and materials poured into Britain as the Atlantic convoys braved the German wolf-packs, and the elements to bring vital supplies needed to sustain the British war effort. Naas man Matty O'Rourke served as a Chief Petty Officer on Atlantic and Murmansk convoys and was sunk four times. His brother, Michael, served as a driver in the RAF.

The Russian port of Murmansk was the primary port for Allied Arctic convoys bringing much needed supplies to Russia. Unfortunately, it was only a few miles up the Kola Inlet on Russia's Barents Sea coast, and well within range of bombers from the German airfields at Petsamo and Kirkenes. Able Seaman John Blake,

Fortress Europe

Newbridge, was on board the escort carrier HMS *Avenger* when it was sunk on November 15 1942. After the disaster which befell Convoy P.Q.17, when 19 out of 30 merchantman were sunk, the Royal Navy provided P.Q.18 with a more powerful escort, which included *Avenger*. Despite this 13 of the 40 vessels that then sailed from Hvalfjord were lost compared to 4 German submarines and 41 aircraft. John Blake was among the many dead.

RAF Coastal Command played a major and unsung part in the

Photo: J. GREHAN.

Jack Grehan, Naas, RAF Coastal Command. Note pre-1939 pilot and observer insignia above breast pocket.

Fortress Europe

defence of Britain. John, or Jack, Grehan served with the Coastal Command in those most crucial days. Jack Grehan was born in Naas in 1918 and left his job as a legal apprentice to begin a career in the RAF in March 1939. He signed on for 10 years and passed out as an Acting Sergeant and Acting Air Observer. He was assigned to 215 Squadron Coastal Command based at Honington and later served in Malta. On May 15 1942 he was a awarded the Distinguished Flying Cross, for a sustained effort in battle. The role of Coastal Command was long-range maritime patrol and convoy escort, air-sea rescue of downed pilots and U-boat sorties. The major operational aircraft were the excellent Sunderland flying boat and the Catalina. After four years active service Jack Grehan was placed on the reserve, where he continued serving throughout the war as an instructor.

Britain, fighting a war on two fronts - Italy and the Far East - was still under pressure and felt it was not ready to invade France until at least mid-1944. The armed forces had attained the limits of its growth and the population, after over four years of conflict were war weary. Nevertheless, the invasion represented an opportunity for Britain to return to France and expunge the ghost of Dunkirk.

In the early hours of June 6 three Allied airborne divisions were dropped over targets in Normandy. The British 6th Airborne were dropped between the Orne and Dives rivers while the American 82nd and 101st Airborne Divisions were dropped further west over the Cotentin peninsula. They were to seize key objectives and link up with the advancing troops who stormed ashore several hours later. Pte. Jack McCormack, Newbridge, was serving with the 8th Regiment, 6th Airborne Division. The 6th Airborne's objectives were to capture intact the bridges across the Orne and its canal between Bénouville and Ranville and to destroy the Merville battery and the Dives bridges between Troarn and the coast. The 8th Regt. dropped northwest of the village of Touffréville.

Fortress Europe

Like many of the British troops in the invasion force Jack McCormack was arriving back in France after been brutally expelled four years earlier. Jack McCormack was with the 2nd Irish Guards in the summer of 1940 and had fought through Holland and France before been evacuated from Boulogne. Anxious to get back into action Jack had transferred to the airborne forces. Now he was on one of the toughest of all D-Day jobs. As in all amphibious operations the Allied invasion of Fortress Europe depended on the weather. The paratroops and glider-borne infantry needed a late-rising moon. Their surprise attack depended on darkness up to the time they arrived over the drop-zones, followed by a late-rising moon. (The land force needed low tides to expose beach obstacles.) The paratroops of the 6th Airborne dropped over a huge area, victims of navigational errors, planes forced off courses by ground fire, badly marked drop zones and gusty winds. Some were fortunate to land on target, but hundreds fell miles from the drop zones. Dozens were lost in the waters and swamps of the flooded Dives. Troops were loaded down with guns, ammunition and heavy equipment and many drowned while others were shot as soon as they landed.

Despite the obstacles and heavy losses the 6th Airborne performed well, capturing or gaining all their objectives. Several hours later an assault force of 176,000 Allied troops landed on five designated beaches - three British and two American. The British beaches were code-named Gold, Juno and Sword, the American beaches were Utah and Omaha. The latter soon became known as 'Bloody Omaha' when the Americans suffered over 2,000 casualties against strong German resistance. On the whole, the Normandy landings had been successful, but the Allies had nowhere gained their prescribed objectives for the evening of D-Day. The British 2nd Army had been assigned Bayeux, Caen and Troarn (nine miles east of Caen) as its D-Day objectives. While the British were near all their objectives, none were reached and some, like Caen, were not taken until July 19.

Fortress Europe

The Normandy *bocage* (mixed woodland and pastureland) favoured the German defenders and the Allies paid dearly for every yard of ground taken. The Allied tanks were also no match for the German panzers - the Mark V (Panther) and the Mark VI (Tiger). The German units facing the British 2nd Army were a formidable foe and included the 12th S.S. Panzer Division, the *Panzer-Lehr* Division and the Waffen-S.S. I Panzer Corps. Despite the German counterattacks the Allied beach-heads were cleared and by June 12 all the Normandy bridgeheads were linked, giving the Allies a front of 50 miles. It would be another two months before the Allies broke out of the Normandy bridgehead, with the bulk of the German army escaping through the 'Falaise Gap'.

Photo: F. McCORMACK.

Paratrooper, Jack McCormack, Newbridge.

Fortress Europe

Paratrooper Jack McCormack was involved in the heavy fighting in the Normandy *bocage*. His unit was dropped with one days supply of food and water, as they were supposed to link up with the invading land forces on D-Day. Instead it was six days until they were relieved and they had to drink water out of ditches. The paratroopers were under constant German attack. Jack McCormack recalled the most nerve racking experience was under mortar fire. He was wounded twice in the fierce fighting. The first time a bullet winged his nose, chipping off a slight piece of bone and flattening his nose. The second wound was more serious. A German sniper, hidden in a bell tower, shot him in the left arm, blowing off the bicep muscle. He was taken out of the combat area and sent back to England. He lost some power in his arm and would have to wear a brace for the rest of his life.

Joe Walsh, from Athy, arrived in France in late June. He had joined the Irish Army in 1940 at the age of twenty. "Conditions in the Irish army were very poor." he said. "I deserted from the Irish army and joined the RAF in October 1942 in Belfast. I wanted to be a rear gunner. We travelled from Larne to Stranraer. As far as I could make out, there were dozens of Irish army deserters joining the British forces. We were sent to Padgate, near Warrington, for training. All airforce personnel went through Padgate. After eight weeks training, I passed out as an Aircraftman, which is the same as a private in the army. Orders came through that all personnel were to do a navigational course, or some other course. This was in 1943.

"After the navigational course, and that, it was into 1944. I eventually caught up with my unit, 715 Motor Transport and Light Repair Unit, around D+9 or D+19, in London. I was rearing to get to France to see some action. The Irish were not worried about the danger. They always went for the most dangerous jobs; tanks, tail-gunners and paratroops - the paras were full of Irish. We were sent to France and reached there about the time of Falaise. We did not see much action.

Fortress Europe

I remember a V1 rocket landing in a field beside us once, though it didn't cause any casualties."

Leading-Aircraftman Michael Coady was also sent to France with the RAF after the Normandy invasion with a close-support squadron, but was "only there a short time before being recalled to England, for 'special duties' at No.2 Experimental Station, Boscombe Down, Wiltshire. Everything was 'special duties'. You never knew what was happening. You just did what you were told."

After the breakout from Normandy the Allies quickly crossed the Seine (Allied forces entered Paris on August 25) and isolated and reduced the Channel ports. As the German northern front disintegrated Allied armour tore a 75 mile gap in the line, leaving Germany's vulnerable north-west frontier open and undefended. The British 2nd Army driving into Holland could outflank the Siegfried Line and swing into the Ruhr, the industrial heart of the Reich. In September Field

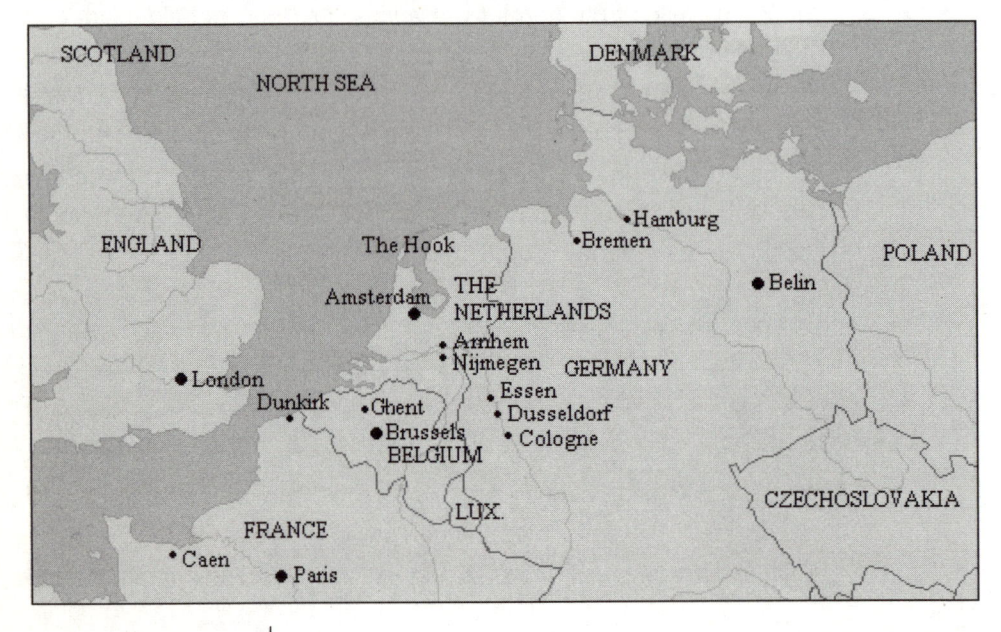

Fortress Europe

Marshall Bernard Montgomery, one of the most cautious of Allied commanders, proposed an ambitious plan, a combined airborne and ground offensive, to do this and end the war by Christmas. He proposed to drop three and a half airborne divisions to seize a succession of river crossings in Holland ahead of ground troops with the major objective being the Lower Rhine bridge at Arnhem. The surprise airborne attack would open a corridor for the Allied armour which would race across the captured bridges to Arnhem, cross the Rhine, wheel east, outflank the Siegfried Line and dash into the Ruhr.

On Sunday September 17 1944 5,000 fighters, bombers, transports and more than 2,500 gliders began the airborne phase of Operation Market-Garden, the dropping of an entire Allied airborne army, complete with vehicles and equipment, behind the German lines. An hour later, the massed tanks of the British 2nd Army, spearheaded by the Irish Guards Armoured Group, made up of an armoured battalion (2nd) and a mobile infantry battalion (3rd) of the Irish Guards, preceded by artillery and led by swarms of rocket-firing fighters, began a dash along a strategic route the paratroopers were already fighting to capture and hold open. Unfortunately Allied intelligence was unaware that the II S.S. Panzer Corps, recouping its losses after Falaise, was in the Arnhem area and the British 1st Airborne Division landed right amongst them. All went well for the US 101st Airborne Division, except for the Son bridge over the Wilhelmina Canal which it could not save from destruction. The US 82nd Airborne managed to capture the Grave Bridge, but failed in its first attempt on Nijmegen, which was later taken in a joint assault with the Guards. On September 18 the S.S. II Corps counterattacked against the British in Arnhem. Bad weather and a breakdown in communications hampered the British in Arnhem and despite being reinforced by the 1st Polish Parachute Brigade, they eventually had to evacuate to the left bank of the Neder Rijn. Over 1,200 British soldiers were killed and 3,000 captured in what was one of the greatest feats of arms in WWII.

RAF Sergeant Jim Cullen, Naas, was on his first combat flight during the Arnhem battle. Sgt. Cullen had trained as an air-gunner and was on board an Avro Lancaster which came under heavy ground fire. "We were told not to expect any opposition but the British dropped right on top of a whole German tank Corps who were well hidden. I was in the tail-gunners position, but our pilot wouldn't let our stick of paratroops jump. I was very pleased, as the Germans were just shooting them as they came down. I don't think any Englishmen even got to the far side of that bridge in Arnhem."

The Irish Guards Armoured Group spearheaded the ground offensive. The Guards Armoured Division had been fighting steadily since the breakout from Normandy and had received few replacements, in men and tanks, for the staggering losses they had endured. From the Seine to Antwerp the Guards had averaged 50 miles a day, but since the beginning of September the advance had slowed down as German resistance stiffened. It had taken four days for the Guards to advance ten miles and capture the vital bridge over the Meuse-Escaut Canal near Neerpelt from which the attack into Holland would begin.

The Guards Armoured Division consisted of Irish, Grenadier, Coldstream, Scots, Welsh and Royal Horse Guards units. The commander of the Irish Guards Group was the renowned Lieutenant-Colonel J.O.E. ('Joe') Vandeleur. He personified the devil-may-care attitude of the Guards officers. Vandeleur's typical dress was black beret, camouflaged parachutist jacket and corduroy trousers tucked into high rubber boots. He always wore a .45 automatic strapped to his hip and tucked into his jacket, which had become a symbol for his tankers, was a flamboyant emerald green scarf. The commander of XXX Corps, Lieutenant-General Brian Horrocks had once admonished him "If the Germans ever get you, Joe, they'll think they've captured

Fortress Europe

a peasant." Joe's cousin, Lieutenant-Colonel Giles Vandeleur, commanded the 2nd Battalion, Irish Guards.

Within minutes of kicking-off the Irish Guards had lost nine tanks to German gunners. The drive up the corridor consisted of mad dashes forward and sharp deadly firefights. The disabled tanks were quickly pushed aside and the advance would then continue. By the time the Irish Guards had blasted their way to Eindhoven and linked up with the American 101st Airborne they were seriously behind time. It was September 20 before they linked up with and supported the 82nd Airborne in their fight for the Nijmegen bridgehead. The armoured column was finally halted within six miles of the beleaguered British and Polish paratroopers in Arnhem. The massed tanks of the Germans proceeded south to halt the Allied drive while the Arnhem pocket was systematically obliterated.

The great dash ended only six miles short of Arnhem as the German resistance stiffened and the attacking forces were so busy defending themselves that it was no longer possible to continue the attack. The Irish Group were sent to help stem the attacks by the German 9th and 10th S.S. Divisions on the east flank of the Nijmegen bridgehead. The Germans had vowed to destroy the Nijmegen bridge and continued bombing and shelling the area. Eventually, they succeeded. The Germans still kept up the pressure and Irish casualties mounted. On October 1 the Guards received their most valuable reinforcement - Major John Kennedy. As shells exploded around Headquarters at the height of a battle Kennedy walked in. He was wearing a cap-comforter and a blue sailor's jersey and had an American M1 carbine slung over his shoulder. "I have come," he announced. "Never was a man so welcome," said Joe Vandeleur. "His battle record was second to none in the Regiment. He was one of those rare persons who really enjoyed war. It did us all good to see him." Major Kennedy had left his draft in England, to get on without

Fortress Europe

Lieut. Robin O'Reilly, Straffan, killed in action with the Irish Guards in Holland, 1944.

Photo: MRS. C. CLEMENTS.

him, hitched a plane ride and lorry-hopped through Belgium and Holland.

The Germans were making a serious attempt to eliminate the Nijmegen bridgehead using flame-throwers and Tiger and Panther tanks. The Guards resisted stubbornly inflicting heavy losses on the Germans. The next day the Guards were taken out of the line for some valuable rest and much earned leave. They returned to the lines again around the beginning of November to a reasonably quiet stretch of the front around the Sittard-Gangelt area.

The 3rd Irish Guards were to relieve an American unit in the line and the Irish reconnaissance parties were astonished at the 'live and let live' atmosphere around the front line. However, on November 15,

Fortress Europe

as the Guards were moving in the Germans fired one shell. This one shell killed Lieutenant Robin O' Kelly and Sergeant Mathews of the Intelligence Section and wounded two more officers. Lieut. O' Kelly, was only nineteen and from Millbrook, Straffan. He had only joined the battalion several months previously. Lieut. O' Kelly was educated at Ampleforth College, Yorks, and was there during the Blitz. There was talk at the time of sending the students to America or Canada, but young Robin insisted he would be staying. When he was eighteen Robin was commissioned into the Irish Guards.

Robin O' Kelly's sister, Mary, was in Antwerp, at the time of her brothers death, with the Catholic Women's League. The CWL handed out tea and sandwiches and organised entertainment at officers and enlisted men's clubs. Shortly after her brothers death, Mary O' Kelly made the trip to his grave, at Sittard, accompanied by Major John Kennedy, who was a family friend and whose homeplace, at Bishopscourt, was just a few miles from Millbrook.

In a letter to Mary O'Kelly, John Kennedy said: "It hit me like a brick when I learned he was dead. Although we have been neighbours so long, only recently did I get to know Robin and more I regret it. I can't tell you how much I miss him here as he was one of the very few human beings on this front. He was always himself as he managed despite the odds and always preserved his own individuality which in one word was charming."

Aircraftman Joe Walsh, Athy, was with the RAF in northern Europe as the Allies approached the German border. "My unit moved into Dietz (December 1944). We were a unit of fitters and mechanics. We knew something was about to happen. (On December 16 the Germans launched the beginning of their offensive known as the Battle of the Bulge.) That night a German plane attack put out of action all our vehicles that had only been repaired that day. Four of our

Fortress Europe

British tank crossing the Albert Canal as a Dutch solider of the Princess Irene Regiment and an Irish Guardsman guard the bridge.

men were machine-gunned in a jeep, but I don't know whether they lived or died. You never really found out. They were taken away and that was that. We pulled out, back to Ghent. We ran short of food and we were eating German biscuits then. We stayed in Ghent for a few weeks and didn't advance much further after that."

Christmas in the line was always hard on the troops. Maj. Kennedy wrote, "It seems a long time since I have written to you (his sister, Toby) but it was Christmas here and I always try to make it as good a Christmas as possible. This one was no exception. We pulled into a small town here and since then have been having a most wonderful time. I took up residence in the château and lived in great style. Big bed, clean sheets, running water etc. We all put our Christmas cards on the mantelpiece in the big room, started up the central heating and for a time had to ignore the war. It was almost too good to last.

"One could not help feeling homesick at times because it really was too much like home. I fixed the men up with a pretty good spread also.

"Did I tell you that I went for the funniest cross-country chase on

Fortress Europe

an old cart-horse here one day before Christmas. After it I was unable to move as I was so stiff."

Even though the end of the war was in sight volunteers from Ireland kept on arriving in Britain. Jimmy Sheridan, 4 Caragh Road, Naas, joined the RAF as soon as he was eighteen in early 1945. (Jimmy's older brother Jackie was killed in action in Italy the previous year. His death did not deter his young brother from enlisting.)

The 3rd Irish Guards were still facing stiff resistance around Nijmegen in 1945. On February 21 they were ordered to clear a group of scattered farmhouses and a château at Terporten, on the German/Dutch border, some 2,000 yards ahead of the front line. Major John Kennedy was again in charge of No. 3 Company, which he had taken over when its commander was wounded. He regarded this as providence as this was the company in which he had always served. The Germans were well dug in and the Guards lost three Bren Gun carriers to mines straight away. The rest were quickly bogged down. The area was water-logged and the attacking troops were more often than not knee-deep in water. The Guards wireless sets were also down preventing them from calling down supporting fire. However, the Guards chased the Germans from ditch to ditch and house to house all the time under intense fire. When the leading platoon of No. 3 Company reached the village château they found it held by superior forces. As Maj. Kennedy reached the château at the head of the platoon, Germans streamed out of the back door and hopped into trenches. "Come on, lads." he shouted, "We've got them now." He ran to the trenches in front of everyone else and walking back and forward he shot down Germans with his revolver. He soon used up his ammunition and was about to jump into the trench when a single shot hit him from behind, killing him instantly. The outnumbered Guardsmen had no choice but to break off the attack and retreat. In the attack the battalion lost 175 men from Numbers 1 and 3 Companies, including

Fortress Europe

both company commanders and all the platoon commanders. No loss was more keenly felt, than that of the heroic Kildareman, Maj. Kennedy.

In February 1945 Allied troops reached and broke through the Siegfried Line. A month later they crossed the Rhine river, Germany's last natural barrier. On March 28 the Allied objective was switched from Berlin to Leipzig and the British 2nd Army began its drive towards the Elbe. On April 24 the Red Army entered Berlin and after six days of heavy fighting reached the Reichstag building. On April 30 Adolf Hitler committed suicide in the Chancellery bunker. On May 7 Colonel-General Alfred Jodl signed the instrument of unconditional surrender of all German forces at Allied Headquarters at Rheims. The war in Europe was over.

Major Charles Clements, 4th Hussars, of course was still in Germany, as the end of the war in Europe approached. Captured in Greece in 1941 Maj. Clements had spent the last four years in POW camps in Germany. His first camp was Bibarach in Bavaria where he had only remained for a few weeks. He was transferred to Warburg (1941-42) and then to Rotenburg (1942-45). In Warburg he was head of the escape committee and was mentioned in dispatches for arranging escapes. The German government, as a signatory to the Geneva Convention of 1929, which safeguarded the rights of prisoners, treated most Western prisoners correctly. (The same could not be said of their treatment of prisoners captured on the Eastern Front.) Officers and NCOs did not have to work, but as many troops as possible were pushed out into farms, coal-mines and factories to free German workers for a more active part in the war effort.

Conditions in most German prison camps were bearable. Medical treatment was not a great problem and supplies of Red Cross food, clothing and tobacco parcels arrived regularly. The men in the camps

Fortress Europe

organised their own entertainment and schooling. Some camps had vegetable and flower gardens and facilities for football and cricket. These activities did not prevent much attention being devoted to the POWs most popular past-time - escape. Many attempts were made and most camps had escape organisations, with escape officers. All escape activity was co-ordinated and there were many successful Allied escapes - the most famous being that from Stalag Luft III in 1944 when 76 POWs escaped through tunnels.

In the second week of April 1945 the German guards marched the Allied POWs out of the Rottenburgh camp and headed east, away from the advancing American 1st Army. The POWs were rescued by an advance column of Americans at Eisleben on April 13, in what would later become part of the Russian zone. Maj. Clements was later flown back to England. He was promoted to Lieutenant-Colonel and later wound up commanding a German POW camp in Bridgend, Wales, housing over 200 German generals and admirals, including Field-Marshall Karl von Runstedt, General von Senger, the defender of Cassino, and Luftwaffe General Seidel. Lieut.-Col. Clements felt no animosity towards his German captives and in his treatment of them he tried to repay the excellent treatment he had received by his first captor, the Governor of the German held island of Anti Kithrya. His treatment of his German captives was favourably acknowledged by General von Senger in his memoirs, 'Neither fear, nor hope' (MacDonald and Co. London.1963).

In 1948 it was decided to release the last German POWs and Lieut.-Col. Clements accompanied some of his captives home. He wrote "It looked like being a rough crossing and I asked one general if he was a good sailor. He said that he had never been on board ship in his life. Apparently he had been flown to England. I was astonished and said so to General Seidel. 'It is not surprising at all,' he replied 'you will probably find that some of the admirals have never been to sea either'."

The entourage of escort and prisoners arrived at the Hook, in Holland and travelled from there across Germany, where the scenes of desolation awaited them. "It was Whit Sunday," Charles Clements wrote. "What was left of the buildings were decorated with oak leaves and the undernourished children, dressed as smartly as they could manage, welcomed the generals home, at the numerous stops.

"We detrained at Munster Lager, where the discharge formalities were quickly got through. I can not quite remember the process, but I think the generals were fitted out in civilian clothes, given a small amount of money and probably a travel warrant to their homes. Not one single general whose home was in the Russian zone, elected to return to it. I was unable to dissuade my own servant (one of the German orderlies) from going there. I had a car laid on, to take me to Hanover and was able to give a lift to General von Senger und Etterlein and two of his comrades."

Lieut-Col. Clements retired from the British Army in 1948 and returned to Ireland. "So ended my war experiences and army career," he wrote "as after having had a Field-Marshall and nearly 200 generals and admirals under my command I could hardly expect any future appointment to equal it."

The end of the war in Europe was welcomed by the population in Ireland - though de Valera upset many by calling on the German Minister to express condolences on the death of Hitler. Many of the young Kildaremen in the British armed forces chose to stay on. Sergeant Mickser Mahon, Naas, served in Austria and Palestine and then travelled to Hong Kong, where he patrolled the Chinese border for three years. He returned to Naas in 1952.

Fortress Europe

Joe Walsh, Athy, serving with the 715 Motor Transport Light Repair Unit, "was stationed in Hamburg and did a few weeks in Berlin after the war was over. I finished up a Leading-Aircraftman. I was demobbed in June 1947, though I was home for five weeks holidays that May. The only regret I had was I didn't go sooner. I might have had seen more action. I would have loved to have been an air-gunner and wouldn't have minded the risks."

LAC Michael Coady, Naas, was posted to Austria after Germany surrendered. "We were sent to Austria just to keep the Russians out. The Russians had no respect for anything," he said. "You could go up with a beer label and show it to them as your pass. We celebrated Christmas with the Austrian's. The Russians didn't even know what

Photo: B. MARTIN

CSM Fred Kelly, Newbridge, pictured in 1958 with his nine medals.
1. M.B.E.
2. D.C.M.
3. 1939-45 Star.
4. Italian Star.
5. Defence Medal.
6. War Medal.
7. Coronation Medal.
8. Long Service/ Good Conduct Medal.
9. Meritorous Service Medal.

Fortress Europe

Christmas was." Later he was sent to Germany to the 26th Group Transport Command for the transportation of food supplies during the Berlin Airlift. Michael Coady left the RAF in 1952 and returned home to Naas. "I never regretted it. You always look on the good side and forget the bad side."

LAC Brendan Conlan, Newbridge, stayed in Palestine until 1947 when he was demobbed. On leaving the RAF he was presented with "a complete outfit; suit, hat, mackintosh, underwear and socks."

Cpl. Dennis Carroll, Maynooth, remained in Hong Kong until 1949. He retired from the British Army due to ill-health. Dennis suffered a perforated ulcer which he blamed on the conditions in the Italian campaign and drinking water out of shell-holes in Italy.

Michael 'Barreller' Byrne, Naas, finished up in Northern Italy and transferred from the Royal Artillery to Prince Albert's Own 11th Hussars. He retired from the British Army a Warrant Officer.

Paratrooper Jack McCormack, Newbridge, returned home in 1946, invalided out of the army after been wounded in Normandy. A sniper had blew the muscle off his left arm. He died in 1966, age 57, from a perforated ulcer brought on by drinking water out of ditches in France, when his unit was cut off. His wounds had shortened his life and when he died in Leopardstown Hospital he looked twenty years older.

The long-term effects of the wounds Fred Kelly received in Italy also forced him to retire from the army in 1959. He had served in Austria, Germany (where he was awarded the MBE as garrison Sergeant Major in Berlin) and Gibraltar after the war. He died at the age of 84 in 1996 in England. In a letter to Fred's wife, Major-General Purdon described Fred as "the finest example of the best of Irish fighting soldiers."

CHAPTER 16

The Far East

On December 7 1941 Japan launched a surprise attack on the American Pacific Fleet at Pearl Harbour. Almost simultaneously Japanese bombs fell on Singapore. The following day Britain and the United States declared war on Japan. When the Japanese landed at Singora in Siam, not far from the Malaya frontier two British battleships, *Prince of Wales* and *Repulse*, with an escort of four destroyers, sailed to try and take them by surprise. While en route Japanese planes were sighted and the British commander, believing his intentions were known, decided to return to Singapore. At 1100 hours on December 10 Japanese bombers attacked. The capital ships, *Repulse* and *Prince of Wales*, were both sunk. The loss of the two vessels left Malaya with no powerful maritime defence and the Japanese Navy could now operate around the peninsula with almost complete impunity. On the night of December 9-10 Japanese troops stormed the defences on Kowloon peninsula and forced the British back on to Hong Kong island after three days of heavy fighting. Gunner Peter Delahunt, 7th Battery S.H.A.A. Regimental Royal Artillery was killed in action on December 19 during another Japanese

The Far East

attack. Gnr. Delahunt, aged 26, was from Ballysax, Curragh. His body was never recovered and he has no known grave. The vastly outnumbered British continued to resist until they ran out of ammunition. The garrison capitulated on Christmas Day 1941 after losing 4,400 men in action and another 7,450 as prisoners-of-war.

By the end of December the Japanese were on the Burma frontier after being welcomed in Siam as the new masters of Asia. On January 11 1942 they entered Kuala Lumpur, in Malaya. Five days later, after

Photo: A. DORAN.

John Thompson, Newbridge, who died in a Japanese P.O.W. Camp in 1943.

The Far East

Photo: K. MAHON.

The Bridge over the River Kwai, built from the sweat and blood of Allied POW's.

almost a month of bombing raids against Rangoon and other military installations, Japanese land forces invaded Burma. By the end of the month the British forces in Malaya had withdrawn into Singapore, demolishing the causeway linking the island fortress and the mainland. Reinforcements of two Indian Brigades and the British 18th Division arrived, but it was too late. Singapore had adequate defences against attack from the sea but the land front had been neglected as it was thought impossible for an enemy to attack through the thick jungles of Malaya, which is exactly what the Japanese did. Severely outnumbered, and with their backs to the wall, the British garrison had no other choice but to surrender. On February 15 General Percival surrendered. The 80,000 prisoners were marched off to captivity - first in he comparative comfort of Changi Jail, but later, for thousands, amid the horrors of the "Death Railway" in Siam.

The Far East

Lance-Corporal John Thompson, Newbridge, died while a prisoner of the Japanese. He was born in 1918 and left Newbridge in 1936, when the new Liffey bridge was being built. He enlisted in the Manchester Regiment and was sent to the Far East with the 1st Battalion. Lce/Cpl Thompson was captured at Singapore. He was reported missing and for several months his family was unaware of his whereabouts. Then word came that he was a prisoner. In the Japanese the Western powers found a formidable and cruel foe. The Japanese were callous, brave and skilful. They despised weakness and did not understand how a soldier who could still fight would choose to surrender. So they treated their prisoners as something beyond contempt, (Japan was not a signatory to the Geneva Convention) forcing them to work on the "Death Railway" and the infamous bridge over the River Kwai. The Japanese had a work quota to achieve each day and they did not care how this was accomplished. Men were beaten to work harder, or taken from the hospitals in the camps and made work, even if they were to lie on a stretcher and hold a rock-boring tool while another prisoner hit it. Men who fell by the wayside, and showed no hope of recovery, were left to die or were bayoneted. Captured escapees were beheaded in full view of the other prisoners. And, if that was not enough, the food was meagre and the conditions in the camps and the tropics unbelievably foul. Allied POWs died in their thousands from the cruelty and hardship and the hatred towards the Japanese from surviving prisoners remains as real today as it was over fifty years ago. Conditions in most POW camps were dreadful and prisoners had an appalling time. John Thompson died, from malaria, on March 29 1943, aged 25.

On March 6 1942 Rangoon fell. The 1st Inniskillings were flown into Magwe and moved directly to Prome. The battalion was about sixty per cent Catholic and the majority were from Southern Ireland. By the time the Skins reached India, two months later, only a hundred men of their original strength remained. Lashio, the southern terminus

The Far East

Photo: A. DORAN.

John Thompson, Newbridge, second from the right.

of the Burma Road - China's lifeline - was captured on April 29. The fall of Lashio was a crushing blow to the Allied supply line. Not to be deterred they established the airlift over the Himalayan "Hump" from India to China. The Allied commanders realised they could no longer hold any line against the Japanese in Burma and ordered a withdrawal to India, undertaking a 20-day journey of hard foot-slogging through 140 miles of jungle and mountain. By the end of May, though temporarily checked by monsoon rains, the Japanese were poised to attack either India or China.

Father Thomas Murphy, from Naas, was in Burma when the Japanese invaded. Thomas Murphy was born into a large family in 1906 and lived at Kilcullen Road, Naas. After school he became apprenticed to the bar and grocery trade in Staples Dowlings public

The Far East

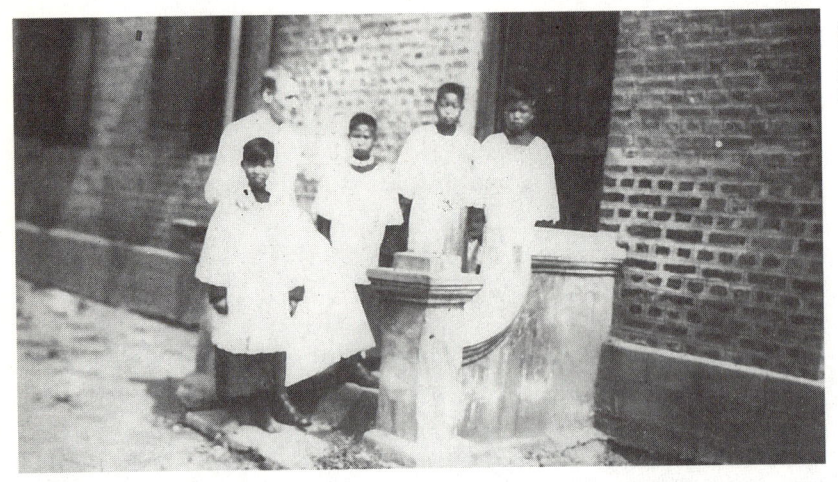

Photo: E. TRAPP.

Fr. Murphy, Naas, in Burma.

house. He was a devout practitioner of his religion and after a late vocation - and with the help of local support - went to Mungret College, Limerick, for clerical education. Tom Murphy was ordained into the Columban Fathers' on December 21 1935 at Dalgan Park in Galway and left for the Mission to Burma the following year.

It took six weeks by freighter-passenger ship to reach Calcutta from London. Fr. Murphy and five fellow Columbans travelled to Rangoon and then on to Bhamo by paddle steamer on the Irrawaddy River. The missionaries first task was to learn the language and customs of the local people. 1938 saw the first medical dispensary in Nanghlaing and the following year saw a big project in the building of an orphanage for girls in conjunction with a group of sisters. This building was financed by the presentation money from the people of Naas. The following years were difficult for the lives of missionaries having to contend with wet and dry seasons, the constant threat of malaria, typhoid and other fevers and the danger of encountering tigers, elephants or cobras.

On May 3 1942 Japanese troops entered Bhamo. As the Japanese

page number 234 | *far from the short grass*

The Far East

were approaching the retreating British advised the Columban Fathers to leave. The priests decided to stay with their parishioners and take charge of Bhamo Civil Hospital. The Japanese, in turn, arrived to take over the building, and the Columbans were placed under 'Protective Custody' in Bhamo Jail. Asked why they did not run away to India with the British the Irish priests tried to explain their neutrality. "English, Irish, all the same," the Japanese replied to the chagrin of the Irish priests. In Bhamo Jail they fared well as outside friends brought in milk and food and smuggled in books. The priests set up two altars and had daily Mass. They kept fit by drilling and devised their own games to pass away boredom.

On June 18 1942 the Columbans were released from jail to find the town a scene of great desolation. In October, in response to representations from the Vatican, an order came from Tokyo that the Columbans were to be specially protected. They were ordered by the Japanese Commander in Bhamo to go to Mandalay. Fr. Tom Murphy and eighteen other priests with six native helpers journeyed down the Irrawaddy from Bhamo to Mandalay by riverboat. On reaching Mandalay the priests came upon a scene of terrible desolation. When the British fled earlier in the year the town had burned unceasing for three weeks. Now all was rubble as far as the eye could see. It was a far cry from what the priests could remember of a few years earlier. The Columbans were surprised to see that in the midst of the ruins there was one sector untouched: the palace and grounds of the Kings of Burma, in the heart of Mandalay. The Japanese had never bombed it, and the fleeing arsonists had also left it alone. The missionaries were given the use of a fine house at Mandalay Agricultural College well outside the city, where they remained until the following year.

The Japanese 'Blitzkreig' continued until it was halted on New Guinea in the southeast and the India-Burma frontier in the east. The Americans were still established on Midway Atoll, the western extrem-

The Far East

ity of the Hawaiian chain. The tide of the Japanese advance was finally checked at the naval battles of Coral Sea, and at Midway on June 4-5 1942, when the Japanese lost four carriers to one American carrier in one of the most decisive battles of the war. Within weeks the Allies would go on the offensive in the Pacific and in Burma.

In Burma the monsoon season, which lasts about five months and brings some 200 inches of rain, gave the British a welcome respite after their long retreat. However, the Allies wanted to regain the initiative as soon as possible and in October went on the offensive in an attempt to capture Akyab and reoccupy the upper Arakan. (October-May are the dry season in Burma). The superior British forces, though many were untried and untested troops, were roundly defeated by the battle-hardened and expert jungle fighters of the Japanese army. The only advantage gained by the British was that the RAF had begun to attain air superiority throughout the whole front. Morale, especially in the Indian Army, was at an all time low. However, the appointment of Lord Louis Mountbatten, as overall commander of South-East Asia, and the reorganisation of the Allied forces, produced better results when the two sides met again.

Fr. Tom Murphy, Naas, and the rest of the Columban priests were still in Japanese-occupied Mandalay. However, the house they were assigned to, Mandalay Agricultural College, was surrounded by Japanese units and attracted the attention of Allied bombers. Drums of gasoline stored all about did not contribute to peace of mind, as the air raids continued day and night. In October 1943 the Japanese said they wanted to occupy the house and moved the Columbans to the nearby St. John's Leper Asylum. By moving out of the military camp the Columbans thought they would be safe from air raids. How wrong they were. The leper asylum got it's fair share and on one day alone the Allies bombed them thirteen times. Somehow an American Airforce major learned about the prisoners in the leper asylum and

The Far East

passed the word among the pilots, and from that day on no bombs fell within a mile of St. John's.

In February 1944 the Japanese decided the best means of defence of Burma was to attack and launched an offensive against the British who were slowly moving down the Arakan. Only the superior numbers of the British halted the Japanese offensive and the Allies abandoned any idea of a counter offensive in the area in the dry season of 1944-45. The Japanese troops were brave, hardy, well-trained and intelligently led. Throughout the war they fought to the last and with sav-

Photo: M. ECCLES.

Charlie Rogers, Ballymore-Eustace, and Indian friend, Burma.

The Far East

age, yet disciplined fanaticism whether defending or attacking. In March 1944 the Japanese 15th Army crossed the Chindwin and attacked Imphal laying siege to Imphal and Kohima, where heavy fighting continued until the Japanese retreated losing 53,505 of 88,000 men engaged. Victory at Imphal and Kohima would probably not have been possible without absolute air superiority, air supply, and close air support.

Charlie Rogers, from Ballymore-Eustace, was with the RAF in Burma. Charlie joined the RAF in 1943 and after training in Padgate, Lancashire, was sent to RAF Burma Command in 1944. His convoy went through the Mediterranean, Suez and the Red Sea and docked at Bombay. Aircraftman Rogers was stationed at Brahmaputra, Burma. Working conditions for the RAF in Burma were usually difficult. The weather, of course, dictated everything. Disease was a big factor too, and destroyed beyond recovery a large portion of the armed forces each year.

Tom Dillon, from Rathfield, Newbridge, was with 355 Squadron, South East Asia Command, as the Allies went on the offensive. He joined the RAF in February 1943, when he was 20. After training in Padgate, he went to No. 4 Gunnery School in Marpeth, where he trained with Anson aircraft. From there he went to Harwell, practising bombing formation and gunnery with Wellington bombers. Tom remained at Harwell until February 1944, when he was assigned as an air gunner to 355 Squadron, SEAC. "I was a sergeant." He recalled. "You got your stripes a few months after finishing your courses. We sailed to Calcutta, passing through the Suez Canal. It took us a month to get there." 355 squadron was based at Darjeeling, India, and flew American Liberator bombers. "The Liberator was a good plane, very manuverable. They had .50 calibre's in the front and .303's in the rear. I was a front gunner, a nose gunner."

far from the short grass

The Far East

Photo: T. DILLON.

Flight Sgt. Tom Dillon, Newbridge, pictured in Darjeeling, India, 1944.

"There were no Irishmen from the 26, (Counties) a few from Northern Ireland and every other nationality; Australian, Canadian, Scotch, Welsh and English. I joined up with two Northern Irishmen. One was killed by a blade. (an accident with a propeller) We had just three or four attacks, (by Japanese fighters) Betty's, Zeros and Zekes. No 'certs', several 'probables'- these had to be verified. We lost 5 crews; 2 crashes; 1 tangled in the air; 1 crashed on take-off and 1 shot down. We were bombing ammo dumps, railways and troop concentrations and were sometimes 16 hours in the air; 8 hours to target and 8 hours back."

The Far East

Sgt. Dillon's older brother, Davey, was also in the RAF and spent some time in India on ground crews. He returned to England with chest problems. The heat and humidity in India was hard on men. "You got used to it after awhile." Sgt. Dillon said. "The weather was very warm and dry. You looked forward to the monsoons to give you a break." As the Allied offensive in Burma continued 355 Squadron flew more and more missions over Burma. Here is an extract from Sgt. Tom Dillon's log-book for March 1945:

March 7. Ops. Martban. Target. Docks & jetties.
Bombed as briefed. Bomb load 6,000.
No. 2 engine caught fire on run up to target.
Bombed on three engines. No. 4 losing oil.
Crossed bay on 2 engines. Restarted No. 4 for landing.

March 9. Ops. Rangoon. Target. Dumps & stores.
Bombed as briefed. Bomb load 7,500.

March 17. Ops. Rangoon. Target. Dumps & stores.
Bombed as briefed. Bomb load 8,000 lb.
Height 14,000.

March 19. Ops. Ma-Miem. Target. Railway warehouses.
Bombed as briefed. Bomb load 4,500 lb.
Height 2,500'

March 24. Ops. Moulmein. Target. Dumps &
stores at Pa-Aug. Bombed as briefed.
Bomb load 4,500 lb.
Height 4,000'

March 29. Ops. Moulmein. Target. Bridge 27. Rly.line between
Moulmein & Bangkok. Bombed as briefed.

The Far East

Height 300. Bomb load 7,000 lb. Holed by A/A fire, on run in. Running fight with an Oscar for 15 min, at 2,000 ft. Enemy shot down and definitely destroyed. (Single sortie).

With the defeat of the Japanese 15th Army, at Imphal and Kohima, the Allies were now on the dry plains of Burma where tanks, artillery, and aircraft could be used to maximum effect. The time was ripe for the ejection of the Japanese from all of Burma and the Allies began the advance on Mandalay and then Rangoon. In Mandalay the interned Columban Fathers found their liberation was the most trying time of all. When the British were moving in to recapture Mandalay, the Japanese placed a large artillery piece in front of the leper asylum drawing the British fire. The strain on the priests, and the 300 or so

The Far East

lepers, in the compound, began to tell as there was hardly a moment free from the sound of shells, machine guns and grenades. Since the Japanese invasion three and a half years ago the Columbans had survived through the harshness of war. It would be so unfortunate to die now when freedom was so close.

Suddenly on March 15 1945 came the news that a British unit had dug in at the corner of the asylum grounds. Within minutes the soldiers were handing out chocolate and cigarettes. On the morning of March 16 the priests arose around 5a.m. as was usual and started their first round of Masses. Air shells began exploding close up. Towards the end of Mass another explosion took place nearer to them, so they decided to wait a while before starting the next round of Masses. Father Lyons wrote: "We waited some time and then more or less decided that the particular shelling had subsided for the time being. Five priests, including Father Murphy, started the second round of Masses with five other Fathers serving. Two other priests were making their thanksgiving in the little chapel. I myself was serving Mass and was sitting on a seat only two or three feet away from Father Murphy."

Fr. Tom was saying the Epistle when a stray shell exploded right over the part of the zinc roof directly over his head. Of the twelve priests in the room several were injured, none seriously, except Fr. Murphy. He was wounded seriously in the stomach and the right foot. The others knew he was badly wounded and moved him to the asylum dispensary, where the Sisters and a local doctor did everything they could. Only major surgery would save Fr. Tom's life and Fr. McEvoy cautiously slipped out the back and waded through a canal to reach a British outpost. The officer commanding sent a radio message to headquarters for help, who promised that if necessary they would fly Fr. Murphy to India within two hours.

The Far East

Fr. Lyons wrote: "He had the happiness of receiving all the Sacraments while he was fully conscious, before leaving us at St. John's Leper Asylum, Mandalay. His last words to us before leaving were, 'Please forgive me, if I have offended any of you in the past.'" As he was in such a critical condition the stretcher bearers decided to save time and bring Fr. Tom down the main road. The Japanese held their fire and the group arrived safely at the British outpost. A gun carrier was waiting to transport Fr. Murphy a few miles to an advanced dressing station and thence to hospital. Every care was taken, but after reaching the first dressing station Fr. Tom died through loss of blood and also because of the serious stomach wound he had received.

The British sent trucks back to the asylum for any of the prisoners who could reach an assembly point three miles away. Several of the priests and sisters stayed behind to look after the lepers, but about 160 internees slipped out the back way to reach the British trucks and freedom. Fr. Tom Murphy was laid to rest in the British War Cemetery in Mandalay. (In 1984 Naas Urban District Council decided to name newly-built houses, near to the Church grounds at Sallins Road, as Fr. Murphy Place, in honour of the Columban priest who died so far away from his native town.)

Mandalay fell on March 20 and the 14th Army was now all set for its dash to capture Rangoon and obtain a port before the monsoon. In May Rangoon fell to a combined air and seaborne attack. By now the Japanese army's organisation had disintegrated and their morale was crumbling. More and more Japanese soldiers began to surrender, a thing unheard of in the previous months and years. The Japanese Army high command was despondent. Germany had surrendered, and it was obvious that the British and Americans were planning to redeploy all their military strength for a final invasion of the Japanese home islands.

The Far East

Photo: E. TRAPP.

Fr. Thomas Murphy, Naas.

RAF Sergeant Jim Cullen, Naas, was engaged in England in tow-firing practice "for Americans going to the Far East for the invasion of Japan. After one incident when the tug was hit and the cable snapped back it got too dangerous and I left to go to the chemical warfare group."

On August 6 1945 the Americans dropped an atomic bomb on Hiroshima. Three days later a second atomic bomb devastated

far from the short grass

The Far East

Nagasaki, and the Soviet Union declared war on Japan. On August 15 Japan surrendered unconditionally to the Allies. General Numata arrived in Rangoon, from Saigon, on August 26, for the signing of the preliminary agreement for the surrender of all Japanese forces in South East Asia. The formal act of surrender took place in the throne room of Government House, Rangoon. AC Charlie Rogers, Ballymore Eustace, was with an RAF unit in Rangoon when the Japanese party led by General Numato arrived.

Sgt. Tom Dillon, Newbridge, flew with 355 Squadron as a nose gunner from May 1944 to April 8 1945, when he completed his operational tour. From then until the end of the war he flew as a D.D.T operator, again on Liberator bombers. He left the RAF in 1947, retiring a Warrant-Officer.

After recovering from wounds suffered in Italy, Corporal Dennis Carroll, Maynooth, was sent back to England. He was promoted and

Photo: M. ECCLES.

Japanese surrender of SE Asia, taken by Charlie Rogers, Ballymore-Eustace.

The Far East

Photo: T. DILLON.

began training young Dutch troops. He was home in Kildare for three months leave in 1946, but felt out of place and signed on for another five years. He was sent with his battalion, 2nd/6th Inniskillings, to India in 1947. "It was March," he said "as I remember there was a heavy snow in Omagh. They were partioning India and Pakistan. I was there until the latter half of 1947. We sailed from Madras. There was a beautiful hotel there, the Connemara Hotel. It was a beautiful place and is still there. We went to Rangoon and picked up some Jap POWs and continued on to Hong Kong. Tens of thousands were waiting to go back to Japan, but there was a shortage of shipping. The Japs were cheeky bastards. You wouldn't think they were prisoners."

Flight Sgt. Tom Dillon, (second right), pictured with friends at Tiger Hill, near Mt. Everest.

far from the short grass

The Far East

The end of the war in Southeast Asia signalled the end of the British Empire in the East. The Asian people had witnessed the British defeats by the Japanese and many countries now sought to overthrow their British rulers once and for all. The success of Communism in China heralded the spread of revolutionary politics to Asian countries like Malaya and Korea. India had supplied valuable troops and important raw materials to the Allied war effort and felt its reward should be independence from British rule. But ending British rule was to be no simple matter. Deep religious divisions existed between the majority Hindu population and the minority Sikhs and Muslims. The last Viceroy of India, Lord Louis Mountbatten, decided the best solution was to divide India into separate Hindu and Muslim states, with the Hindu state retaining the name India and the Muslim states becoming East and West Pakistan. All this did not go off peacefully and British troops had to maintain order until the independence of both India and Pakistan on August 15 1947. Many of the Kildaremen in Far Eastern Command stayed on in the British armed forces, witnessing the changeover of power in the former British Empire.

Charlie Rogers, Ballymore-Eustace, poses with Japanese fighter bomber, Burma.

Photo: M. ECCLES.

APPENDIX 1

Deaths in action – WWI.

*Denotes servicemen are brothers.

Henry Adams, ...Kildare.
Maurice Adams, ... Kildare.
Rodney Ahearne, ... Newbridge.
Thomas Ahearn, ... Newbridge.
Frank Alcock, ... Athy.
Thomas Alcock, ... Athy.
S.F. Alfort, ... Newbridge.
Michael Ambrose, ... Newbridge.
Horace Andrews, ... Kildare.
Robert Angus, ... Newbridge.
G.K. Ansell, ... Co. Kildare.
H.L. Anthony, ... Newbridge.

F. Baldry, ... Naas.
Christopher Baker, ... Curragh.
Patrick Bambrick, ... Athy.
E.N. Banks, ... Naas.
Henry Barber, ... Curragh.
Frank Barnes, ... Curragh.
John Barton, ... Kildare.

William Bateman, ... Curragh.
George Bates, ... Curragh.
James Baxter, ... Kilcock.
Richard Baxter, ... Kilcock.
George Beale, ... Newbridge.
Michael Bearns, ... Celbridge.
James Bedding, ... Newbridge.
Thomas Behan, ... Eadestown.
Thomas Belford, ... Suncroft.
Matthew Bell, ... Athy.
William Bell, ... Brownstown.
R.B. Bennison, ... Curragh.
Joseph Bermingham, ... Naas.
Thomas Bermingham, ... Allen.
Thomas Blackburn, ... Curragh.
C. F. Blacker, ... Johnstown.
William Blakely . . . . .Kildare.
Robert Bloomer, ... Athy.
Michael Bolger, ... Kilberry.
G. F. Bolster, ... Co. Kildare.

Appendix

Walter Borrowes, ... Barrettstown.
Eustace Bourke, ... Co. Kildare.
Michael Bowden, ... Athy.
H. K. Bradbury, ... Co. Kildare.
Patrick Bradley, ... Curragh.
George Byers, ... Naas.
Anthony Byrne, ... Naas.
Christopher Byrne, ... Rathangan.
Cornelius Byrne, ... Castledermot.
James Byrne, ... Kildare.
James Byrne, ... Athy.
John Byrne, ... Athy.
John Byrne, ... Newbridge.
Joseph Byrne, ... Athy.
Joseph Byrne, ... Moyvalley.
M. Byrne, ... Monasterevan.
M. Byrne, ... Athy.
Martin Byrne, ... Kildangan.
Patrick Byrne, ... Maynooth.
Patrick Byrne, ... Naas.
Thomas Byrne, ... Athy.
Vivian Bradley, ... Curragh.
James Brady, ... Kilcullen.
Joseph Brady, ... Naas.
Michael Brady, ... Ballymore.
Simon Brady, ... Barnawal.
Chris Brannigan, ... Brownstown.
Thomas Brazlin, ... Newbridge.
James Brennan, ... Curragh.
James Brennan, ... Athy.
Arthur Brewer, ... Curragh.
Chris Bride, ... Monasterevan.
James Brien, ... Kilcock.
Patrick Brien, ... Naas.
William Brilly, ... Kilbrook.
Albert Brown, ... Curragh.
Andrew Brown, ... Curragh.
Chris Brown, ... Cookstown.
James Brown, ... Naas.
Patrick Brown, ... Clane.
Patrick Browne, ... Arlis.
C. H. Browning, ... Co. Kildare.
Reeves Browning, ... Newbridge.
H. Brunskil, ... Curragh.
William Bryant, ... Curragh.

Hugh Buckley, ... Celbridge.
Thomas Burdett, ... Naas.
D. J. Burgess, ... Naas.
H. W. Burgess, ... Co. Kildare.
D. Burke, ... Naas.
D. J. Burke, ... Naas.
J. Burke . . . . Maynooth.
James Burke, ... Curragh.
L. Burke, ... Maynooth.
Michael Burke, ... Blacktrench.
Peter Burke, ... Kilcullen.
Thomas Burke, ... Naas.
W. Burke, ... Athy.
William Burke, ... Prosperous.
Charles Burns, ... Curragh.
Horace Burrell, ... Kildare.
John Burrows, ... Kildare.
William Burt, ... Curragh.

Patrick Cahill, ... Kilcullen.
Thomas Cahill, ... Naas.
James Callaghan, ... Sallins.
C. H. Cameron, ... Naas.
Michael Campion, ... Ballyadams.
Maurice Cane, ... Celbridge.
William Cantwell, ... Athy.
Peter Carberry, ... Ballyroe.
D. A. Carden, ... Straffan.
James Carey, ... Castledermot.
Leonard Carolan, ... Ballysax.
Frank Carroll, ... Newbridge.
Patrick Carroll, ... Monasterevan.
Peter Carroll, ... Monasterevan.
William Carter, ... Curragh.
James Cash, ... Straffan.
Thomas Cherry, ... Newbridge.
J. F. Church, ... Curragh.
George Claxton, ... Curragh.
James Cleary, ... Monasterevan.
John Clegg, ... Newbridge.
W. Clements, ... Naas.
James Coady, ... Clough.
James Coady, ... Naas.
Joseph Coghlan, ... Suncroft.

Appendix

Alfred Cole, ... Curragh.
Patrick Condron, ... Athy.
Nicholas Conlan, ... Rathangan.
John Conlan, ... Monasterevan.
E. Connally, ... Newbridge.
Thomas Connell, ...Athy.
Edward Connolly, ...Curragh.
James Connolly, ... Newbridge.
Patrick Connolly, ...Monasterevan.
Thomas Connolly, ...Monasterevan.
Thomas Connolly, ...Kildare.
Patrick Conville, ...Clough.
William Cook, ...Curragh.
John Cooke, ...Kilcullen.*
William Cooke, ...Kilcullen.*
Edward Cooper, ...Newbridge.
John Cooper, ...Curragh.
William Corcoran, ...Athy.
William Cornelius, ...Kildare.
Henry Cornpolth, ...Kildare.
William Corrigan, ...Athy.
Patrick Cosgrove, ...Naas.
Peter Coughlin, ...Naas.
Allan Coupar, ...Monasterevan.
Arthur Coupland, ...Kildare.
Alfred Coyle, ...Nicholastown.
Thomas Coyle, ...Nurley.
Patrick Coyne, ...Newbridge.
J. G. Crawley, ...Co. Kildare.
G. O. Creed, ...Maynooth.
Hubert Crichton, ...Ballymore.
Samuel Crone, ...Kildare.
Maurice Cullen, ...Foxhill.
Walter Curley, ...Finstown.
John Curtis, ...Athy.*
Lawrence Curtis, ...Athy.*
Patrick Curtis, ...Athy.*
Patrick Cusack, ...Monasterevan.
John Collomy, ...Monasterevan.

John Delaney, ... Athy.
William Delaney, ... Crookstown.
Edward Dempsey, ... Celbridge.
J. J. Dempsey, ... Kildare.

P. Dempsey, ... Celbridge.*
Thomas Dempsey, ... Celbridge.*
Thomas Dempsey, ... Leixlip.
Michael Devoy, ... Athy.
Johnson Digby, ... Naes.
James Dillon, ... Athy.
Patrick Dillon, ... Clane.
John Doherty, ... Athy.
George Dolan, ... Ballaghmoon.
Patrick Dolan, ... Vicarstown.
Christopher Donnelly, ... Newbridge.
James Donnelly, ... Curragh.
Michael Donnelly, ... Newbridge.
Patrick Donnelly, ... Robertstown.
Jeremiah Donohoe, ... Brownstown.
Michael Donohoe, ... Newbridge.
Michael Donohoe, ... Celbridge.
Murtagh Donohoe, ... Naas.
Patrick Donohoe, ... Athy.
John Doody, ... Castledermot.
Laurence Dooley, ... Athy.
William Dooley, ... Naas.
Christopher Doran, ... Kildare.
John Doran, ... Celbridge.
Joseph Doran, ... Monasterevan.
Patrick Doran, ... Ballymore.
Edward Dowling, ... Athy.
J. Dowling, ... Kilcullen.
John Dowling, ... Kilberry.
Joseph Dowling, ... Kildare.
M. Dowling, ... Kilberry.
M. Dowling, ... Naas.
Michael Dowling, ... Robertstown.
J. Downey, ... Ballymore.
Patrick Downey, ... Robertstown.
A. Doyle, ... Naas.
Charles Doyle, ... Kilcullen.
John Doyle, ... Monasterevan.
John Doyle, ... Newbridge.
John Doyle, ... Suncroft.
Joseph Doyle, ... Kilcullen.
Moses Doyle, ... Athy.
Patrick Doyle, ...Kilcock.
Francis Daly, ... Carbury.
John Daly, ...Newbridge.

Appendix

Richard Daly, ... Athy.
Thomas Daly, ...Monasterevan.
Michael Davis, ...Adamstown.
James Deay, ...Bonabreena.
John de Burgh, ...Naas.
John de Courcey, ...Kilcock.
Michael Deegan, ...Ballymore.
Thomas Deegan, ...Ballymore.
Andrew Delaney, ...Crookstown.
Daniel Delaney, ...Athy.
J. Delaney, ...Ballitore.
Patrick Doyle, ...Athy.
Thomas Doyle, ...Castledermot.
Thomas Doyle, ...Naas.
Thomas Doyne, ...Celbridge.
James Duffy, ...Carrisvilla.
Walter Duffy, ...Naas.
Thomas Dugan, ...Robertstown.
John Dunn, ...Kilcullen.
Joseph Dunn, ...Curragh.
Andrew Dunne, ...Monasterevan.
J. Dunne, ...Athy.
James Dunne, ...Athy.
Joseph Dunne, ...Ballybrittas.
Joseph Dunne, ...Naas.
Michael Dunne, ...Athy.
Patrick Dunne, ...Athy.
Patrick Dunne, ...Naas.
Peter Dunne, ...Allen.
M. Dunphy, ...Athy.
James Dwyer, ...Rathangan.
Joseph Dwyer, ...Newbridge.

Thomas Ellard, ...Athy.
John English, ...Moone.

Christopher Flynn, ... Athy.
Patrick Flynn, ... Athy.
Thomas Flynn, ... Athy.
James Foley, ... Newbridge.
Michael Ford, ...Maddenstown.
John Forde, ... Leixlip.
John Foster, ... Ballymore.

John Foster, ... Monasterevan.
F. Fox, ... Naas.
Thomas Fox, ... Athy.
Richard Foy, ... Curragh.
John French, ... Athy.
Frank Fanning, ...Athy.
Patrick Farnan, ...Castledermot.
Andrew Farrell, ...Naas.
James Farrell, ...Athy.
John Farrell, ...Athy.
Michael Farrell, ...Athy.
Terence Farrell, ...Kildare.
William Feeley, ...Naas.
James Feenick, ...Ballylinan.
John Fenelly, ...Athy.
Hugh Fenlon, ...Athy.
James Fennell, ...Maynooth.
Patrick Fenneral, ...Allen.
C. Fennessey, ...Newbridge.
Thomas Fingleton, ...Monasterevan.
Chris Fitzpatrick, ...Monasterevan.
John Fitzpatrick, ...Monasterevan.
John Fitzpatrick, ...Newbridge.
William Fitzpatrick, ...Newbridge.
Bernard Fitzsimons, ...Kilcock.
Thomas Fitzsimons, ...Co. Kildare.
Patrick Flanagan, ...Celbridge.
Joseph Fleming, ...Naas.
Johnn Flood, ...Naas.

John Gallery, ... Curragh.
Walter Galligan, ... Prosperous.
Frederick Galway, ... Curragh.
William Gamble, ... Newbridge.
James Gannon, ... Suncroft.
James Garland, ... Newbridge.
H. Garrett, ... Curragh.
James Garry, ... Monasterevan.
Michael Gaynor, ... Leixlip.
Patrick Gibney, ... Kilcock.
William Gibson, ... Rathangan.
Gerald Gilbank, ...Curragh.
Michael Ging, ... Cookstown.
W. Ging, ... Rathangan.

Appendix

Christopher Gleeson,	Athy.
Charles Goble,	Curragh.
Henry-Chapman Goldie,	Curragh.
Frederick Good,	Kildare.
Stephen Goodall,	Naas.
Alfred Goodman,	Kill.
John Goodman,	Kill.
David Goodwin,	Whitechurch.
John Gorman,	Curragh.
J. J. Gorry,	Naas.
William Gorry,	Kildare.
John Gott,	Newbridge.
Thomas Goucher,	Straffan.
Maurice Granger,	Eadestown.
John Green,	Curragh.
Eric Greer,	Curragh.
Christopher Grimes,	Kilcullen.
Thomas Grimes,	Narraghmore.
James Grogan,	Moone.
James Grogan,	Celbridge.
Peter Grogan,	Clane.
Matthew Homan,	Ballymore.
James Hooks,	Naas.
R. Hornridge,	Naas.
Michael Houlahan,	Curragh.
Albert Hubbard,	Curragh.
Thomas Humphrys,	Newbridge.
Martin Hurley,	Athy.
William Hurley,	Athy.
Martin Hutchinson,	Ballickmoyler.
Martin Hyland,	Athy.
Robert Hackett,	Athy.
Joseph Hall,	Co. Kildare.
Martin Halloran,	Crookstown.
Mark Halligan,	Naas.*
Matthew Halligan,	Naas.*
Michael Halligan,	Naas.*
Christopher Hanlon,	Athy.
Daniel Hannigan,	Curragh.
Henry Hannon,	Athy.
Ian Hannon,	Athy.*
John Hannon,	Athy.
Norman Hannon,	Athy.*
Thomas Hannon,	Athy.
W. Hannon,	Dunnstown.
Peter Hanphy,	Athy.
Richard Harding,	Kilcock.
John Harrington,	Kildare.
John Harrington,	Naas.
Michael Harrington,	Naas.
Henry Harris,	Curragh.
Samuel Harris,	Naas
W.T. Hart,	Kildare.
Thomas Harvey,	Kildare.
Frederick Haseltin,	Kildare.
Patrick Haughey,	Doonane.
John Hayden,	Castledermot.
Thomas Hayden,	Kilcullen.
Charles Haywood,	Curragh.
Edward Healy,	Kill.
Michael Heffernan,	Eadestown.
S. Hemingway,	Newbridge.
Gerald Hendrick,	Kerdiffstown.
Aloysius Heydon,	Athy.
Patrick Heydon,	Athy.
Joseph Hickey,	Athy.
Alfred Hicks,	Athy.
Dennis Higgins,	Rathangan.
Edward Higgins,	Ballitore.
Ralph Hindes,	Naas.
Herbert Hirst,	Curragh
Samson Hockley,	Newbridge.
George Holbrook,	Maynooth.
C. C. Holland,	Newbridge.
P. Holohan,	Athy.
John Holton,	Carbury.
William Ingram,	Curragh.
William Irwin,	Celbridge.
James Jackson,	Celbridge.
Joseph James,	Kilcullen.
James Jaynes,	Curragh.
Henry Jeanes,	Kildare.
Charles Johnson,	Kildare.
John Johnston,	Athy.
Philip Johnston,	Naas.

Appendix

Thomas Johnston, ... Naas.
William Johnston, ... Maynooth.
Vincent Johnston, ... Athy.
R. A. Jones, ... Co. Kildare.
T. C. Nowlan-Jones, ... Kilcullen.
Michael Judge, ... Celbridge.
Thomas Judge, ... Nurney.

Peter Kane, ... Athy.
Peter Kane, ... Naas.
John Kavanagh, ... Eadestown.
John Kavanagh, ... Kilcullen.
Michael Kavanagh, ... Naas.
Patrick Kavanagh, ... Naas.
James Kaye, ... Ballymore.
John Kearney, ... Kilcullen.
Christopher Keefe, ... Athy.
Michael Keegan, ... Monasterevan.
W. Keegan, ... Ballymore.
Martin Keenan, ... Kildare.
Christopher Kelly, ... Athy.
David Kelly, ... Kildare.
Denis Kelly, ... Athy.
Frank Kelly, ... Kilcullen.
Gilbert Kelly, ... Athy.
John Kelly, ... Athy.
Joseph Kelly, ... Monasterevan.
Larry Kelly, ... Athy.
Owen Kelly, ... Athy.
Thomas Kelly, ... Castledermot.
Thomas Kelly, ... Leixlip.
William Kelly, ... Leixlip.
Charles Kemish, ... Newbridge.
Ronald Kennedy, ... Straffan.
Dominick Kennedy, ... Allenwood.
Herbert Kennedy, ... Naas.
Michael Kennedy, ... Allenwood.
R. B. Kennedy, ... Anntown.
Simon Kennedy, ... Maynooth.
Edward Kenny, ... Kildare.
W. Kent, ... Naas.
Patrick Keogh, ... Kildare.
Michael Keogh, ... Naas.
Joseph Keogh, ... Cookstown.

Peter Keogh, ... Ballindrum.
Michael Kiernan, ... Caragh.
Patrick Kiernan, ... Caragh.
Patrick Kilduff, ... Leixlip.
Thomas Kilroy, ... Curragh.
Edward Kinahan, ... Kilcullen.
G. Kinahan, ... Straffan.
Patrick King, ... Monasterevan.
William King, ... Crookstown.
Michael Kinsella, ... Castledermot.
William Kirwan, ... Celbridge.
Joseph Knott, ... Newbridge.

Thomas Lynam, ... Kilcock.
Kieran Lyons, ... Kilcullen.
George Larner, ... Kildare.
George Lattin, ... Naas.
Thomas Lawler, ... Arles.
Thomas Lawler, ... Athy.
William Lawless, ... Straffan.
Thomas Lawlor, ... Athy.
Michael Lawlor, ... Athy.
Patrick Lee, ... Kildare.
James Leech, ... Cloncurry.
J. Leonard, ... Naas.
Patrick Leonard, ... Athy.
William Leonard, ... Manor Kilbride.
Michael Lewis, ... Naas.*
Patrick Lewis, ... Naas.*
Christopher Libbiter, ... Curragh.
James Lonergan, ... Curragh.
John Loughlin, ... Naas.
A. C. Loveband, ... Naas.
James Lowery, ... Kildare.

F. W. J. MacDonnell, ... Kildare.
James Maher, ... Newbridge.
Martin Maher, ... Athy.
Patrick Maher, ... Co. Kildare.
Sydney Maher, ... Curragh.
Thomas Maher, ... Athy.
Michael Mahon, ... Ballymore.
Michael Mahoney, ... Naas.
J. Malloy, ... Naas.

far from the short grass

Appendix

Thomas Mangan, ... Ballymore.
Joseph Manning, ... Curragh.
Eustace Mansfield, ... Lattin.
James Marsh, ... Naas.
John Martin, ... Kilcock.
John Martin, ... Monasterevan.
Michael Martin, ... Co. Kildare.
Patrick Martin, ... Newbridge.
Thomas Martin, ... Leixlip.
William Martin, ... Curragh.
Patrick Masterson, ... Naas.
William Masterson, ... Naas.
William Matterson, ... Glassealy.
Horace Maxfield, ... Kildare.
Robert Maxwell, ... Naas.
Stephen Mealy, ... Clough.
B. McAuley, ... Kilcock.
Fred McCann, ... Celbridge.
Michael McCann, ... Rathangan.
John McCormack, ... Naas.
Edward McCormick, ... Kilcock.
Bernard McDermott, ... Derrinturn.
Dermot McDermot, ... Carbury.
P. McDermot, ... Ballylinan.
Robert McDonagh, ... Naas.
James McDonald, ... Leribys.
John McDonald, ... Kildare.
F.W. McDonnell, ... Kildare.
Martin McDonnell, ... Kiimeague.
Thomas McEnery, ... Athy.
Owen McEntee, ... Celbridge.
Christopher McEvoy, ... Kildare.
William McEvoy, ... Kildare.
D. McFarlane, ... Leixlip.
Andrew McGarr, ... Ballymore.
James McGrath, ... Naas.
J. McGuire, ... Naas.
Thomas McGuirk, ... Monasterevan.
George McKenna, ... Allen.
Peter McLeish, ... Straffan.
James McMahon, ... Kildare.
T. McNally, ... Drehid.
W. J. McVeigh, ... Naas.
Robert McWilliams, ... Athy.
Stephen Mealy, ... Athy.

Patrick Mearns, ... Monasterevan.
George Medlicott, ... Dunmurry.
Joseph Meehan, ... Monasterevan.
James Merrin, ... Mullaghmast.
John Milbanke, ... Co. Kildare.
Robert Millar, ... Cookstown.
Michael Mills, ... Allen.
James Mitchell, ... Ballagh.
Michael Mius, ... Allen.
Lawrence Molloy, ... Rathangan.
Martin Moloney, ... Athy.
Edward Mooney, ... Kildare.
J. Mooney, ... Monasterevan.
John Mooney, ... Newbridge.
Patrick Mooney, ... Moyvalley.
Richard Mooney, ... Naas.
David Moore, ... Kildare.
James Moore, ... Courtwood.
Percival Moore, ... Curragh.
Reuben Moore, ... Curragh.
Thomas Moore, ... Arles.
William Moore, ... Doonane.
D. Moran, ... Kildare.
Daniel Moran, ... Ballyadams.
Edward Moran, ... Kilcock.
James Moran, ... Naas.
James Moran, ... Prosperous.
William Moran, ... Athy.
M. Morrin, ... Naas.
Matthew Morrin, ... Naas.
William Morris, ... Clane.
Mattie Morrison, ... Naas.
James Morrissey, ... Kildare.
John Mulhall, ... Athy.
Patrick Mulhall, ... Athy.
Richard Mulhall, ... Kildare.
James Mullaly, ... Newbridge.
Albert Mullen, ... Kilberry.
James Mullen, ... Kilcock.
Laurence Mulligan, ... Maynooth.
Albert Murphy, ... Newbridge.
Andrew Murphy, ... Newbridge.
Andrew Murphy, ... Clough.
John Murphy, ... Maynooth.
John Murphy, ... Naas.

Appendix

Joseph Murphy, ... Athy.
Joseph Murphy, ... Maynooth.
L. J. Murphy, ... Kildare.
Martin Murphy, ... Moone.
Patrick Murphy, ... Newbridge.
Patrick Murphy, ... Kildare.
Patrick Murphy, ... Monasterevan.
T. Murphy, ... Newbridge.
T. Murphy, ... Naas.
Patrick Murray, ... Celbridge.
Thomas Murray, ... Curragh.
Walter Murray, ... Celbridge.
James Myers, ... Newbridge.

Harry Naylor, ... Newbridge.
G. H. Neely, ... Monasterevan.
Joseph Neill, ... Suncroft.
Patrick Neill, ... Blackchurch.
Thomas Neill, ... Kilcullen.
John Nelligan, ... Co. Kildare.
Philip Nestherfield, ... Kildare.
Arthur Nevitte, ... Naas.
John Newman, ... Newbridge.
Joseph Niland, ... Newbridge.
Charles Noble, ... Timahoe.
Edward Noble, ... Kilcullen.
Edward Nolan, ... Kilcullen.
Fenton Nolan, ... Athy.
James Nolan, ... Castledermot.
Michael Nolan, ... Maddanstown.
William Nolan, ... Ballymore.
William Nolan, ... Athy.
William Norris, ... Rathangan.
Henry Notley, ... Ballymore.

P. Butler-O'Brien, ... Naas..
John O' Brien, ... Naas.
Joseph O' Brien, ... Naas.
Michael O' Brien, ... Athy.
Thomas O' Brien, ... Naas.
Thomas O' Brien, ... Athy.
William O' Brien, ... Naas.
James O' Connell, ... Athy.

Christopher O' Connor, . . Castledermot.
Hubert O' Connor, ... Celbridge.
John O' Connor, ... Kill.
Patrick O' Donnell, ... Naas.
William O'Halloran, ... Co. Kildare.
John O' Hara, ... Kildare.
Michael O' Hara, ... Ballymore.
Michael O' Keefe, ... Athy.
Michael Oldham, ... Kiidare.
John O' Leary, ... Naas.
Patrick O' Mara, ... Kildare.
Denis O' Neill, ... Kildare.
D. J. O'Neill, ... Ladytown.
Joseph O' Neill, ... Kilcullen.
Thomas O' Neill, ... Naas.
William O' Neill, ... Kildare.
Joseph O' Reilly, ... Kildare.
Patrick O' Reilly, ... Maynooth.
James O' Rourke, ... Kildare.
Thomas O' Rourke, ... Kildare.
Patrick O'Toole, ... Kilcullen.

George Paisley, ... Naas.
Albert Patterson, ... Curragh.
Henry Payne, ... Barrowhouse.
John Payne, ... Curragh.
C. W. Peel, ... Co. Kildare.
Andrew Pender, ... Ballyadams.
Joseph Pender, ... Athy.
Christopher Power, ... Athy.
Christopher Power, ... (16273) Athy.
Henry Price, ... Ballitore.
James Price, ... Athy.
Michael Price, ... Ballitore.

James Quaile, ... Naas.
Patrick Quinlan, ... Robertstown.

John Reilly, ... Kilcock.
Thomas Reilly, ... Newbridge.
W. Reilly, ... Monasterevan.
David Rice, ... Curragh.

Appendix

Ralph Richardson, ... Curragh.
W. Ripton. . . . . Naas.
Nicholas Robinson, ... Naas.
William Robinson, ... Curragh.
James Roche, ... Co. Kildare.
John Rochford, ... Athy.
John Rogers, ... Naas.
George Ronaldson. . . . . Naas.
Patrick Rourke, ... Clane.
William Rouke, ... Suncroft.
Patrick Rowan, ... Ballyadams.
William Rowan, ... Wolfhill.
Edward Ryan, ... Newbridge.
Michael Ryan, ... Athy.
Thomas Ryan, ... Athy.
Thomas Ryan, ... Newbridge.
John Rafferty, ... Maynooth.
Cornelius Rafter, ... Harristown.
Henry Ransome, ... Monasterevan.
Benjamin Raybould, ... Curragh.
John Reaney, ... Curragh.
Francis Reddy, ... Monasterevan.
Lawrence Reddy, ... Allen.
John Redman, ... Co. Kildare.
Arthur Reeves, ... Athgarvan.
James Regan, ... Maynooth.
Andrew Reilly, ... Maynooth.
Christopher Reilly, ... Naas.
James Reilly, ... Naas.
John Reilly, ... Athy.

Frederick Sanders, ... Curragh.
John Sangster, ... Curragh.
George Sanure, ... Kildare.
Noel Scott, ... Monasterevan.
David Scully, ... Naas.
Thomas Shaughnessy, ... Rathangan.
Patrick Shea, ... Naas.
Edward Sheenan, ... Naas.
John Sheridan, ... Kildare.
Patrick Sheridan, ... Naas.
James Sherlock, ... Monasterevan.
Matthew Sherry, ... Leixlip.
Edward Shiel, ... Castledermot.

Henry Shilcock, ... Curragh.
Edward Shirley, ... Curragh.
Jeremiah Shirley, ... Athy.
Henry Sibley, ... Naas.
Walter Slight, ... Curragh.
Henry Smith, ... Newbridge.
Robert Smith, ... Jigginstown.
William Smith, ... Kilcock.
William Smith, ... Curragh.
John Smullen, ... Rathangan.
Laurence Smullen, ... Rathangan.
Laurence Smullen, ... Naas.
Michael Smyth, ... Co. Kildare.
H.M. Soames, ... Co. Kildare.
George Speed, ... Curragh.
Thomas Spencer, ... Newbridge.
John Spicer, ... Curragh.
Hugh Spittle, ... Newbridge.
James Spooner, ... Kilmeague.
Henry St. John, ... Athy.
Edward Stafford, ... Athy.*
Thomas Stafford, ... Athy.*
V. Stanley, ... Carnalway.
Thomas Steedman, ... Curragh.
Charles Stephens, ... Curragh.
Donald Stuart, ... Kildare.
Bertram Stroud, ... Newbridge.
William Supple, ... Moone.
John Swift, ... Kilmeague.

C. Teehan, ... Kill.
Alfred Telford, ... Arcreigh.
Michael Territt, ... Athy.
Nathaniel Thom, ... Cookstown.
James Thompson, ... Celbridge.
William Thompson, ... Kildare.
Michael Thorogood, ... Naas.
William Tice, ... Newbridge.
James Tierney, ... Kildare.
P. Tierney, ... Castledermot.
Patrick Tierney, ... Athy.
William Tobin, ... Newbridge.
Ernest Tomlin, ... Curragh.
William Treacy, ... Kildare.

far from the short grass

Appendix

Samuel Trehearne,	Harristown.
Edgar Tristram,	Curragh.
James Tuite,	Johnstownbridge.
William Tuite,	Johnstownbridge.
Patrick Tyrell,	Kilcock.
D. Underwood,	Sallins.
Joseph Underwood,	Naas.
John Veitch,	Newbridge.
John Watson,	Kilcock.
Anthony Weldon,	Athy.
Arthur Weldon,	Forenoughts.
Thomas Welsh,	Kildare.
John Wheeler,	Naas.
William Wheeler,	Newbridge.
Christopher Whelan,	Athy.
Patrick White,	Kilcullen.
Bernard Whitman,	Kildare.
Patrick Willen,	Curragh.
A. Williams,	Kildare.
Francis Williamson,	Celbridge.
William Wilmot,	Brownstown.
Edward Wolfred,	Milemill.
Maurice Wookey,	Leixlip.
William Wray,	Naas.
James Wright,	Ballymore-Eustace.
F.F. Waldron,	Melitta Lodge.
Robert Walker,	Kilcullen.
William Wall,	Athy.
William Wallace,	Clough.
Patrick Walsh,	Maganey.
Thomas Walsh,	Naas.
W. Walsh,	Monasterevan.
Michael Walker,	Kilcullen.
George Ware,	Kildare.
Alfred Warmington,	Naas.

APPENDIX 2

Deaths in Action – WWII.

Ian Blacker, ...Kilcullen.
John Blake, ...Newbridge.
Michael Breen, ...Naas.
James Burns . . . . .Currgh.

Peter Delahunt, ...Ballysax.
Adrian Dooley, ...Castledermot.
Murtagh Doyle, ...Curragh.

George Fawcett, ...Straffan.

Robert Gill, ...Naas.
Stephen Glespan, ...Athy.
William Gormanstown . . . . .Naas.

John Harmon, ...Moone.
James Holland, ...Naas.
Terence Hosie, ...Athy.
Christopher Hynes, ...Leixlip.

Darby Michael Kennedy, ...Kill.

James McGowan, ...Suncroft.
Denis McLoughlin, ...Sallins.
Raymond Morris, ...Athy.
John Mulpeter, ...Rathangan.

Frederick Nixon, ...Kildare.
Edward Nettlefold, ...Maynooth.

Robin O'Kelly, ...Straffan.

John Rice, ...Monasterevan.
Norman Robinson, ...Carbury.
John Sheridan, ...Naas.
William Simpson, ...Kildare.
Patrick Donnelly-Swift, ...Kildare.

John Thompson, ...Newbridge.

Francis White, ...Athy.

far from the short grass

Bibliography

NEWSPAPERS AND PERIODICALS.

The Leinster Leader, Naas.
The Kildare Observer, Naas.
The Blue Cap, Dublin.

BOOKS.

World War I. Susan Everett. Bison Books. 1980.

Orange, Green and Khaki. The story of the Irish regiments in the Great War. 1914-18. Tom Johnstone. Gill and Macmillan. 1992.

World War II. Lt. Col. Eddy Bauer. Orbis. London. 1972.

Clear the Way! A history of the 38th (Irish) Brigade, 1941-47. Richard Doherty. Irish Academic Press. 1993.

History of the Irish Guards in the Second World War. Major D.J.L. FitzGerald, Gale and Polden. 1949.

Major D.M. (John) Kennedy, M.C. A Tribute. Robert Jocelyn. 1993.

A Bridge Too Far. Cornelius Ryan. Coronet. 1975.

Images of war. The Real Story of World War II. Marshall and Cavendish. 1988.

Mission in Burma. The Columban Fathers Forty-three years in Kachin County. Edward Fischer. Seabury Press. 1980.